The Irish voter

The Irish voter

The nature of electoral competition in the Republic of Ireland

MICHAEL MARSH, RICHARD SINNOTT, JOHN GARRY AND FIACHRA KENNEDY

Manchester University Press
Manchester and New York

distributed exclusively in the USA by Palgrave

Copyright © Michael Marsh, Richard Sinnott, John Garry and Fiachra
Kennedy 2008

The right of Michael Marsh, Richard Sinnott, John Garry and Fiachra Kennedy to
be identified as the authors of this work has been asserted by them in accordance
with the Copyright, Designs and Patents Act 1988.

Published by Manchester University Press
Oxford Road, Manchester M13 9NR, UK
and Room 400, 175 Fifth Avenue, New York, NY 10010, USA
www.manchesteruniversitypress.co.uk

Distributed exclusively in the USA by
Palgrave, 175 Fifth Avenue, New York,
NY 10010, USA

Distributed exclusively in Canada by
UBC Press, University of British Columbia, 2029 West Mall,
Vancouver, BC, Canada V6T 1Z2

British Library Cataloguing-in-Publication Data
A catalogue record for this book is available from the British Library

Library of Congress Cataloging-in-Publication Data applied for

ISBN   978 0 7190 7731 9 *hardback*
ISBN   978 0 7190 7732 6 *paperback*

First published 2008

17 16 15 14 13 12 11 10 09 08   10 9 8 7 6 5 4 3 2 1

Typeset in 10.5/12.5pt Sabon
by Graphicraft Limited, Hong Kong
Printed in Great Britain
by The Cromwell Press Ltd, Trowbridge

Contents

List of tables

List of figures

Preface

We count ourselves extremely lucky to be around when funding for the social sciences in Ireland has at last been substantial enough to sustain a full election study. Public money was made available under the Programme for Research in Third Level Institutions (PRTLI) in 2000, and we are grateful to those in TCD and UCD who supported our successful application to run the post-election survey in 2002 that is the basis for this book. The data is now deposited with the Irish Social Science Data Archive at UCD and we hope it will provide fertile soil for future researchers. This project was co-directed by Michael Marsh in TCD and Richard Sinnott in UCD, while John Garry and Fiachra Kennedy each won post-doctoral scholarships to work on the design and implementation of the surveys. The interviews were carried out by the Economic and Social Research Institute (ESRI) and we are deeply grateful to James Williams and Dorothy Watson of the ESRI for their patience and support, which went well beyond what could reasonably be expected.

A draft of the questionnaire was discussed at a conference in 2001. Thanks are due to John Curtice, Cees van der Eijk, Roger Jowell and Phil Shively for coming to Dublin to take part in this and giving so unselfishly of their time and experience. Thanks also to those at TCD and UCD who attended this and other planning meetings: Ken Benoit, John Coakley, Michael Gallagher, Gail McElroy and Michael Laver. Michael Laver's particular contribution to this project is immense, as a senior administrator at TCD in 2000, as a strong voice for social science funding, and as the most generous of colleagues.

A further conference was held in September 2006 to discuss the study of the 2007 election on the basis of the findings of the 2002 study as detailed here. We are grateful to all those who attended. We owe particular thanks to Heinz Brandenburg, Wouter van der Brug, Ray Duch, Cees van der Eijk, David Farrell, Jeff Karp and Kathleen Knight for their comments on an earlier draft of this book, to Jane

Suiter and Zbyszek Zalinski for organisational help and to the Institute for International Integration Studies at TCD for its financial support. Thanks are also due to those who have sat through the many conference presentations and seminars given by the authors on aspects of this work in recent years and offered wisdom and encouragement.

Michael Marsh would also like to thank a number of individuals and institutions for support in the initial phase of analysing the data: the Irish Council for the Humanities and Social Sciences (IRCHSS) gave a scholarship to fund sabbatical leave in 2003–04 during which the first drafts of many chapters were written: André Blais provided inspiration and hospitality at the Centre for Electoral Research at the University of Montreal, and Geoff Evans and Chris Wlezien arranged for a research fellowship at Nuffield College, Oxford. He would also like to acknowledge the contribution made by Kathryn Marsh in preserving the English language in some of his text. Richard Sinnott wishes to thank IRCHSS and the European Commissions Fifth and Sixth Framework programmes for their support for a series of studies of voter turnout. He would like to acknowledge his intellectual debts to the participants of those projects.

Earlier versions of Chapters 2 and 8 were first published by Michael Marsh as 'Candidates or Parties? Objects of Electoral Choice in Ireland, *Party Politics* 13(2) (2007): 500–27; Chapter 4 as 'Party Identification in Ireland: An Insecure Anchor for a Floating Party System', *Electoral Studies* 25(3) (2006): 489–508; and Chapter 7 as 'None of your Post-modern Stuff Around here: Grassroots Campaigning in the 2002 Irish General Elections', in Roger Scully *et al.* (ed.), *British Elections and Parties Review*, Vol. 14 (2004), pp. 245–67 (www.informaworld.com). We are grateful to Sage, Elsevier and Taylor & Francis respectively for permission to use material from those publications.

Michael Marsh
Richard Sinnott
John Garry
Fiachra Kennedy

1

Introduction

This book reports the analysis of the first full-scale election study conducted in Ireland.[1] Voting behaviour has by now been the subject of studies in most countries of the democratic world. Such studies address universal questions, such as why people vote, why they vote as they do, and whether their choices vary from election to election or tend to be fairly stable over the long term. There is a very substantial literature that offers general answers to such questions and a book on voting behaviour in Ireland can fruitfully draw on this existing literature and assess how conventional explanations can contribute to an understanding of contemporary Irish voting behaviour. However, there are also several features of Irish elections that make the link between the universal questions and the conventional answers of interest well beyond Ireland. The study of electoral behaviour should aim to extend our understanding not simply by looking more deeply into each election, or by looking at more elections, but by examining elections in a wider variety of contexts so as to better understand the power and limitations of established theories (Marsh, 2002). The Irish context is a rich one for a number of reasons.

The first is that elections in Ireland are fought using an electoral system known as Proportional Representation-Single Transferable Vote (PR-STV).[2] This system was introduced at the foundation of the state, with the aim of maintaining a link between members of parliament (the Dáil) and their constituents, while at the same time allowing for a degree of proportional representation in order to ensure representation of minorities, in particular of the Protestant minority. The PR-STV system employs multi-member districts and voters are asked to rank the candidates on offer within those districts in order of preference. They vote, at least formally, for candidates rather than parties. There is nothing in the ballot or electoral system that forces them to vote on party lines. Nonetheless, the Irish experience has been that candidates have not, for the most part, been independents, but rather have been members of highly disciplined parties. This has been achieved because the electorate has been loyal primarily to parties and also because parties have been sensitive to the voters' desires to support local candidates (Mair, 1987: 67–74). However, the evidence of voting records suggests that party loyalties are declining (Gallagher, 2003: 105). Moreover, non-party candidates ('Independents') have done well in the recent general elections, indicating the difficulties parties have in maintaining their control over the electoral process.

If the Irish electoral system was unique, the study of Irish electoral behaviour might be no more than an interesting activity of no real concern to anyone but the electoral 'anorak'. However, while only one other country uses the STV system for national elections, the system is growing in popularity as an *adoptable* electoral system, a system that several countries are seriously considering implementing.[3] More importantly, the process of electoral system change over the last decade or so in old and new democracies has increased the number of countries using electoral systems that have much in common with the Irish one.[4] Under some electoral systems individual candidates have a strong incentive to differentiate themselves from other candidates in their party and to develop a personal following (Cain et al., 1987). Carey and Shugart (1995) explained how this stimulus would be higher where the vote was cast for a candidate and not a party and where that vote had a significant effect not just on which parties won seats, but on which candidates did so (see also Katz, 1986a; Marsh, 1985b). Many countries use a system of proportional representation that allows voters to choose individuals from a list and, by doing so, to influence and in some cases determine who is elected to fill party seats. In many other countries, the use of separate votes for a constituency candidate and for a regional party list also allows for the clear separation of candidates and their parties. The Irish case may be an extreme one, but it is an extreme case of a widespread and growing institutional phenomenon and so provides an ideal opportunity for the study of the importance of individual candidates who have an incentive to identify themselves as separate from, even if attached to, their parties.

A second significant characteristic of Irish electoral politics is the nature of the party choice offered to voters. The party system is the product of a centre versus periphery cleavage (centre and periphery being understood in a British Isles context) that divided the Irish political parties not into nationalists and anti-nationalists, but into strong nationalists and moderate nationalists. The two major Irish parties – Fianna Fáil and Fine Gael – that emerged from this nationalist struggle do not conform to the European model, where parties are usually distinguishable in terms of being Christian Democratic, Social Democratic, or Liberal. Also, at least until the late 1960s when it began to advocate clearly economically left-wing policies, the long established, but smaller, Irish Labour Party did not really fit into the European mainstream. The sort of class cleavage that typified politics elsewhere was in Ireland

- overshadowed by the nationalist conflict;
- sidelined by the prevailing conservative religious ethos; and
- further marginalised by the decision of the Labour Party not to contest the 1918 election (Sinnott, 1995).

Thus, the social and ideological fault lines that seem to underlie most of the older European party systems have not been seen as very relevant in the Irish case, leading Whyte, in the first systematic analysis of Irish voting behaviour, to observe that Irish politics were 'without social bases' (1974: 619).

While this makes the Irish case unusual in historical terms, the social differentiation that once characterised party systems has declined markedly in most countries over the last half century (Franklin *et al.*, 1992), although this has not been a linear development, and there are countries, and certainly elections within countries, that stand out from this trend. However, there seems little doubt that the sort of social cleavages that Lipset and Rokkan (1967) identified as underpinning party systems in the 1960s, cleavages which had done the job since at least as far back as the 1920s, and often much longer, have lost much of their significance, just as Lipset and Rokkan suggested they might. While all parties have certainly not become 'catch-all' (Kirchheimer, 1966), most now spread their electoral net much more widely than they once did. In such a situation, the Irish experience also becomes far less unusual. As Gallagher (1981) observed, Irish parties were catch-all before the term was invented. For these reasons, a study of how voters choose between such parties has much to offer the wider world of electoral analysis – arguably parties in many countries in the world are increasingly becoming like Irish parties.

A third characteristic of Irish elections reinforces those already mentioned: the electorate is dealigned. That is, the connection between voters and parties is weak. The bond between voters and parties in Europe has typically been seen to be either ideological, or sociological, characterised by the term 'cleavage' (Lipset and Rokkan, 1967; Bartolini and Mair, 1990). Cleavage explanations of voting assert that voting is underpinned by long-standing, well-structured and relatively stable conflicts.

An alternative view of this bond between voters and parties is that it is one of *party attachment*, also known as party identification or partisanship. This concept has been a defining and enduring preoccupation in voting behaviour studies since Campbell *et al.'s The American Voter* (1960). Party attachment is a predisposition towards a political party that would normally manifest itself in a vote for the party in question and that could also act as a filter, excluding or de-emphasising some political signals and highlighting others. The fact that vote can diverge from partisanship has been crucial to the argument, and Converse's (1966: 14) 'normal vote' analysis developed this point. Carty (1983) argues strongly that such identification is a critical factor in explaining voting behaviour in Ireland, precisely because the sort of cleavages established by the civil war have not endured. The party system is in one sense free-floating and it is party attachment that provides an anchor. The same point could be made with respect to the USA. What makes the Irish case so interesting is the evidence that party attachment itself has been declining for some time and by the early 1990s had reached an exceptionally low level. Even allowing for problems with the evidence, which was largely derived from Eurobarometer surveys, it is clear that there has been a substantial decline in party attachment in Ireland over many years (Sinnott, 1995; Mair and Marsh, 2004). By 1994 the Republic of Ireland had the lowest level of attachment to parties among the then twelve member states of the EU (Sinnott, 1998). The electorate thus is increasingly dealigned, free of cleavages and now even of party loyalties, a feature that gives added interest to the potential differentiation of candidates and parties already discussed above.

A fourth interesting feature of the Irish case is that the economy has grown at a remarkable rate since the mid-1990s (Barry, 1999). Ireland has changed from having a huge national debt, high taxation, high unemployment and chronically high levels of emigration, to a country which in 2002 had a low national debt, low direct taxation, low unemployment and, increasingly, significant immigration. Such growth may solve old problems, but it also creates new ones as the public services and planning process has so far failed to keep pace with new demands. While the economic boom certainly predated the 1997 election, many of the benefits were less apparent at that time, with unemployment still over 10 percent. Arguably, the 2002 election was the real political assessment of the legacy of the so-called 'Celtic Tiger'. There are now hundreds of international studies on the importance voters attach to government performance, and particularly to its performance in economic terms (Lewis-Beck and Stegmaier, 2000). From this we would certainly expect that a government that presided over one of the most remarkable economic success stories of the post-war world would be rewarded richly at the polls. However, prior to the election, the air was full of predictions that the election would be decided by the downside of the economic boom (inadequate road network, poor public transport, intolerable traffic congestion and declining quality of life), by healthcare and hospital issues or by politicians and parties being called to account in relation to a number of political scandals. As things turned out, the government was returned with a marginally increased vote, and a lot more seats – a victory, but not perhaps such a large victory as might have been expected. It is thus critical to assess fully how these various issues played out with the electorate.

These four features underline the significance of Ireland in developing our understanding of electoral processes in general. There are some additional features of the Irish case, that mark out Irish elections as particularly rewarding cases for study. The first is the role of political leaders. Election commentary focuses on the party leaders almost everywhere, minutely analysing their performance, dissecting their debates, speculating about their longevity as leaders should the election go badly for their party and, after the election, allocating praise or blame for victory or defeat (Poguntke and Webb, 2005). In Ireland, where more conventional bases for party choice – cleavages or party identification – are weak or absent, leaders might be expected to play a particularly significant role. This is the argument put forward in rather different ways by those who focus on the implications of declining party attachment (Dalton *et al.*, 2000) and declining or absent social cleavages (Kitschelt, 2000).

A further important feature of Irish politics is the style of campaigning: extensive door-to-door canvassing by party workers and the candidates themselves. In Ireland, this feature is strongly related to the electoral system, combining small districts in terms of population with the previously discussed incentives for candidate differentiation. The level of canvassing is exceptionally high in European terms (Karp *et al.*, 2003). It merits further study in itself, but it also demands study in the context of the candidate versus party balance that we have discussed.

Finally, Irish elections are also marked by the fact that a substantial number of electors do not take part in them. Turnout is low, at least by the standards of the well-established European democracies, and is in steady decline. Given the sometimes startling revelations that have emerged from two tribunals of inquiry into what is generically referred to as 'payments to politicians', it would not be surprising to find widespread cynicism and alienation among the electorate (O'Halpin, 2000).

Plausible as this expectation is, we also need to consider the possibility that abstention may not simply be a result of alienation, but may also be related to the dealigment already observed (Wattenberg, 2000).

We begin by homing in on the details of the 2002 election and examining how people voted. We first contrast 2002 with 1997, asking how people voted in the two elections and assessing how far the different outcome was the result of a few voters changing their mind. Given the arguments made above about the lack of the usual underpinnings for a stable party system, how far is electoral choice itself stable? We then move on to look more closely at the manner in which voters made use of the PR-STV system. This provides our first look at the question of candidates versus parties, but we also examine the ways in which people may be said to have voted for the government.

In Chapter 3, we test the conventional wisdom that there is little or no cleavage basis to Irish voting. How valid is Whyte's conclusion, noted above, that Ireland has 'politics without social bases' (1974). Is it really the case that there is no socio-economic or socio-cultural basis to Irish party choice? Our exploration of the possible cleavage basis to Irish voting takes two forms. We begin by focusing on the social bases of voting. One key advantage of using our Irish National Election Study (INES) is that it facilitates a comprehensive and reliable analysis of the possible class basis of Irish voting. The study by Whyte (1974) – in common with almost all subsequent analyses – used as a measure of class the conventional social grades (AB/C1/C2/DE/F) employed by opinion polls. Included in the INES survey is a more appropriate measure of social class. Specifically, we use the Goldthorpe schema, which is widely used internationally in studies of class and voting. Unlike the social grades categories, which are based on income and lifestyle, the Goldthorpe approach takes into account important aspects of a person's position in the labour market: Are they employed or self-employed? How much autonomy do they have at work? Are they in charge of other employees? Using this theoretically grounded measure of social class we explore the class basis of voting in Ireland and assess the extent to which we can uncover a social basis that was not obvious when relying on the less appropriate class measures from the opinion polls.

Next, we assess the extent to which there are ideological underpinnings to voting. Are citizens' political values (or political attitudes) a good predictor of who they vote for? Value conflicts, originating in political and social divisions well before the early twenty-first century, are seen as important determinants of the vote in many countries. Typically, they also help us to understand how social divisions turn into political ones. There has been little opportunity until now to explore the impact of values on Irish electoral behaviour. Opinion polls carry very few, if any, questions on political values and, although academic surveys that have focused extensively on values have been fielded (most notably three waves of the European Values Survey), they have not tended to be carried out close to an election, a time when political competition maximises the correspondence between parties and values.

One approach to take when addressing the question of cleavages is to place Ireland firmly in a comparative perspective and assess the extent to which Lipset and Rokkan's framework for the analysis of party systems and voter alignments in Western Europe applies to the Irish case (Lipset and Rokkan, 1967). They identify a range of cleavages common across European party systems, which relate to divisions arising from economic development and from the development of states. We examine how far underlying divisions or conflicts in the Irish case can be interpreted using this comparative lens and we identify a range of possible cleavages based on attitudes to economic management, Church–state relations and attitudes to Northern Ireland. We also seek to position the Irish case in the context of new political cleavages that have arisen in many democracies in recent years: the materialist–post-materialist cleavage and related attitudes to environmental and quality of life issues (Inglehart, 1977, 1990) and those arising from European integration. The INES survey contains a very wide range of questions covering attitudes to redistribution and privatisation, the EU, the environment, Church–state relations and Northern Ireland.

Asking such a comprehensive range of questions enables us to generate high quality measures of the attitudes in question. When we use these comprehensive measures of underlying attitudes does it emerge that Irish voting is based on values? We also provide, for the first time, a comprehensive assessment of where voters think the parties stand on key attitudinal dimensions. Do they perceive much difference between the parties in terms of views on economic management, the EU, the environment, abortion and Northern Ireland? This discussion about voter and party positions is supplemented using original data on voters' descriptions of their 'image' of each party. Do voters have a clear idea of what each of the parties stands for? Do they share the same ideas of what a party stands for? Is there much variation between parties in terms of what they are perceived to stand for?

In Chapter 4, we move on from our discussion of cleavages to a discussion of the other possible 'long-term' factor shaping Irish voting, namely party identification. We assess the link between this, which is also often referred to as partisanship or party attachment, and vote choice. A voter's party identity is believed to arise out of early adult experience; many voters are brought up – socialised – to believe in one party rather than any other. Thus, in Irish terms, many voters may come from 'a Fianna Fáil family' and many others come from 'a Fine Gael family'. Voters who identify with a party may also vary in terms of the strength of that identity, with some being very strong and others less strong partisans. We explore the extent to which such partisanship is rooted in family background. Is the party that a respondent identifies with also the party that one or other or both of their parents usually voted for? Crucially, we also identify the proportion of voters who have no party identity at all. If this proportion turns out to be high then the usefulness of party identity in terms of explaining vote choice will be fairly minimal.

We also consider the extent to which this concept of party identification is useful in terms of understanding the stability of voter behaviour in Ireland. Are voters who loyally vote for a party at subsequent elections likely to be strong identifiers and are 'switchers' who vote for one party at one election and another party at the next election likely to have either weak or no party identity? The notion of party identification may also help us understand how extensively voters support the candidates of a particular party. One of the key advantages of the INES survey is that respondents were not just asked who they gave their first preference vote to, which is the question usually asked in previous studies. Instead, voters were presented with a mock ballot paper which was essentially the same as the ballot paper used in the election. They were asked to fill in this survey ballot just as they did the real one at election time. Thus, the full ranking of candidates by each respondent is available for analysis. We can, therefore, identify those who vote consecutively for all the candidates of the same party. For example, a Fianna Fáil voter in a constituency with three Fianna Fáil candidates might give their first, second and third preference vote to these three candidates. Alternatively, a voter might give their first preference to one of the Fianna Fáil candidates but then give a second preference to the Labour candidate and then return to their original party to give a third and fourth preference to the two remaining Fianna Fáil candidates. These differences in what Gallagher (1978) called 'party solidarity' are akin to the existence of straight and split ticket voting in many other countries. The level of solidarity has declined over the last 30 years (Gallagher, 2003), but we know little of the individual correlates of different patterns of voting, and what it means for the individuals who vote for all, or only for some of a party's candidates. Knowing the partisanship of voters may help us understand what different types of voters may exist. The INES data allow us to examine to what extent voting a 'straight ticket' is associated with partisanship.

We then turn our attention to 'short-term' factors: influences on vote choice that can change quite fluidly over a fairly short period of time. Specifically, we concentrate on matters relating to government performance on the economy and other issues (Chapter 5), and on the role of party leaders (Chapter 6). Commentators and electoral analysts often lament the low level of political knowledge and political interest voters seem to have. Surely dangerous consequences for the state of democracy must flow from such ignorance and indifference among the voters? Surely a high quality democracy requires the input of a reasonably knowledgeable and sophisticated electorate who choose on the basis of careful consideration of the policy proposals of each of the parties? However, it is now a long time since V. O. Key (1966) argued that while the voters may not know very much, they know enough. Specifically, they are well placed to make rational and coherent decisions about politics once they know whether things are, generally speaking, getting better or worse. If things are going badly in the country then voters will blame the government and it will be ejected from office. If things are going well, the incumbent will be rewarded and will be returned to government office. Placing the issues relating to the Celtic Tiger economy centre stage, Chapter 5 examines the question of policy or issue-voting, and seeks to determine which issues, if any, affected the election outcome. The extensive range of questions that we were able to ask in the survey allows us to test a comprehensive model of party-evaluation voting under which voters would punish the government if they

1 evaluated a state of affairs (such as the economy, or the health service or transport service) as being poor;
2 blamed government policies for the decline;
3 thought someone else would do better.

Conversely, voters would reward a government where a situation had improved as a result of government policy and they thought no other party could have done better.

Another 'short term' electoral factor relates to political leadership. Conventional wisdom would say that party leaders are very important and that to a significant extent the electorate votes on the basis of whether or not they like, or are impressed by, the different party leaders on offer. Many observers suggest that leaders are replacing parties as objects of voter choice, but there is another body of scholarly literature that finds very little evidence to support the idea that they are important (King, 2002). Thus, there is a genuine problem about whether we can reconcile common belief with current evidence. What is the situation in Ireland? Are party leaders important or unimportant? Certainly the governing parties in 2002 were seen to be favoured in that the Fianna Fáil Taoiseach (prime minister) Bertie Ahern and his Progressive Democrat Tánaiste (deputy prime minister), Mary Harney, were both held in high regard by the public, while Michael Noonan, the Fine Gael leader and potential alternative Taoiseach, was held in very low regard.

How far this reflected, rather than determined, levels of party support is another question. We explore leadership effects on voting in Chapter 6. In our analysis we seek to tease out a range of various possible ways in which leaders influence party choice. Following Bean and Mughan (1989) we focus on the perceived competence of leaders as an important factor. Given Ireland's recent history of tribunals of inquiry into alleged wrongdoings by politicians we also assess the impact of voters' perceptions of the relative honesty of each of the main party leaders. Our aim then is twofold: do leaders matter? And, in so far as they do, what is it that matters most – perceptions of their competence or of their honesty?

All of the explanations outlined so far – social characteristics, political attitudes, party identification, policy evaluation and party leaders – are party-based. In Chapter 7 we shift the focus away from parties and back towards candidates by looking not at the election campaign fought by party leaders in the media, but at the activities of local parties and candidates, at the grass roots. The general international trend in campaigning is towards greater control by central party headquarters and towards the increased use of experts at the national, rather than local, level (Norris, 2002; Denver and Hands, 2002). To some extent these centralising trends are observable in Irish campaigning. In 1970, Chubb described centralised Irish campaigning as very limited, but in 2002 Collins observed national party headquarters as having a very significant impact in terms of using focus groups and various other marketing devices, particularly in relation to Fianna Fáil (Chubb, 1970; Collins, 2003).

There are two campaigns: the national and the local. Most analyses have focused on the national level (e.g. Collins, 2003; Brandenburg and Hayden, 2003), but despite the glossy posters of party leaders, the extensive use of opinion poll and focus group research, the central management and the sometimes extensive teams of media watchers and controllers all seeking to shape the agenda, the bulk of campaigning is probably still done at the local rather than the national level. One of the key ways in which the local element is influential relates to candidate selection. The parties place great importance on identifying the appropriate candidates for each constituency and they must do so under quite strict local constraints. Crucially, the local party organisation retains control of who runs where, and there is an overwhelming tendency for them to be local figures (Galligan, 1999, 2003). The essential style of campaigns in Ireland remains personal, with individual candidates seeking to make an impact and doing so for the most part by the traditional method of meeting 'the people'. This typically involves knocking on doors, distributing leaflets, putting up posters and canvassing at shopping centres, railway stations and the like. Several international studies have highlighted the importance of local campaigning (Bochel and Denver, 1971; Gerber and Green, 2000; Denver *et al.*, 2002). Evidence in the Irish case is rare (but see Gallagher and Marsh, 2002; and Benoit and Marsh, 2006). We carry out a systematic analysis of what happens locally once the election is called. Our main concern is to explore a key feature of Irish local campaigning about which very little is currently known: what exactly is the impact of local campaigning and, in particular, what exactly is the impact of local campaigning by the individual candidates?

This leads us to look more closely at the candidates as objects of electoral support, and even loyalty (Chapter 8), returning fully to the question about the importance of candidates first addressed in Chapter 2. Typically, analyses of voting behaviour in any given country focus on parties and ask why some vote for one particular party and others for a different one. In many countries there might be a 'personal' aspect to the vote, some sense of connection between the voter and the particular candidate who they want to represent them, but, by and large, it is the connection between the voter and a party that is seen as being of crucial importance. As in other countries, political parties are important in Ireland; they are highly disciplined in the Dáil and are the crucial building blocks of government. It is parties that are commonly regarded as important in terms of voter choice and voters at election time are typically described as choosing between the parties contesting the election. However, individual candidates play an important electoral role. We explore, in much greater detail than has previously been possible, the relative importance of party and candidate. Their relative importance has implications for our evaluation of the quality or otherwise of the democratic process. If people vote for candidates and not for parties then it is difficult to interpret elections as approving, or legitimising, a particular government.

We then bring together all aspects of vote choice in Chapter 9, where we carry out multivariate analyses of both party and candidate choice, using as explanatory variables the factors discussed in earlier chapters. Multivariate analysis is one in which the impact of several explanations of vote choice can be assessed simultaneously. This is done in order to deal with the fact that several of our explanatory variables (such as age and religiosity, or attachment and judgements of competence) may be quite strongly related to each other. Such inter-relationships lead to the problem that the unique impact of each explanatory variable can only be isolated in the context of an analysis in which the effects of all explanatory variables are assessed simultaneously, thus controlling for the inter-relationships. For each party in turn, we assess, in a single comprehensive model, the influence of our range of party-based explanatory factors. This allows us to do two things.

First, such an analysis enables us to get a sense of the relative importance of all the explanatory factors. Which particular explanations of voting are most powerful if we control other explanations? Second, this multivariate analysis allows us to assess the extent to which a model containing party related factors works much better on some voters than on others. Specifically, we use a party-oriented versus candidate-oriented index, developed in Chapter 8, to explore whether party based models perform much better when applied only to those voters who are party-oriented rather than candidate-oriented. The behaviour of those who are party-oriented may be relatively well explained by conventional party based models of electoral behaviour. For candidate-oriented voters it may be that different sets of explanatory variables, firmly based on candidate characteristics, have to be used in order to explain the variation in their vote choice successfully. Thus, in a separate analysis, we focus explicitly on candidate choice and assess the relative importance of a range of explanations for one candidate being preferred to another.

Notes

1 Full details of the survey can be found in Appendix I.
2 The electoral system is described in more detail in Appendix II.
3 STV was approved by 58 percent of voters in a referendum in British Columbia, but was not adopted as the required 60 percent was not obtained. It will be considered again in 2008. It has also been adopted recently for local elections in Scotland and New Zealand.
4 A review in 2004 identified 10 states with such strong preferential voting (Chile, Cyprus, Estonia, Finland, Greece, Liechtenstein, Luxembourg,

Poland, San Marino and Switzerland, plus a further four with candidate votes that are not automatically pooled at party level: Ireland, Malta, Mauritius and Vanuatu (Karvonen, 2004: 208). Shugart also includes Brazil and Peru, but sees Estonia's list system as more strongly determined by party ordering. In addition, recent changes have increased the importance of the preferential vote in Austria and Belgium (Shugart, 2005: 41–3).

2

How people voted

The primary function of this book is to attempt to answer the question: *why* do people vote the way they do? However, we must also address the question of the vote itself: *how* did people vote? We know what the result was and how many first preference votes were cast for the different parties, but in the Irish system there is so much more to know in terms of the full range of preferences expressed. Moreover, that knowledge gives us important guidance in making sense of the result. In simple electoral systems – such as the plurality system used in UK general elections, or many of the systems of proportional representation used across Europe – to ask how people voted would seem an unnecessary question as voters simply put a tick beside the party they wish to vote for. The Irish Proportional Representation (Single Transferable Vote) system is a good deal more complex, with voters allowed to indicate a preference for a wide array of candidates. Large parties typically nominate a number of candidates to run in a given constituency, so voters may choose not merely between parties but also between a numbers of candidates from within the same party. In many constituencies there are also Independent candidates, who are not nominated by any party. Voters rank the candidates on the ballot paper. They give a '1' (first preference vote) to the candidate they most prefer, a '2' (second preference vote) to their second favourite candidate, and so on down the list of candidates (as far as they want to go).[1]

We explore here some key features of *how* voters voted in the 2002 election: what were the choices on offer and what was the extent of the preferences indicated? One particular aspect studied relates to whether there is any evidence of what may be termed 'government voting'. Did voters who gave a first preference to one of the two governing parties (Progressive Democrats and Fianna Fáil) tend to give a second preference to the other governing party subsequently?

One of the key stories of the 2002 election was the re-election of the government, something that very rarely happens in Irish politics these days. In fact, an incumbent government had not been returned by the Irish electorate since 1969. Examining the relationship between first and subsequent party preferences will give us some indication as to whether the return of the Fianna Fáil–Progressive Democrats coalition was deliberately intended by many voters, and particularly by Fianna Fáil and Progressive Democrats voters, or was simply the result of other factors such as people voting for parties independently of each other, or perhaps voters not voting on the basis of party considerations at all but rather on the basis of candidate-related factors.

The result of the 2002 Irish election can be simply summarised. The incumbent minority government was returned with a decisive majority. Fianna Fáil and its small coalition partner – the Progressive Democrats – each won more seats, with Fianna Fáil pushing its vote up from 39.3 to 41.5 percent, its highest share since 1989, and the Progressive Democrat party doubling its seat total to 8 with a marginally smaller share of the vote. The main opposition parties did poorly, with Fine Gael losing 5.5 percent of the vote and dropping to its lowest level of support since 1948. Even worse, its Dáil contingent was reduced by more than a third, as 23 seats out of 54 were lost. Labour stood fairly still, but even that was a considerable disappointment as the previous election had seen a big swing against the party and it had hoped to retrieve some of the ground lost in 1997, aided by a merger with Democratic Left. There were important gains by the smaller parties and by Independents. The Greens won four more seats with a slightly increased share of the vote, while Sinn Féin also won four new seats, and increased its vote share to 6.5 percent, making it the fourth largest party. Non-party or Independent candidates also did well, gathering more than 10 percent of all votes cast and obtaining 14 of the 166 seats.

Voting in 1997 and 2002

We start by establishing some estimates of the stability of vote choice, putting to one side the question of the use of single transferable vote and the expression of lower preferences and asking simply about first preferences and how these changed from the previous election in 1997. Respondents to the 2002 election study were asked whether or not they voted in 1997 and, if they did vote, which party they supported. Table 2.1 shows the pattern of response by vote in 2002.[2] First, there are the 34 percent who voted the same way in both elections, to which we can add the 22 percent who did not vote in either of them. Next are the 12 percent who voted in both elections, but who switched their party preference between the two elections. Finally, there are the 32 percent

The Irish voter

Table 2.1 Voting and non-voting in 2002, by voting
and non-voting in 1997

2002	FF	FG	Green	Lab	PD	SF	Ind	Did not vote	Total
				Recalled vote in 1997					
FF	15.3	1.4	0.2	0.6	0.2	0.1	1.2	6.7	25.6
FG	1.0	9.2	0.1	0.3	0.2	0.0	0.1	3.0	13.9
Green	0.1	0.1	0.8	0.4	0.0	0.0	0.2	0.7	2.3
Lab	0.2	0.5	0.0	3.6	0.3	0.0	0.3	1.7	6.6
PD	0.4	0.4	0.0	0.2	0.8	0.0	0.0	0.6	2.4
SF	0.6	0.0	0.1	0.2	0.0	1.3	0.2	1.7	4.0
Ind	0.7	0.7	0.2	0.3	0.0	0.1	2.8	1.9	6.6
Did not vote	6.3	4.8	0.5	2.5	1.4	0.1	1.3	21.7	38.6
Total	24.4	17.0	1.8	8.0	3.0	1.6	6.1	38.1	100.0

Note: the data are weighted so that the table marginals reflect the 1997 and
2002 results.

who moved between voting and non-voting. Obviously, any change
between 1997 and 2002 has to come from only two of those groups,
those who switched allegiance, and those who moved into, or out of
the group of those voting. This means that 56 percent of voters in 2002
were doing what they had done in 1997, but that a large minority,
44 percent, were behaving differently – at least if we assume that the
electorate is constant (we return to this point later).[3]

There is a strong element of stability in the vote, but a strong element
too of instability. This balance of stability and instability also applies
to turnout. While many, indeed a majority, voted in at least one election, there is a very significant number who seem to drop in and out
of voting. It is hard to pin down effectively the numbers who do so as
we cannot be sure what the turnover is in the electorate.[4] If we allow
for the fact that around 10 percent of our transition matrix effectively
comprises people who could only vote on one occasion, we can see
that stability may be underestimated. However, it is also the case that
recalled vote has a stability bias: panel data, where we have independent
accounts of voting on both occasions, tend to show more instability.

How did these patterns of stability and change affect the 2002
result? Looking first at stability, in each row and column we can see
that the highest figure is that which indicates those who behaved in the
same way on both occasions. Stable voters thus make the largest single
contribution to each party's support, and all parties are more likely to

have retained voters from 1997 than to have lost them to another party
or to abstention. This does not mean most support is stable. If we read
across the rows and ask how great a contribution to each party's vote
share is made by its its stable voters, we see Fine Gael, Fianna Fáil
and then Labour appearing more stable than the smaller parties and
Independents/others. If we ask a slightly different question and look at
the extent to which each party *retained* its 1997 support, we get a
fairly similar answer, although there are striking differences with respect to two smaller parties. The Progressive Democrat party kept only
a quarter and Sinn Féin kept three quarters of their respective 1997
supporters.[5] There is a mathematically generated tendency in tables like
these to show larger parties as being slightly more stable (van der Eijk
and Niemoller, 1983: 103) even when each party loses the same proportion of voters, but the Progressive Democrats turnover is still large
while Sinn Féin's stability is doubly impressive.

Table 2.2 shows the contribution of the different sorts of change to
the result. It indicates the net effect on its support of party switching
and of differential turnout for each party. These numbers indicate shares
of the electorate, not shares of the vote. They are smaller than the more
familiar shares of the vote and would need to be adjusted upwards by
a factor of approximately 1.6. In the case of Fianna Fáil, we see that
the party gained a net 0.7 percent of the electorate due to party switching and a further 0.4 percent through what we have called turnout
differences and that this adds up to 1.1 percent overall.[6] Vote switching
and turnout change each make similar contributions to overall support
for Fine Gael and Labour. The Progressive Democrats gained little from
vote switching and lost due to turnout changes. The fact that they ran
fewer candidates may be a factor here. Sinn Féin gained rather more
from turnout than from switching, a result that suggests that those who
see Sinn Féin as mobilising new voters may be right. The same seems
to be true of Independents. Overall, though, we see that the net effects
from each process are small. Nowhere are they much above 2 percent

Table 2.2 Impact of different types of change on party support in 2002

	FF	FG	Green	Lab	PD	SF	Ind
Net gains from vote switching	0.7	−1.4	0.9	−0.7	0.9	0.8	0.0
Net gains from turnout	0.4	−1.8	0.2	−0.8	−0.8	1.6	0.6
Overall net gain	1.1	−3.2	1.1	−1.5	0.1	2.4	0.6

Note: calculated from Table 2.1.

of the electorate, but the changes in party support were also, of course, quite small for the most part.

Choice options and number of preferences

It emerges that 32 percent of respondents were offered what may be regarded as a 'full choice' on the ballot paper in 2002:[7] nominees from *all* of the six main political parties (Fianna Fáil, Fine Gael, the Labour Party, the Green Party, the Progressive Democrats and Sinn Féin) as well as independent candidates and one or more small, or micro, parties.[8] A further 31 percent were presented at election time with a choice between all these options except the Progressive Democrats. The remaining 37 percent of respondents were faced with one or other of a range of possible options (see Table 2.3). Most notably, for 11 percent, the options on the ballot were the two big parties as well as Labour, Sinn Féin and a micro party/Independents.

Most voters were also offered considerable choice *within* some parties. Typically, Fianna Fáil put up three candidates and Fine Gael two. The other parties (except the Progressive Democrats) tended to nominate one and there were usually three independents or others. Labour did nominate more than one candidate in several constituencies, normally where Democratic Left, which had merged with Labour during the 1997–2002 parliamentary term, had an incumbent Teachta Dála (TD). This allowed 17 percent of voters a choice between Labour Party

Table 2.3   Voters' options

	Sample %
All	32
All but PDs	31
FF FG Labour SF Other	14
FF FG Labour Other	4
FF FG Labour Green PD Other	4
FF FG Green PD SF Other	4
FF FG Green SF Other	3
FF FG Labour PD Other	2
FF FG Labour Green Other	2
FF FG Green Other	2
FF FG Labour Green PD	2

Note: voters only.

candidates. Usually, voters were given the option of expressing preferences across several parties as well as across candidates from the two largest parties.

Given these options, and the freedom to rank many candidates, what did voters do? Only 6 percent of them cast what may be termed 'a minimal ballot', giving just a first preference. The overwhelming majority of voters took advantage of the provisions of the PR-STV system to express at least a second preference. The average number of preferences expressed was 3.9, a figure inflated by the fact that a few expressed a dozen or more. Where there are more candidates, voters tend to give more preferences. Where between six and nine candidates stand, the average number of preferences expressed is less than four; where 10 or more stand it is (with one exception) greater than four (see Table 2.4). Just under 8 percent of voters expressed preferences for all available candidates, a practice more common where there were fewer candidates; the six constituencies with only six or seven candidates (representing just 12 percent of respondents) account for over 30 percent of such ballots.[9]

With some parties nominating several candidates it could be that the average voter ranks only the candidates of a single party and does not go on to vote for those of any other party. If this were true it would suggest that candidates themselves were subsidiary to party in the minds of most voters, but in fact most voters do vote for candidates from more than one party. This is evident in Table 2.5, which shows the average number of parties voted for according to the options provided

Table 2.4 Average number of candidate preferences cast by length of ballot

Candidates on the ballot	Average number of preference votes	N
6	3.5	50
7	3.8	64
8	3.2	71
9	3.3	80
10	4.3	113
11	4.6	88
12	3.9	94
13	4.7	28
14	4.0	185
15	4.3	164
17	4.7	65
All	3.9	1808

Table 2.5 Numbers of different parties voted for
by number of options (%)

	3	4	5	6	7	All
			Number of parties standing			
1	32	23	16	17	17	18
2	48	31	37	35	30	34
3	20	26	28	27	31	28
4		20	6	9	14	10
5			13	4	3	5
6				8	2	4
7					4	1
Total	100	100	100	100	100	100
Average	2.0	2.7	2.7	2.9	3.0	2.8
N	29	139	466	645	529	1808

(micro parties are grouped with Independents). For example, when there
are three parties standing in a constituency, 32 percent of voters merely
indicate a preference (or preferences) for candidates of one party and
have nothing to do with any other party. But most voters indicate a
preference for candidates from more than one party. Almost half give
a vote at some stage in their ballot to candidates from a second party.
One fifth of voters give preferences to all three parties. It is again
apparent that as the number of parties increases so does the number
given a preference vote of some kind. For instance, when there are five,
six or seven parties standing in a constituency only 16 or 17 percent of
voters plump for a single party. However, a majority of voters express
a preference for more than two parties only when all seven party options
are available – which, as we have seen, is the case in only about one
third of instances.

Table 2.6 shows which parties win these successive preferences, allowing us to examine across parties the distributions of votes for second,
third and fourth parties and so on.[10] Lower party preferences are certainly distributed more evenly than is the case with first preferences.
Fianna Fáil – necessarily perhaps – does not dominate second and third
choices as it does first ones. Even so, the party does very well out of
second party preferences given that only 58 percent have not already
voted for them. Twenty-one percent of the support of the remainder (at
least of those who have a second party preference) constitutes a remarkable tally. Almost two-thirds of voters give support to Fianna Fáil as

Table 2.6 Distributions of successive party preferences

	First choice party	Second choice party	Third choice party	Fourth choice party	Fifth choice party	Sixth choice party	Seventh choice party	Eighth choice party	Any choice
FF	42	21	17	14	9	9	10	0	72
FG	23	20	19	11	8	12	19	8	53
Labour	11	19	17	17	16	8	0	13	41
Ind	9	17	16	21	22	13	2	3	38
Greens	4	8	13	17	16	9	13	8	23
SF	7	7	6	7	11	13	21	39	20
PDs	4	7	7	7	4	14	13	9	16
Others	2	2	5	6	13	34	22	18	12
N	1837	1652	997	428	218	113	66	44	

their first or second party. Irish politics has often been described as being fought between Fianna Fáil and the rest, but this is not at all apparent here. In 1997 and again in 2002, the aggregate figures suggest Fianna Fáil did much better out of transferred votes than in previous years, not so much because they attracted more lower preferences than other parties, but because they started to pick up as many as other parties. These figures underline this pattern and show how hard it is for other parties' candidates to make up the deficit on Fianna Fáil candidates after the initial counts. Transfers still cost Fianna Fáil a net 5 seats in 2002, but in 1992 they cost the party 15 seats (see Gallagher, 2003, 1993).

Labour and Independents are relatively successful at winning second and third party preferences (that is, second and third preferences for a candidate with a different party label – we will refer to these as second *party* preferences). Each is much more popular as a second choice than as a first choice. The same is true for the Progressive Democrats and Greens. Fine Gael is less successful but, like Fianna Fáil, its initial share is larger. Of the smaller parties, Sinn Féin does relatively badly at attracting second preferences. This helps explain why this party won a smaller proportion of seats than of votes in 2002. It is also notable that Sinn Féin and the small group of 'other' minor parties appear much more often as the low preferences, a standing which suggests an antipathy towards them by some voters who will complete the ballot paper in order to put their candidates in the bottom places. Fine Gael is also prominent among sixth and seventh choices, so for a small group of voters it too is an object of considerable disapproval.

Also shown in Table 2.6 is the total share of all preference votes won by each party as a percent of those voting. Fianna Fáil gets a vote from

72 percent of all voters, Fine Gael from 53 percent and Labour from almost 40 percent. It is important to understand what this means. Fianna Fáil is clearly very popular, but not all mentions are favourable. The fact that a party attracts lower preference votes – particular those for a fourth or fifth party – may indicate its unpopularity as voters take the opportunity to place it firmly near the bottom of the pile. A high number of preferences indicates that a particular party is salient to most voters, rather than that it is popular. It is necessary to look closely at the stages at which that party wins its lower preferences – is it the second, third or fourth party? In the case of Fianna Fáil, it is clear that its preferences stem overwhelmingly from popularity.

Party solidarity

So far we have seen that most voters give several preference votes and that most give some measure of support to the candidates of more than one party. This makes the Irish case very unusual in comparative terms. Voting tends to mean ranking one party or candidate above all others. Those who study voting get little information as to what a voter thinks about the other parties from their choice. However, in the Irish case, thanks to the sophistication of the options offered by the STV system, we do know something of the ordering of parties in the voter's mind. We also get some indication of how strong the commitment to any one party is, at least where a party fielded more than one candidate, since we can see how many of a party's candidates are supported, and whether they are supported before those of any other party. This tells us something about how voters see the respective parties, but also it suggests that the voter is not choosing parties at all, but instead is selecting candidates. The ballot itself does not provide as much help to those who want to vote on party lines as it might. Certainly it would facilitate, and even encourage, party voting if it were structured in a series of columns, by party, as it is in other, similarly preferential electoral systems, rather than as an alphabetically ordered long ballot (see Darcy and Marsh, 1994). Party names have been on the ballot since 1965, and party logos now also appear, but the voter will still have to scan a list of around a dozen or more candidates carefully if he is to organise all his preferences along party lines.

How would people mark their ballot if party were to be the dominant criterion? There has been considerable analysis of the patterns of voting using the aggregate material at constituency level available from official results (see for instance Gallagher, 1978, 1993, 1999, 2003; and Sinnott, 1995). However, the information this gives is limited to those votes that do transfer, either when a candidate is eliminated or when a candidate has more votes than he or she needs to be elected. Moreover, the original preference of those voters whose vote is transferring can soon be obscured. Ideally, we would know how each voter voted and this is what our simulated ballot tells us. In a pioneering analysis of such data, drawn from European Parliament elections and by-elections, Bowler and Farrell (1991a, 1991b) discussed how the information from simulated ballots could shed light on the importance of party (see also King, 2000). The strongest sign that party matters would be that whenever a voter voted for a candidate he subsequently voted for all the other candidates of that candidate's party in sequence. In other words, the ballot record would show no sign that candidate was ever more important than party. This would be a 'pure' party preference structure. Candidates could well matter, but only nested within party preference.

Whether or not support should also be confined to one party is a matter for debate. Bowler and Farrell (1991a, 1991b) question whether partisan voting, as envisaged by American and British students of electoral behaviour, is really compatible with voting for several parties, but this is another matter. Certainly there is an important strand in current research on voting behaviour that argues for a much more nuanced view of voter-party relationships (van der Eijk *et al.*, 2006). What is clear is that someone who votes for all the candidates of Fianna Fáil, followed by those of Fine Gael, followed by those of Labour is voting on party grounds just as much as someone who stops after Fianna Fáil. A similar, if weaker, sign would be that all the running mates of the first placed candidate would be supported before any other candidate. Bowler and Farrell called this an 'unravelling' party vote, in the sense that a single set of party preferences comes first, and then a mixture of candidate and party preferences may follow for the less significant votes. Weaker still is what Laver (2004), in an analysis of the full record from the three constituencies using electronic voting in 2002, has called 'complete' party votes, where all of a party's candidates receive a preference vote, even if these are not cast in sequence.

This approach infers the importance of party for the voter from a preference pattern that favours a particular party's candidates. One problem in applying this sort of framework is that where a party runs a single candidate it is not possible to see any difference between a party vote and a personal vote. Someone who picks the sole Labour candidate as No. 1, the sole Green as No. 2 and the sole Progressive Democrat as No. 3 may be voting on party grounds, but may also be choosing on some other basis. We cannot tell simply on the basis of the simulated ballot. We can analyse voting patterns where a party fields

Table 2.7 Patterns of sequential and complete party voting
in multi-candidate situations (%)

	First preference vote		
	Fianna Fáil	Fine Gael	Labour
Voting for all the candidates of first preference party in sequence	51	38	31
Voting for all the candidates of first preference party	65	58	52

Note: table includes only instances where a party fielded more than one candidate.

more than a single candidate and generalise from that situation to others. This is not wholly unproblematic since most multi-candidate situations involve either Fianna Fáil or Fine Gael and their voters may be more loyal, more party-centred, than those of other parties. However, some contrasts between Fianna Fáil, Fine Gael and Labour are apparent and will be considered when generalisations are made to the wider electorate.

Table 2.7 examines the patterns of voting in situations where a party fields more than one candidate and so allows voters to show what Gallagher (1981) called 'solidarity' – a vote for all a party's candidates in sequence. It also shows the proportions of voters who cast a complete vote for their first preference party: 51 percent of voters giving their first preference to Fianna Fáil cast a complete, and sequential, ballot – a classic 'straight ticket'. The figure is lower for the other parties. However, a majority of voters vote for all of the candidates fielded by their first preference party. Moreover, many of the departures from a strict sequence are small, involving the interpolation of a single candidate. Overall, a majority of first preference votes for parties translate into votes for the whole party slate, and the majority of the latter are cast in sequence. It should be remembered that this is based on the behaviour of two-thirds of those voting and it may be that, were more parties to run more than one candidate this figure would fall.

Government voting

Most voters support more than one party. As indicated earlier, this shows the election analyst something more than simply which party was ranked first. It also conveys information on the voter's attitude to the other parties. Most voters do not feel it worthwhile to rank all parties or candidates but, to the extent that they do rank at least two parties, we can ask whether there are common patterns in the pairs of choices. Is there, for instance, a tendency for voters of one party to give a second party preference to another particular party (and vice versa) or is there no obvious pattern? Certainly, if candidates were primary in the voters' calculations we would see little of such a pattern. If parties were primary we would expect to see Fianna Fáil and the Progressive Democrats, fighting on their record in government, or Fine Gael and Labour, commonly government partners, attracting one another's supporters in relatively large numbers.

Table 2.8 shows the eight most popular combinations, first for all voters and then for that subgroup of voters who were given a full slate to pick from. As might be expected in view of Fianna Fáil's dominance, the most common pairs tend to include Fianna Fáil. The largest set of voters are those who give at least one vote to Fianna Fáil, but give no support to any other party – the pattern known as 'plumping', always considered to be particularly common among voters of that party. Fianna Fáil's traditional anti-coalition stance has been seen as encouraging this form of behaviour and it persists despite the pragmatic abandonment of the principle in 1989 (see Laver and Arkins, 1990; and Farrell, 1990).

Next most common is the Fianna Fáil/Fine Gael sequence and the Fine Gael/Fianna Fáil sequence. Seventeen percent of all voters select this pair of parties in one order or another. The frequency of this pattern is perhaps unexpected, in as much as these two parties, despite their similarity, are the twin poles of alternative governments and might

Table 2.8 Most common patterns of party choice

First party	Second party	All constituencies %	Constituencies where all parties stood %
FF	None	11.3	9.8
FF	FG	9.1	5.9
FG	FF	7.9	5.8
FF	Independent	6.7	3.0
FF	Labour	6.5	3.4
FG	Labour	4.7	2.6
FG	None	3.7	2.9
FF	PD	3.0	6.9
All other pairs		47.1	59.7

have been expected to be almost mutually exclusive in electoral terms. This is obviously not the case. Not only do many observers see the parties as close (and our analysis in Chapter 3 will analyse their proximity further), but it appears that many electors also prefer both to any others. In contrast, only 5 percent voted for Fianna Fáil and the Progressive Democrats as their first two parties, and only 12 percent for any two of the putative Rainbow Coalition of Fine Gael, Labour and Greens. Of course these choices were not always available. Table 2.8 also shows the combinations picked when all options were available. Most notable here is that the Fianna Fáil/Progressive Democrats option is much more popular, with 7 percent voting (1) Fianna Fáil and (2) Progressive Democrats; and 4 percent (1) Progressive Democrats and (2) Fianna Fáil. Fianna Fáil voters in such constituencies were more likely to transfer to the Progressive Democrats than to any other party, but the number doing so was still a relatively small minority of Fianna Fáil voters and more voted for no other party than selected a Progressive Democrat candidate. The 'Rainbow' options again attracted only 12 percent, with Fine Gael voters choosing to give no further preferences rather to than voting Labour.

While there is a pattern here then, it is obviously not a strong one. The top eight options in Table 2.8 account for a little over 50 percent of all voters; the figure falls to 40 percent in constituencies where all options are possible. What this means is that knowledge of the party to which a voter gives a first preference provides little indication of the destination of the second party preference. One measure of 'predictability' of this sort, Kendall's tau, records a score of only 17 against a minimum of zero and maximum of 100.

The election of 2002 did not provide a very clear context for patterns of party choice, since the Rainbow parties were very loose allies and even the Progressive Democrats and Fianna Fáil ran quite separate campaigns. In addition, the possibility of an overall Fianna Fáil majority might have made the (1) Progressive Democrats (2) Fianna Fáil sequence less attractive. There is another possibility. The ordering of preferences can differ across voters even though each is determined by exactly the same perception of parties. If voters support the party closest to them on a single underlying dimension, then support the next closest and so on, this would give a varied set of paired votes which might look as if there was nothing regular about the overall pattern. A strong underlying structure of this sort would imply that those who voted, for instance, for Fianna Fáil should divide their second preferences between those parties either side of it. The same would be true in the case of any other party. However, while the transfers suggest some ordering, it is obviously not a clear one. Looking just at those constituencies in which all parties fielded a candidate, all Fianna Fáil voters divide almost equally between Progressive Democrats (21 percent) and Fine Gael (18 percent), but, leaving aside the 31 percent who give no second party preference, another 30 percent divide across the remaining parties. Much the same is true of Fine Gael. Fianna Fáil gets 34 percent of the second preferences and the Progressive Democrats 16 percent, with 16 percent also going to Labour and 33 percent to other parties. In the case of Labour only 57 percent of second preferences go to two, possibly adjacent, parties. Arguably Independents complicate matters as they vary by constituency, but even if we left them out altogether, and left out the 'plumpers', only two-thirds of second preferences go to two parties and the further third is spread across three more. These sort of patterns can be explored systematically using a technique known as 'unfolding', examining the whole set of voter preference orderings to see how well they fit such a deterministic pattern. Analyses of this sort on Irish data do suggest some underlying pattern, but it is a comparatively weak one (Marsh, 2006; see also van der Brug *et al.*, 2000).

What would account for the lack of any strong pattern? There are several possibilities. The first is that each voter has a different view of what issues are important, and the second is that there is little uniformity of opinion on what the different parties stand for (see Chapter 3), or of their perceived capabilities (Chapters 5 and 6). A third possible reason is that many voters may look at the candidate rather than the party. The first two of these interpretations would suggest that while parties are very salient, the party system is not doing a good job for electoral democracy. Parties, in democratic theory, are supposed to simplify the electoral decision for voters and to promote a democratic decision via the aggregation of party preferences. However, if people support a party for very different reasons, and perhaps even for reasons that are contradictory, it is not clear that an election can convey any clear message beyond: put party X in charge. The third interpretation, which suggests that parties are not salient, and that candidates are the attraction, would mean that the message of any election for the composition and mandate of a government is even less clear.

We take up this last possibility in Chapter 8. First, we explore the party side of voting, assessing a number of possible explanations why people support a particular party in the light of the evidence we have from our survey. Initially, in Chapters 3 and 4, we examine explanations that emphasise the relatively enduring nature of partisan commitments. According to these explanations parties are seen in terms of enduring patterns of political conflict within Irish society, which themselves give rise to loyalties which may endure across generations. We look at what sort of people vote for the different parties, their values, and the images they have of the parties, as well as at the evidence that voters have long-term commitments to a particular party. Then we move on to look at those explanations which deal more with change between elections as government parties run on their record and opposition parties do their best to expose that record as inadequate. Many observers feel that leadership matters a lot here; many also feel that the activities of parties and candidates 'on the ground' may also be critical. Hence, we look at respondents' evaluations of the issues, the leaders and the local campaigns for evidence of the extent to which each was important in 2002. Then we turn to the consideration of the candidates themselves and assess the evidence that many, if not most, voters are much more interested in picking a local candidate to represent their needs than selecting a government and a Taoiseach to run the country.

Notes

1 More detail on the electoral system is given in Appendix II.
2 We have weighted this analysis so as to ensure the marginals for the table, the party vote shares and turnout in 1997 and in 2002, are accurate. This was done using the routine 'surwgt' within Stata. Those who could not remember whether or not they had voted, or were unsure of who they voted for, were excluded from the analysis.
3 This gives us a matrix showing the transition of votes (and no votes) from 1997 to 2002. This is a simplification since it pictures the electorate as fixed from 1997 to 2002. Obviously, we cannot reconstruct the 1997 electorate, some of whom would have died, or gone off the electoral register for 2002 and could not form part of our 2002 sample. There are also those in the 2002 sample who for one reason or another – generally on the grounds of age – were ineligible to vote in 1997. Even so, it allows us to see the contribution that is made to the 2002 outcome by three separate groups of voters.
4 However, over 9 percent of our 2002 sample were too young to vote in 2002 when the electorate was also expanded by net migration, or at least returning emigrants, who made up 2 percent of our sample. In fact, the 2002 electorate is about 9 percent larger than the 1997 electorate (2,744,000 up to 3,000,000). The gains would have been discounted somewhat by losses, with about 4 percent of the 1997 electorate lost through death. But this would still mean that a substantial proportion did make some kind of decision to vote in one election but not in the other. We take up the question of why they might do so, and of why a larger number did not vote in either election, in Chapter 10.

5   This does not change much if we look only at those constituencies running a PD candidate in 2002.

6   It appears as 1.2 percent in the marginals. The difference is due to rounding errors.

7   These figures reflect perfectly the figures in the official results, as 32 percent of voters were from constituencies in which there was a complete choice. The same figures show a further 30 percent were given a choice of all but the PDs, compared with 31 in our survey. Eighteen percent were confronted with all but the PDs and Greens, compared with only 14 percent in our sample.

8   All respondents were provided with something very like the ballot they would have been faced with on Election Day and asked to fill it in as they did at that time or, in the case of those who said they did not vote, how they would have done had they voted. They were also offered the option of filling in the ballot and placing in a sealed envelope. In all, 86 percent of all respondents and 91 percent of those who voted completed the ballot. We should be a little sceptical about how well people can remember exactly how they voted, given that many preferences might be expressed. Obviously many people may misremember details. However, it is assumed here that people filled in these using the same rationale and it is this that is of most interest here. However, our ballots lacked the candidate photographs and party logos of the real thing, though they did feature clearly party names. They thus resembled closely the pre-2002 style of ballot. Three constituencies used electronic voting machines but voters in those districts were given the same information and asked to make the same judgements as those voters using the old-fashioned methods.

9   It is worth comparing these figures with those from the full record of electronic voting in three constituencies at the same election. These were analysed by Laver (2004) who found the average number of preferences cast was 4.7 in Meath (12 candidates), 4.4 in Dublin West (9 candidates) and 5.0 in Dublin North (14 candidates). On average this is almost one candidate more than is estimated from the election survey, a difference outside the bounds of expected sampling error but in line with previous work using simulated ballots (Bowler and Farrell, 1991a, 1991b). However, Laver also found that about eight percent completed the whole ballot, figures ranging from four percent (in Meath) to 13 percent in Dublin West, a figure in line with that estimated here. Moreover, the most common number of preferences is three, as Laver found, a figure which is characteristic irrespective of constituency size. (The only exception was the set of three eleven-candidate constituencies where the modal number was 4.) Overall, we can have a reasonable level of confidence in the evidence from the simulated ballot, subject to the proviso that many people in practice would give one more vote in a real election. The advantage of the survey data, of course, is that it also gives information about

the individual voters themselves which can provide evidence for why people behaved as they did.

10   It is important to stress that these figures do not summarise second and third preferences as such but only lower preferences *when they are cast for a different party*. In fact, 82 percent vote for at least two parties and 48 percent for at least three, although only 1 percent vote for all seven parties and groupings.

3

The evidence for cleavage politics

The question of the impact of socio-economic or socio-cultural cleavages on vote choice in Ireland provides a prime example of the way in which analysis of the Irish case often gives a particular twist to a universal theme in the international research on electoral behaviour. In this instance the twist arises from the *prima facie* impression that, in stark contrast to many other countries, cleavages play no role in determining Irish voting behaviour. The no-cleavages interpretation, famously captured in Whyte's 'politics without social bases' phrase, is bolstered by the manifest electoral weakness of socialism in Ireland, a puzzle that has preoccupied political scientists for decades (Whyte, 1974; for an overview see Mair, 1992).

Is it in fact the case that Irish politics really is unusual? Does Ireland have politics without social bases? This begs the question of what we mean by 'social bases' and, more broadly, of how we go about identifying which bases or which cleavages to expect in particular cases. The, now standard, answer to this question in the Irish case is to apply the Lipset and Rokkan (1967) framework for the analysis of party systems and voter alignments in Western Europe.[1] Doing so leads to a number of key observations. The first is that the dominant cleavage at the foundation of the party system was a centre versus periphery cleavage (centre and periphery being understood in a British Isles context) that divided the Irish political parties not into nationalists and anti-nationalists but into moderate nationalists and strong nationalists (Fine Gael and Fianna Fáil, respectively). The second is that any potential church–state cleavage was excluded from the foundations of the party system by the smothering consensus of an overwhelmingly Catholic society. The third is that any substantial agrarian–industrial conflict was avoided because the vast bulk of the economy of the new state was agrarian. The fourth and final observation deriving from the Lipset and Rokkan approach is that the owner–worker conflict was:

- overshadowed by the nationalist conflict;
- sidelined by the prevailing conservative religious ethos;
- further marginalised by the decision of the Labour Party not to contest the 1918 election.[2]

What all this adds up to is that cleavages in the Irish party system and in Irish electoral alignments can indeed be mapped on to the standard European cleavages provided we recognise that this has to be done in a highly particular fashion.

The configuration of cleavages just described formed the basis of the party system and voter alignments in Ireland for a substantial part of the twentieth century. However, Ireland underwent enormous change in the last third of that century, particularly in its last two decades, whether this is looked at in economic, social or political terms. These changes cannot but have affected the roles played by nationalist issues, by church–state (or confessionalist–pluralist issues), and by the owner–worker (capital–labour or left–right) cleavage. The question to be addressed in any analysis of contemporary voting behaviour is: What is the current configuration of cleavages at the mass level and how, if at all, do they affect vote choice? Is there any evidence that other cleavages (for example, those around attitudes to environmental and quality-of-life issues or issues related to European integration and European treaty changes) may be beginning to emerge? This chapter focuses first on the question of the impact, if any, of social class and other socio-demographic factors that might point to underlying cleavages. It then analyses the more ideological and attitudinal indicators of potential cleavage-based politics, namely revisionist versus traditional nationalism, secular-liberal versus religious-conservative orientations, pro-environment versus pro-growth, left–right socioeconomic ideology and left–right self-identification.

The socio-demographic evidence

Though it may be subject to some methodological debate (see below), the kind of socio-demographic evidence that would support or refute a class-cleavage interpretation of Irish vote choice is obvious and comes mainly from occupation-based measures of social class. This chapter begins by sifting through these indicators and the different bodies of data in which they are found, with a view to arriving at a clear assessment of a major aspect of the perennial debate as to whether Irish politics has or has not got 'social bases'. Social class is generally measured in opinion polls by using information on occupation to classify respondents into one or other of the following groups: AB (upper middle class/middle class), C1 (lower middle class), C2 (skilled working class), DE (working class/lowest levels of subsistence), F50+ (farmers owning 50 acres or more), and F50− (farmers holding less than 50 acres). Most of the analysis of the relationship between class and voting in Ireland to date has explored the link between these 'social grades' and party choice.[3] Figures 1–3 present the breakdown of support for the three main parties by social grade for all elections since 1969, using the opinion poll conducted closest to election day itself.[4]

The first thing to note – see the left-hand side of Figure 3.1 – is the cross-class nature of support for Fianna Fáil in 1969. This was the main finding that underpinned Whyte's 'politics without social bases' thesis. Fianna Fáil at that election was clearly neither middle class nor working class. It performed best among the lower middle class and worst among the upper middle class, but there was only an 11 percentage point gap in Fianna Fáil support between these two groups (48 versus 37 percent).

This particular intra-class contrast sits uneasily with the standard notion of class-based voting as a matter of middle class versus working class. The elections of the 1980s and that of 1992 were different in that Fianna Fáil support was decidedly weaker among AB voters (see

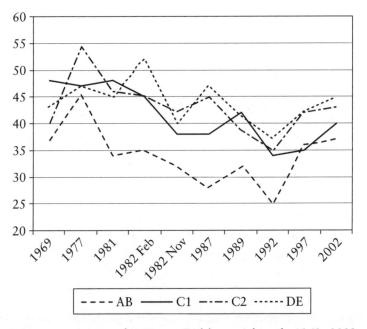

Figure 3.1 Support for Fianna Fáil by social grade 1969–2002

Figure 3.1). However, the elections of 1997 and 2002 saw a return to the more limited class differences in Fianna Fáil support that led Whyte to coin the term 'politics without social bases'. The pattern of class differences in Fianna Fáil support in the 1980s and early 1990s is mirrored and indeed accentuated in Fine Gael support in the same period, especially in the election of November 1982. But there had long been significant class contrasts in Fine Gael support, with the party tending to do better among the middle class than the working class. What happened in the 1980s, and in particular at the high point of electoral achievement for the FitzGerald-led Fine Gael (in November 1982), was an intensification of a well-established relationship. More recently, however, this middle-class orientation shows signs of attenuation (see Figure 3.2). In sum, Fine Gael moved from having significant class contrasts in its support (1969 and 1977), to having quite pronounced contrasts (November 1982), to having practically negligible class-related differences in 2002.

One would expect the Labour Party to attract more working-class than middle-class voters. As Figure 3.3 shows, back in 1969 Labour did indeed have a noticeable class bias – almost 30 percent support in the two working-class categories as against 14 percent in the C1 group

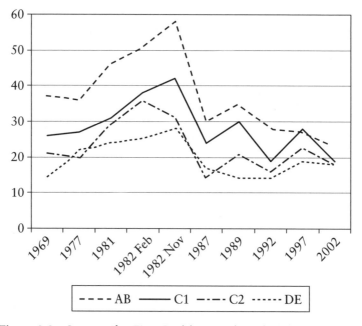

Figure 3.2   Support for Fine Gael by social grade 1969–2002 (%)

Source: Sinnott (1995, 182–3) and authors' analyses of 1997 and 2002
Lansdowne/RTE exit polls

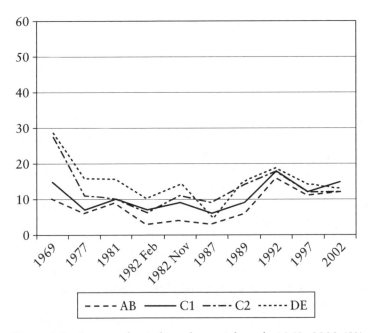

Figure 3.3 Support for Labour by social grade 1969–2002 (%)
Source: Sinnott (1995, 182–3) and authors' analyses of 1997 and 2002
Lansdowne/RTE exit polls

and 10 percent in the ABs. That class contrast was more than halved in 1977 and, far from being reinstated in subsequent elections, has in fact weakened further. Over time, this has resulted in the effective disappearance of any working-class basis to the Labour vote, a trend that culminated in 2002 when Labour got its highest level of support from a section of the middle class (the C1s). In short, Labour Party support has moved from being somewhat class-based (in the late 1960s) to being essentially cross-class in 2002 (but see the further discussion of this issue below). Not surprisingly and with one exception (the 1989 election), the Progressive Democrats have performed best among the uppermiddle class AB group and second best among the lower-middle class C1 group. In 1997 and 2002, the Greens also performed best among middle-class voters. On the other hand, the evidence shows a quite clear working-class bias in the Sinn Féin support in both 1997 and 2002.

Our analysis thus far has set farmers to one side because they are difficult to incorporate into a social class schema. Looking at them separately shows that Fine Gael performs much better among farmers; unsurprisingly, the opposite is true of Labour. But different types of farmers show different levels of support for Fianna Fáil and Fine Gael, with Fianna Fáil attracting a greater proportion of the small farmers' vote (apart from 1977 and 1992). Conversely, Fine Gael emerges clearly as the party most attractive to big farmers. The differences in the support levels involved are – apart from 1977 and 1997 – striking.

Given the key role played by the concept of social class in the study of advanced industrial democracies, it is not surprising that the measurement of social class has generated some quite heated controversy. In particular, sociologists such as Goldthorpe argue for an interpretation of class that is grounded not just in a ranking of occupations, but also in the economic relations that flow from one's occupation, most notably in relation to levels of autonomy in the workplace, levels of security and whether or not one is self-employed.[5] Thus, the Goldthorpe approach distinguishes between different types of 'middle-class' voters. People who own their own business (the self-employed) are distinguished from white collar employees and, within the working class, a distinction is made between those with supervisory power and a certain amount of discretion and autonomy in the workplace and those whose jobs lack these attributes. The former – 'skilled manual/supervisors' – may be seen as a 'blue collar elite' or, essentially, as the 'upper working class', while the latter are rank and file manual workers who are in relatively insecure jobs and are under the authority of others. Finally, the approach distinguishes, within the white collar employee group, between what we might term the upper-middle class ('the salariat' in Goldthorpe terms), consisting of senior managers and administrators plus employed professionals, and the routine non-manual (clerks, secretaries, salespersons and the like).[6]

Applying this alternative class analysis to the 2002 election – see Table 3.1 – confirms the findings noted above for Fine Gael (characterised

Table 3.1　Party choice by Goldthorpe class (7 categories) (%)

	Higher salariat	Lower salariat	Routine non-manual	Self-employed	Skilled manual/ sup.s	Semi/ unskilled manual	Farmers	Total
Fianna Fáil	29	37	39	37	51	46	43	41
Fine Gael	24	20	19	20	22	19	38	22
PDs	9	7	4	4	4	1	3	4
Labour	16	13	18	13	6	10	3	11
Green Party	7	6	6	5	4	1	2	4
Sinn Féin	5	6	4	5	7	9	4	6
Independents	8	9	9	11	7	11	7	9
Others	2	2	2	4	1	4	0	2
Total	100	100	100	100	100	100	100	100
N	185	399	273	119	183	374	174	1707

as having cross-class support), for the Progressive Democrats (having some middle-class bias), for the Green Party (ditto) and for Sinn Féin (being somewhat more working class). However, new insights arise when we use the Goldthorpe schema to analyse support for Fianna Fáil and Labour. Whereas the social grade measure from the 2002 election suggests that Fianna Fáil had consolidated its position as a party with essentially cross-class support, the Goldthorpe-style analysis points to significant imbalances in its support base. The party obtained only 29 percent of the vote of the higher salaried middle class, but won 51 percent support among skilled manual workers and supervisors of manual workers and 46 percent among semi-skilled and unskilled workers. While this does not make Fianna Fáil a working-class party, it does indicate that, in 2002 at least, it was more working class than middle class.

Use of the new class schema throws further light on the role of class in Irish electoral politics by showing that the Labour Party has also a significant class bias, but that this is towards the middle class rather than towards what might be regarded as its natural working-class constituency. As Table 3.1 shows, Labour in 2002 obtained significantly higher levels of support from those in middle-class occupations, especially from the higher salaried middle class and routine non-manual employees and that it received very limited support (6 percent) from skilled manual workers and supervisors.[7] In summary, putting all of this old and new class evidence together shows that there are some social class factors at work in Irish voter alignments, but that, at least on the socio-demographic evidence, this does not add up to a new class-based politics, particularly not given the incongruous nature of Labour Party support in 2002.

There is in fact as much or indeed more variation in the support bases of the parties in terms of age than in terms of social class (see Table 3.2). The age-related nature of party support is particularly evident in the case of the Greens and Sinn Féin. The Green Party won 8 percent of the vote of the under-25s and only 2 percent of those aged 55 to 64 and 0.4 percent of those aged 65+. In the case of Sinn Féin, the spread is from 9 percent among the under-25s to 2 percent among those aged 65+. In 2002 the traditional Labour Party advantage among the young was less in evidence than before, presumably because Labour had ceded ground in this respect to the Greens and Sinn Féin. The corollary of all this is that Fianna Fáil and Fine Gael do less well among the young and better among the older segments in the electorate. But they do so in somewhat different ways. Fine Gael's most distinctive age effect is its greater strength (32 percent) among those aged 65 and

Table 3.2 Party choice by age (%)

	18–24	25–34	35–44	45–54	55–64	65+	Total
Fianna Fáil	26	40	41	44	49	44	41
Fine Gael	22	18	18	23	25	30	23
PDs	4	3	6	4	1	5	4
Labour	14	10	12	12	8	9	11
Green Party	8	6	6	3	2	0	4
Sinn Féin	9	13	8	3	4	2	7
Independents	14	9	7	9	10	8	9
Others	3	1	4	2	2	1	2
Total	100	100	100	100	100	100	100
N	173	282	336	392	320	321	1824

older. Fianna Fáil's most distinctive effect is its weakness in the under 25s, among whom it wins just 26 percent.

This brings us to our third socio-demographic indicator – religion, as measured by adherence to a religious denomination coupled with frequency of religious practice. There is a clear linear pattern to Fianna Fáil support, the party doing better as one moves from those who do not belong to any denomination (20 percent support for Fianna Fáil) to those who attend religious services more than once a week, 51 percent of whom support Fianna Fáil. Fine Gael support also varies across these degrees of religiosity, but the contrasts are not as strong as in the case of Fianna Fáil (see Table 3.3). Support for the Progressive Democrats shows very little variation in this respect On the other hand, Labour, the Greens and Sinn Féin show marked contrasts, Labour, for example, securing only 7 percent of the large 'once a week' group compared to 26 percent among those who say they do not belong to any denomination.

Place of residence, as in urban verses rural, is commonly used in discussions of variations in party support. In fact, there are few instances where a party's support seems to rise or fall steadily with urbanisation. Fine Gael, for instance, does much better among voters living in open country than in Dublin City (31 percent to 12 percent), but it also does better in other cities (25 percent) than in towns of all sizes. Fianna Fáil does worst in Dublin city and county, but does best in large towns and other cities. There does seem to be a Dublin/rest division that is superimposed on any urban–rural division. However, support for Independents declines steadily with urbanisation, and support for the Progressive Democrats rises.

Summarising the socio-demographic evidence, it is clear that there are some limited class contrasts in party support, but that these are

Table 3.3 Party choice by religious observance (%)

	Several times a week	Once a week	1, 2 or 3 times a month	Several times a year	Less frequently/ Never	No religious denomination	Total
Fianna Fáil	51	46	47	37	32	20	42
Fine Gael	23	28	22	13	17	13	23
PDs	5	3	4	8	4	1	4
Labour	8	7	11	10	15	26	11
Green Party	1	2	5	5	8	10	4
Sinn Féin	5	4	2	11	10	18	7
Independents	7	9	8	11	7	9	9
Others	1	0	1	5	7	3	2
Total	100	100	100	100	100	100	100
N	168	891	240	193	178	131	1801

simply not enough to sustain the notion of the belated emergence of a politics with social bases. Other aspects of the socio-demographic evidence, such as the relationship between age or religious practice and voting do, however, leave open the possibility of an emerging secular-liberal versus confessional-conservative cleavage. The socio-demographic evidence is not overwhelming in this regard and the observed relationships are open to other interpretations. In order to go beyond what is no more than suggestive evidence and in order to develop a more detailed picture of the prevailing cleavages and their expression or lack of expression in the party system, we turn to the attitudinal evidence.

Political values and political cleavages

In order to measure the relevant attitudes, we included in the INES questionnaire some 25 items dealing with the following five areas:

- nationalism and the Northern Ireland issue;
- socio-economic left–right ideology;
- secular-liberal versus confessional-conservative outlook;
- attitudes to environmental issues;
- attitudes to European integration.

The large number of items involved enables us to test our expectations regarding the dimensionality of Irish political attitudes by focusing on the extent to which the items we have included hang together to form meaningful attitudinal dimensions, and on the extent to which these dimensions conform to the expectations set out at the beginning of this chapter. We can conduct this test, at least in an exploratory way, by applying factor analysis. This technique begins with the correlations between the items involved and uses these to identify the number and nature of the underlying attitudinal dimensions.

Our factor-analytic results suggest that there are six dimensions underlying the five sets of attitudinal and behavioural indicators (Table 3.4). The first dimension brings together responses to the survey questions relating to abortion, frequency of attendance at religious services, the role of people with a religious outlook in public office, the existence or otherwise of God, and the issue of homosexuality. These items all correlate strongly with each other and suggest an underlying attitudinal dimension that we might label secular-liberalism versus religious-conservatism. The order of occurrence of the factors or dimensions provides some guidance as to the importance of any particular dimension (i.e. importance in the context of the 24 items involved). On this basis, the data provide at least some evidence of the emergence of a secular-liberal versus religious-conservative dimension of socio-cultural cleavage in the Ireland of the late twentieth and early twenty-first century. How significant this cleavage turns out to be will depend on the distribution of respondents on the dimension, on how they see positions of the parties on the issues involved and on how this affects their voting behaviour.

The second underlying attitudinal dimension to emerge from our factor analysis relates to the Northern Ireland issue and captures the historical division between moderate and strong nationalists. The responses to all four questions dealing with Northern Ireland are strongly related to each other (see factor loadings in Table 3.4) Respondents who agree that we should abandon the goal of a united Ireland also tend to agree that 'the British government should continue to have a say' in Northern Ireland. Such respondents also tend to disagree (as shown by the minus signs) with the idea of the British government declaring its intention to withdraw from Northern Ireland and also with the idea that the long-term policy of the Republic should be the achievement of a united Ireland.

The third and fourth dimensions indicated by the factor analysis relate to the environment and to European integration. Thus, respondents who disagree with the idea of accepting a cut in their standard of living in order to protect the environment are also likely to disagree with the notion of paying more tax to protect the environment and to respond in a consistent way to the other two environmental items. Similarly, on the EU dimension, respondents who think that European integration should be pushed further also agree that EU membership is a good thing and disagree that Ireland should prioritise protecting independence over European unity.

Table 3.4 Principal components analysis of political attitude items

	Component					
	1	2	3	4	5	6
Abortion: ban/Available-self	**−0.66**	0.08	−0.06	0.12	0.08	0.13
Religious practice	**0.69**	−0.01	−0.09	−0.04	0.00	0.00
People – strong relig belief held office	**0.63**	−0.01	0.19	−0.01	−0.13	0.01
God: does not/does exist	**0.60**	−0.08	−0.05	0.03	0.12	0.07
Homosexuality: Never/ always justified	**−0.54**	0.14	0.20	0.17	0.09	−0.10
Inst/abandon united irl-self	−0.06	**0.66**	0.03	−0.03	0.19	0.11
Brit govt – intention withdraw from N. Irl	0.09	**−0.77**	−0.05	−0.08	0.03	0.09
Long-term policy N. Irl – Reunify	0.18	**−0.73**	−0.02	0.08	0.05	0.09
Brit govt – continue have say in N. Irl	0.07	**0.67**	−0.04	0.09	0.03	0.03
Cut in stand living to protect environ	−0.02	0.05	**0.78**	0.03	0.06	−0.05
Willing pay higher tax – protect environ	0.03	0.08	**0.71**	0.02	0.05	0.08
Protect environ: damage econ growth	−0.01	0.08	**−0.54**	0.01	0.20	0.00
Claims: environmental threats – exaggerated	0.28	0.01	**−0.47**	0.05	0.03	−0.02
Europe unification: too far/push further	−0.11	−0.01	−0.02	**0.75**	0.11	0.00
Irl mship eU: bad/good thing	−0.02	0.01	−0.02	**0.75**	0.11	−0.02
Irl: unite fully/protect dependence	0.01	−0.05	−0.03	**−0.69**	0.17	−0.01
Business: state/private owned	−0.04	0.01	0.05	0.12	**0.68**	−0.11
Business: run by state/free from state	0.04	0.04	−0.14	0.04	**0.68**	0.05
Services: public/private enterprise	−0.07	0.06	−0.01	−0.11	**0.67**	−0.11
Incr Income Tax – those above avg income	0.13	0.08	0.09	0.00	−0.08	**0.69**
Tax: cut/increase – self	0.13	0.09	0.25	0.14	0.08	**0.52**
Ord people get fair share – nation's wealth	0.22	0.11	0.11	0.16	−0.01	**−0.43**
Nothing wrong – some a lot richer	0.14	0.10	0.10	0.01	0.19	**−0.46**
Left/Right – self	**0.41**	0.04	−0.21	0.20	0.11	−0.17

Notes: Extraction method: Principal component analysis. Rotation method: Varimax rotation with Kaiser normalisation. Rotation converged in 6 iterations. Coefficients above .30 are in bold type.

This leaves one other hypothesised cleavage dimension: that relating to issues of left and right (state and market and equality and redistribution). The first notable aspect of the results in this area is that the substantive items in this domain constitute not one, but two, factors – one related to the role of the state in economic activity and the other to issues of redistribution and equality. In short, there is no comprehensive socio-economic, left–right ideological dimension. Secondly, as can be seen from the factor loadings of the left–right self-placement item (see last row of Table 3.4), the usage of the terms left and right in Ireland have little or nothing to do with socio-economic issues (see the loadings of the self-placement item on factors 5 and 6), being instead associated with issues of religion and morality (see the loading for this item on factor 1).

In sum, this exploratory analysis has confirmed the existence of four of the hypothesised attitudinal dimensions (liberalism-conservatism, strong versus moderate nationalism, pro- versus anti-environmentalism and pro- versus anti-European integration). However, it failed to produce the expected socio-economic left–right dimension. Instead, what emerged were two dimensions, one relating to the role of government and markets and the other to attitudes to economic equality and the distribution of economic resources. The evidence also shows that left–right self-placement is unrelated to either of these dimensions, being instead (weakly) related to the conservatism/liberalism dimension. The questions now are: How are respondents distributed along these various dimension? Are the parties seen to occupy different positions on them? Has this any effect on voting behaviour?

The location of the voters

The distributions of opinion on all 24 items used to identify the six attitudinal dimensions shown in Table 3.4 are presented in full in Appendix IV. In order to summarise this very large amount of information, we focus on the distribution of respondents across six self-placement scales that were included in the factor analysis and are broadly representative of the main dimensions identified in Table 3.4.[8] Thus, the first attitudinal dimension (secular-liberalism versus confessional-conservatism) is represented by the item that asks respondents where they would place themselves on a scale running from 0 to 10 where 0 represents the view that there should be a total ban on abortion in Ireland and 10 represents the view that abortion should be freely available in Ireland to any woman who wants to have one (see question C26.1 in Appendix IV). Similar self-placement scales relating to the other major issues were included in the factor analysis and will be used here to see how respondents are distributed across the various dimensions identified. A major advantage of using this particular set of scales is that respondents were also asked to place each of the six main political parties on each of the scales. This will enable us to compare the placement of respondents themselves with the perceived placement of the parties, comparisons that will be highly relevant when it comes to working out which parties represent which cleavages (if any).

But first we must examine the distribution of respondents themselves across the six scales. We do these using box plots – a graphical technique for comparing distributions across a number of scales. The building block of the box plot is the 'quartile'. This is the value that divides ordered lists into quarters. The box is constructed by identifying the location of the lowest quarter of respondents and the location of the highest quarter, with the area in between being the inter-quartile range. From the point of view of our task here, the crucial information provided by this graphical procedure is the location and spread of respondents across the scale. We begin with the spread. This is represented mainly by the length of the box (see Figure 3.4), which shows the location on

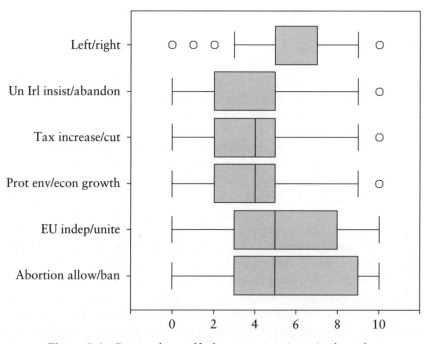

Figure 3.4   Respondent self-placement on six attitude scales

the scale of the middle 50 percent of respondents. Short boxes indicate a bunching together of respondents around two or three points on the scale, reflecting a degree of consensus on the issue in question. A long box shows that respondents are spread out along the scale, indicating that there is a greater division of opinion on the issue.

The distance on either side of the box (including that marked by small circles, if any) shows the location of the lower quarter and top quarter of cases on the scale. Short lines located at one or other end of the scale, or at both, identify concentrations of respondents with strongly held opinions, indicating a degree of polarisation of opinion. In contrast, a long line indicates a dispersal of opinion along that particular segment of the scale and suggests a lack of polarisation. Finally, the line may not extend to the end points of the scale, but may be replaced by a series of small circles. These represent outliers and extreme values and indicate that that area of the scale is very thinly populated.

As well as illustrating the spread of respondents, the box also indicates the location of respondents on the scale since the box itself may be positioned towards one or other end of the scale or at or around the middle (a preliminary glance at Figure 3.4 shows the range of variation across our six scales in this respect). A more precise indication of the location of respondents is given by the median, which is represented by a line in each box indicating the point on the scale at which half the respondents are above the point and half below the point.

The items in Figure 3.4 are arranged from top to bottom in ascending order of the length of the box. The item with the shortest box is left–right self-placement. The consensus indicated by this is confirmed by the fact that the lines to either side of the box are also short and by the occurrence of outliers indicating that there are very few cases at the ends of the scale. Indeed, on the left side, there are very few in the range 0 to 2. In short, the Irish electorate is clearly and consensually located to the right of centre on the left–right spectrum. Two points need to be borne in mind in interpreting the significance of this finding. The first is that approximately 20 percent refused or were unable to place themselves on this scale (the corresponding rate of don't knows for the other self-placement scales was in the range 3 to 5 percent). The second point is that the results of our factor analysis described earlier in this chapter suggest that the left–right spectrum in Ireland has more to do with religious and moral issues than with socio-economic ideology.

The next three items (insist on a united Ireland now versus abandon that aim; tax cuts/reduce services versus increase taxes/spend more on services; and environmental protection versus economic growth) also tend to be fairly consensual issues with majority opinion located broadly to the left of the centre of each distribution ('left' here indicating physical position on the scale with no political connotation). In short, the three scales point to consensual majority preferences for insisting on a united Ireland, for increasing taxes and increasing spending on services and for environmental protection even at the expense of economic growth.

The remaining two issues – European integration and abortion – show quite different distributions of opinion to those considered so far. First of all, both have a greater spread of opinion in the middle of the spectrum (indicated by the greater length of the box), this spread being greatest in the case of abortion. Secondly, while the median on both these items is at the centre of the scale, there is a clear bias towards the right-hand side of the scale arising from the position of a substantial minority in the vicinity of the pro-integration end of the European scale and an even more concentrated minority at or very close to the 'total ban' end of the abortion scale.

In summary, Irish political attitudes are slightly right of centre, moderately pro-united Ireland, moderately pro-increased taxes plus increased spending and moderately pro-environmental protection even at the expense of economic growth. However, attitudes are somewhat more divided on the issue of European unification, although the convinced minority on the pro-integration side is larger than its opposite number on the anti-integration side. And, on the issue of abortion, attitudes are quite polarised, with more than one-quarter of respondents being located at points 9 to 10 (where 10 indicates total support for a ban on abortion) and precisely one-quarter located at points 0 to 3 where 0 indicates full support for the proposition that abortion should be freely available in Ireland to any woman who wants to have one.

The question now is how do the voters see the location of the political parties on the attitude dimensions we have identified? Before proceeding to this question, however, we need to embark on something of a digression in order to explore what kinds of images, if any, the voters have of the parties prior to being presented with our set of issue-scales and being asked to locate the parties on them.

Party images: a digression

In order to examine the spontaneous images of the parties, we asked respondents the following question:[9]

> Thinking in general about the main political parties in Ireland, can you tell me what you think each of the parties stands for [show card]. Take Fianna Fáil first. What do you think Fianna Fáil stands for? Anything else? And what do you think Fine Gael stands for? Etc, etc.

The format of this question differs from that of most of the questions in the INES survey in that it is open-ended – there are no predefined response categories from which the respondent can choose. In certain contexts, this lack of predetermined response categories is a major advantage in that it avoids imposing the expectations of the researcher on the respondent. This is particularly useful in relation to our current concern with discovering the voters' spontaneous responses to the political parties. Rather than simply presenting respondents with a predefined scale and asking them to place the parties on it, thereby running the risk of tapping what are referred to as 'non-attitudes' (Converse, 1964), we first explored the images that come to the respondents' minds as a result of the open-ended question.

The first point to note from the evidence produced by this means is the proportion of respondents who have no image of the parties. Faced with our party-by-party questioning, many voters either had nothing to say or explicitly said they did not know, or were not interested, or that there were no differences between the parties. This lack of image of individual parties varies by party (see Table 3.5). The two parties with the lowest proportion of respondents having no image are Fianna Fáil (28 percent no image) and the Green Party (also 28 percent). At the other end of the image spectrum, 45 percent of respondents have no image of Fine Gael and the same proportion have no image of the Progressive Democrats. Labour and Sinn Féin are in between, but leaning to the high side, with 39 and 37 percent respectively having no image of these two parties.

Some of these inter-party contrasts in what we might call party image formation are surprising and some are not. Thus it is not particularly surprising that Fianna Fáil is one of the parties with a relatively prevalent image. After all, the party has been in government for 40 of the

Table 3.5 Distribution of responses to open-ended questions on what parties stand for, by party (%)

	Fianna Fáil	Fine Gael	Labour	PDs	Green Party	Sinn Féin
None	28	45	39	45	28	37
Ideology	19	12	12	12	2	38
Policy	19	9	10	13	64	5
Groups	18	16	34	10	1	4
Reputation	31	22	12	17	9	19
People	1	1	*	1	*	*
Misc.	4	7	2	10	2	4

last 60 or so years and, in virtue of that simple fact, has been more in the news and more in the minds of the voters. It has also been in the headlines in recent years because of scandals regarding payments to politicians focusing on several senior party figures, including former party leader and Taoiseach Charles Haughey. Since the interviewers recorded negative as well as positive images, this notoriety could be expected to have increased the rate of image formation. The significance of longevity in government and involvement in controversy of the sort indicated as sources of image formation is confirmed by the fact that the largest block of Fianna Fáil images relate to the reputation of the party (see Table 3.5). For example, its achievements in government are reflected in the fairly typical comment, 'They run the country and economy efficiently and improve the infrastructure.' But the negative side is also part of this reputational category, as in: 'A crooked party – Liam Lawlor and Charles Haughey', or: 'Bunch of cowboys, lining their own pockets'.

The most likely reason for the relatively high level of image formation in the case of the Green Party is that it is seen as a single issue party, that the issue in question is quite salient and is clearly encapsulated in the party's name. As one respondent put it, 'I suppose they are mad on the environment.' This interpretation is consistent with the fact that 64 percent of respondents make reference to aspects of policy in answering the question about what the Green party stands for, as in: 'Very strong on the environment. Want more public transport and fewer cars on the road'.

What is surprising about the responses to the open-ended question is the very high proportion of respondents who have no image at all of Fine Gael. The party has been in government on six occasions in the last 60 years or so, most recently from 1994–97. On this basis alone, one might have expected it to have a more widespread image. On the other hand, the lack of knowledge in the electorate of what Fine Gael stands for may reflect the uncertainties arising from the party's frequent leadership changes since the late 1980s and the effects on the image of the party of the traumatic defeat of many of its senior public representatives in the 2002 election. Indeed, some of those who did respond to the question on what Fine Gael stands for highlighted the problem of identity as in, 'They don't know their own identity' or 'They can't decide between themselves what they stand for so how am I supposed to know?'

The relative lack of image formation in the case of the Progressive Democrats may be surprising or not, depending on the way one looks at the matter. Many commentators see the party as having a clear neo-liberal ideological stance (Benoit and Laver, 2005, 2006). Moreover, as of the 2002 election it had completed a long and stable period in a coalition government. One might have thought that these two factors were enough to give the party a clear image in the minds of the voters, but the data refute this expectation. Perhaps the tendency of the party to vehemently deny having a right-of-centre identity confuses the party's image rather than clarifying it. A glance at the content of the images of the party in Table 3.5 certainly confirms the party's success in resisting being categorised in ideological terms – only 12 percent of respondents make any kind of ideological reference in response to the question of what the Progressive Democrats stand for.

Labour and Sinn Féin come next in the strength of the images of their parties. Again, one would have thought that the Labour Party's fairly frequent participation in government and its traditional ideological position would have made what it stands for more obvious to the electorate. As it turns out, almost two in five respondents say they do not know what Labour stands for. And the expectation that it might have an ideological identity in the minds of the voters is not borne out either: only 12 percent spontaneously see the Labour Party in ideological terms – the same proportion as in the case of the ideology-denying Progressive Democrats and a significantly smaller proportion than in the case of pragmatic Fianna Fáil. The one relatively prominent reference in the responses to the question of what Labour stands for falls into the group reference category, with 34 percent of respondents defining the party in terms of group representation, as in the following responses: 'Looking after the working class' or 'Workers' interests at heart'. Some responses in this group reference category did reflect an aspect of the Labour Party that was highlighted in the class analysis earlier in this chapter by making reference to the party standing for 'a balance of worker and business interests' or, in more downright fashion: 'They stand for the middle class.'

Finally, one would have thought that Sinn Féin's prominent role in the politics of Northern Ireland, both before and after the IRA ceasefire and the development of the peace process, would have left far fewer than 37 percent of respondents unable to say what the party stands for. Less surprising is the fact that the bulk of the references that do come to voters' minds are ideological, the ideology in question being nationalism or, in that very specifically Irish sense of the term, 'republicanism'. Sinn Féin's only other significant source of recognition in the minds of the voters comes under the 'reputation' category, in that there are positive references to their reputation on 'local issues' or, as one respondent put it, 'They can change things for the better around here', and negative references to their association with the violence of the past, as in references to 'still in the shadow of the gun' or, simply, 'bloodshed'.[10]

The responses to our open-ended question do not tell the whole story regarding people's perceptions of and relationship to the political parties. The evidence just considered arises from spontaneous responses to an open-ended question. The question was not designed to draw out a comprehensive account of all that the respondent might know or feel about a particular party. Accordingly, it is essential both to take the evidence just presented into account and to supplement it with the responses to structured questions that explicitly ask respondents how they see the parties in terms of this or that issue. We can now turn to that more structured evidence, but we should do so with a certain amount of caution and should bear in mind that not everybody is immediately and always conscious of what Irish political parties stand for.

The location of the parties

In considering the perceived positions of the political parties on the six attitude scales, we follow the order of the attitudinal dimensions indicated by the factor analysis, beginning therefore with the secular-liberal versus confessional-conservative dimension (see Figure 3.5). We have seen that the median voter is located in the middle of the 0 to 10 scale of perceived position on abortion. Judging by the median, that is also where the parties are seen to be located, though the location of the boxes for Fianna Fáil and for Labour indicates a slight tendency for the former to be seen as closer to the 'ban abortion' side and for the latter to tilt slightly towards the side favouring the availability of abortion.

However, what is most striking about the distribution of voter self-placements and the perception of each party's placement on the issue of abortion in Figure 3.5a is the contrast between the position of the respondents and the positions of the parties. While the party placements tend, with some slight nuances, towards the centre of the spectrum and present quite short inter-quartile ranges, voter self-placements are dispersed along the scale, with the middle 50 percent of voters locating themselves across a wide spectrum and with a substantial proportion locating themselves at or near the extreme points of the scale. In short, and returning to the basic theme of political cleavage, there is some evidence of the existence of quite a polarised abortion-based issue cleavage in the society that is not reflected in the party system. The fact that this abortion item is an integral part of the secular-liberal versus confessional-conservative dimension in the factor analysis suggests that this cleavage is not just a matter of the issue of abortion, but that it

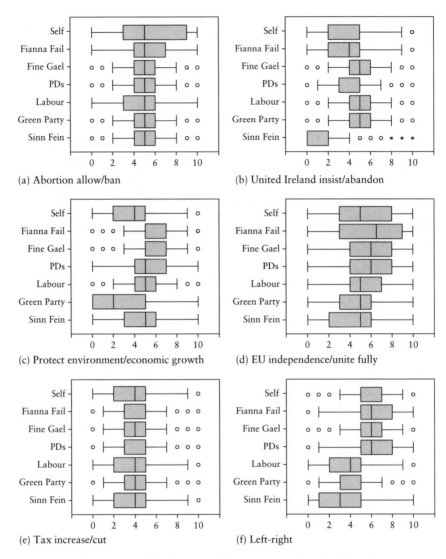

Figure 3.5 Self and party placement on six attitude scales

also includes a wider set of religious/secular and conservative/liberal attitudes.

In the case of the nationalist cleavage, which was dominant at the foundation of the party system and emerges as the second attitudinal dimension in our factor analysis, there is a greater degree of perceived party differentiation than in the case of abortion. The most obvious instance of this greater differentiation is the location of Sinn Féin at the extreme end of the attitudinal spectrum, 55 percent seeing Sinn Féin as being at the most extreme point on the scale. This makes 1 the median value for Sinn Féin and gives rise to the very skewed distribution shown in Figure 3.5b. Fianna Fáil is seen as the next most nationalist party after Sinn Féin, with a median of point 4 on the scale in contrast to the location of Fine Gael, the Progressive Democrats, Labour and the Green Party, whose median values are all located in the centre, at 5.

In summary, perceived party placements on the United Ireland scale give rise to wide variation between, on the one hand, Sinn Féin, which is at the extreme nationalist end of the scale and, on the other, Fine Gael, the Progressive Democrats, Labour and the Greens in the middle of the scale, with Fianna Fáil located in between these two blocks and closely aligned with the position of the bulk of the voters themselves.

We have seen that the voters are clearly located on the pro-protection side of the issue of environmental protection versus economic growth. It is striking, therefore, that, with one major exception, all the parties are seen to be less environmentalist than the voters (see both the median points and the location of the boxes in Figure 3.5c). The exception is, of course, the Green party and its position is indeed very distinctive. The median perception of the position of the Green Party is at point 2 on the scale and approximately three-quarters of respondents locate the party somewhere between 0 and 5. This is quite close to where the voters see themselves, the difference being that the proportion of voters who place themselves at the extreme end of the scale (points 0, 1, 2) is far lower than the proportion of voters who put the Green Party at that extreme point. Accordingly, the median values for the voters' self-placement and for their placement of the Green Party itself are quite different. As we shall see, this discrepancy contributes to the failure of the Green Party to translate the pro-environment instincts of many voters into support for the party.

Mass opinion on the issue of European integration (Figure 3.5d) is relatively dispersed along the spectrum, with the box representing the middle 50 percent of respondents running from point 3 to point 8. The voters themselves all see Fianna Fáil, Fine Gael and the Progressive Democrats as adopting a somewhat more pro-integrationist stance than that which they actually hold. This is particularly true of Fianna Fáil, which emerges as the party seen to be most associated in the minds of the voters with strong pro-integration sentiment. That said, it must be emphasised that perceptions of where Fianna Fáil stands on this issue are also widely dispersed, the box representing the position attributed to Fianna Fáil by the middle 50 percent of respondents extending from points 3 to 9. The parties of the left all show the same median value as that of the voters themselves (5) but, whereas the electorate as a whole tilts towards the pro-integration pole, two of the left-wing parties (the Greens and Sinn Féin) are seen to tilt towards the anti-integration side.

In the case of the issue of tax and spend, there is a remarkably close alignment between the self-placements adopted by the voters and the positions of the parties as perceived by the voters. As can be seen from Figure 3.5e, the boxes are all stacked up in a line, the only variation being the somewhat greater emphasis on tax and spending increases in the voter self-placements and in the perceived positions of the Labour Party and Sinn Féin.

In contrast to the almost negligible differences on the tax and spend scale, the left–right self-placement scale does produce a very clear-cut distinction among the parties, that between the perceived positions of Fianna Fáil, Fine Gael and the Progressive Democrats, on the one hand, and the perceived positions of Labour, the Greens and Sinn Féin on the other. As is clearly illustrated in Figure 3.5f, the former are located towards the right of the centre of the political spectrum, all having median values of 6, whereas the median value for the Labour Party is 4 and that for Sinn Féin is 3. In contrast to all of the other scales considered, there is no overlap between the set of boxes representing the inter-quartile range of the perceived positions of Fianna Fáil, Fine Gael and the Progressive Democrats and the set of boxes representing Labour, the Greens and Sinn Féin (see Figure 3.5f). This suggests that the electorate, or at least the (approximately) 80 percent of it that looks at politics through left–right lenses, can discern a consistent contrast between the self-proclaimed parties of the left and the more reluctant parties of the centre-right. However, there is obviously a certain amount of ambiguity surrounding the exact meaning of this left–right scale and we shall return to this aspect of the matter in exploring how left–right values relate to voting behaviour.[11]

Cleavages and voting

The third key question posed at the beginning of this chapter asked whether such underlying cleavages as might be shown to exist have any effect on vote choice. The evidence as to where the electorate locates the parties is helpful in working out what we might expect. The pictures of the parties in Figure 3.5 suggest that there are two sets of issues in this regard. The first comprises abortion, taxes/social services and the European Union. These stand out as showing little or no inter-party differentiation and, accordingly, one might expect little or no relationship between voters' own views on these issues and their party choice. If the parties present no major differences or alternatives in relation to an issue, then there is no basis for an individual to rely on that issue to choose one party rather than another. The abortion issue illustrates the point: as Table 3.6 shows, there is very little variation in levels of support for the different political parties across the points on the ban/ allow abortion scale. Attitudes in this area simply do not affect party choice. This is not to say that, given the conflict of opinion on this issue revealed by the voter self-placements, they might not do so in the future. The view that there is a non-negligible potential for such a development is reinforced by the findings, reported above, that party choice is related to religiosity, and that party support is also related to respondents' positions on a secular-liberalism versus confessional-conservatism scale that takes all the items in the first factor in our factor analysis into account.[12] However, as argued elsewhere (Sinnott, 1995, 2002), the likelihood of this happening is significantly reduced by the fact that the issues concerned can be insulated from party politics by being channelled through the referendum process.

Tax and spending issues are even less likely to affect vote choice as the positions of the electorate and of the parties on the policy spectrum are practically identical. And the evidence confirms this by showing almost zero relationship between opinions in this area and party support. The same general conclusion holds for attitudes to the European Union. It is true that there is a somewhat wider spread of opinion in relation to this matter (though the spread is not as great as in the case of the abortion issue). However, opinion on where to place the parties is also more dispersed, indicating a good deal of uncertainty about where the parties stand. There is also a substantial level of overlap

Table 3.6 Party choice by respondent self-placement on abortion allow/ban (0–10) attitude scale (%)

	0–2	3–4	5	6–7	8–10	Total
Fianna Fáil	42	38	37	44	43	41
Fine Gael	20	18	23	18	27	23
PDs	4	5	6	3	3	4
Labour	12	15	12	14	7	11
Green Party	3	6	3	5	3	4
Sinn Féin	9	5	6	5	6	7
Independents	7	9	10	8	10	9
Others	3	4	2	3	1	2
Total	100	100	100	100	100	100
N	411	223	325	152	632	1743

Table 3.7 Party choice by respondent self-placement on United Ireland insist/abandon (0–10) attitude scale (%)

	0–2	3–4	5	6–7	8–10	Total
Fianna Fáil	44	41	42	39	38	42
Fine Gael	22	19	22	23	31	23
PDs	1	4	5	9	2	4
Labour	9	11	12	10	10	10
Green Party	2	6	5	5	4	4
Sinn Féin	12	7	3	2	5	7
Independents	8	9	10	6	8	9
Others	1	3	2	6	2	2
Total	100	100	100	100	100	100
N	488	323	570	160	208	1749

across the perceived positions of the parties. In short, the conditions necessary for this particular issue to have an impact on voting choice are just not there and this lack is reflected in the very weak relationship between reported vote and attitude to European integration.[13]

Our second set of issues consists of attitudes to the pursuit of a united Ireland, attitudes to the balance between environment and economic growth, and left–right political orientation. In the case of the first two, there is substantial party differentiation in the form of a minority party (a different one in each case) that is seen to adopt a very distinctive position (see Figure 3.4). The parties, of course, are Sinn Féin and the Green Party. On the left–right spectrum, however, the perceived inter-party differences are less extreme, but more pervasive, in that they involve three parties (Fianna Fáil, Fine Gael and the Progressive Democrats) ranged on the centre-right against three parties (Labour, the Green party and Sinn Féin) on the centre-left.

As all three cleavages in this second set involve at least some degree of inter-party differentiation, one would expect them to have some impact on party choice. And the evidence indicates that they do. Thus, those with strong nationalist views are much more likely to vote Sinn Féin than those with moderate nationalist views. Of course, the fact remains that a near majority of those with a strong commitment to Irish reunification vote Fianna Fáil. But whereas Fianna Fáil support hardly varies at all with variations in attitudes to reunification, Sinn Féin support varies considerably.

In the case of attitudes to environmental issues, there is a slight difference in the rate of Fianna Fáil support between those who put the

Table 3.8 Party choice by respondent self-placement on protect environment/damage economic growth (0–10) attitude scale (%)

	0–2	3–4	5	6–7	8–10	Total
Fianna Fáil	42	35	43	47	45	41
Fine Gael	21	21	23	28	25	23
PDs	3	6	4	3	1	4
Labour	12	13	9	8	8	11
Green Party	6	4	2	2	2	4
Sinn Féin	7	7	8	3	4	7
Independents	8	10	8	7	10	9
Others	1	4	2	3	5	2
Total	100	100	100	100	100	100
N	655	385	459	146	140	1785

emphasis on environmental protection and those who put the emphasis on economic growth, the latter being slightly more likely to vote Fianna Fáil. However, as with Sinn Féin and reunification, the real action lies with the minor party: the Greens get 6 percent support among strong environmentalists and only 2 percent among the go-for-growth brigade. In one sense, these differences in party support for Sinn Féin and the Greens are marginal as they relate to minor parties. In terms of our overall understanding of Irish voting behaviour, however, they are quite significant in that they show that issues and attitudes can make a difference, but only if parties are seen to differ.

This brings us to the left–right dimension, on which the perceived differences between the parties are quite clear-cut, see Table 3.9. The relationship between left–right self-placement and support for each of the political parties is also clear-cut. Support for Fianna Fáil is substantially greater among those who put themselves at the centre or to the right of centre (support ranging from 43 to 53 percent). Among those who put themselves on the left, support for Fianna Fáil ranges from 15 to just under 20 percent. The same relationship holds for Fine Gael though the differences are not quite as strong. Support for the Progressive Democrats comes from almost all points on the spectrum, except from among those who see themselves as most strongly on the left (points 0–2 on the scale). On the other side of the spectrum, Labour gets levels of support from left-wingers that are 3 to 4 times greater than the levels of support it gets from those at the centre or on the right. Differences of almost the same size obtain in the case of the Greens and the differences are sharper again in the case of Sinn Féin.

Conclusion

Does all this add up cleavage politics? This chapter has revealed significant differences in the positions that voters take on certain issues, and/or in how they see the parties, and/or in how these attitudes and perceptions affect the choice they make in the polling booth. The differences we have uncovered relate, in varying degrees, to social class, religious-moral outlook, nationalism, environmentalism and left–right orientation. However, several factors argue against concluding that all or any of this amounts to cleavage politics. First, the differences we have identified are, to say the least, not overwhelming. Second, the spontaneous images of the parties that come to the voters' minds in answer to an open-ended question are, for the most part, not strongly structured by ideology or fundamental underlying issues. Third, none of the issues meets all three of the criteria that must be met if we are to answer the question that opens this paragraph in the affirmative: that voters are divided, that they see the parties as being different and that voters make the connection between their own position and the positions of the parties in deciding how to vote.

The problem with concluding that Ireland has shifted or is shifting towards cleavage politics can be illustrated by reference to the role played by left–right self-identification. Part of the problem is that it is not clear what left and right mean to the Irish electorate. Then there is the problem that the electorate's ability to accurately place the parties on a left/right spectrum may simply reflect a sort of nominalism by which respondents can recognise the left-right usage and apply it to the parties, while at the same time the terms have no real meaning.

Table 3.9 Party choice by respondent self-placement on
left/right (0–10) attitude scale (%)

	0–2	3–4	5	6–7	8–10	Total
Fianna Fáil	15	19	43	45	53	41
Fine Gael	7	19	25	28	23	23
PDs	1	5	4	7	6	5
Labour	30	22	8	7	4	10
Green Party	11	12	4	3	1	5
Sinn Féin	23	11	5	2	3	6
Independents	11	8	10	7	9	9
Others	1	5	3	1	0	2
Total	100	100	100	100	100	100
N	75	157	483	305	317	1337

However, this latter argument does not account for the fact that there is a relationship between the voters' own position on the spectrum and their choice of party, as Table 3.9 indicates. But this raises a further problem, which is that the relationship between left–right self-placement and party choice portrayed in Table 3.9 may be a spurious one created by the fact that some third variable influences both left-right self-placement and party choice, thus creating the false impression that the latter two are causally related. This issue can only be sorted out, if at all, by means of the kind of multivariate analysis undertaken in Chapter 9.

Our overall conclusion in the meantime is that the Irish party system is not based on, and does not appear to be moving towards, cleavage politics, whether cleavage politics is viewed in terms of socio-demographic bases or in terms of socio-cultural bases. We now turn to discuss another possible long term factor that may shape party support and one that is based on a psychological, rather than on a cleavage, interpretation of voting.

Notes

1 For a detailed discussion of the application of the Lipset and Rokkan framework to the Irish case, see Sinnott, 1984.

2 One influential explanation of why Ireland, relative to other countries, has fairly weak levels of class voting is that at a crucial point in Ireland's electoral history – namely the election directly after the last major extension of the franchise (the 1918 election, following the Representation of the People Act in 1918) – politics was dominated by 'the national question'. The Labour party, instead of highlighting class-related political issues, actually opted out of this election allowing it to be dominated by issues relating to national independence. Sinnott argues that Labour's non-participation at this key election meant that class conflict 'was not translated into political form' (1984: 302). Similarly, Farrell regards the Labour party decision to opt out of this election as 'the real foundation of contemporary Irish politics' (1970: 501). Adshead notes the common perception that 'Labour's withdrawal from the contest enabled the line of political representation to be completely defined in relation to "the national question" [and denied Labour] any significant role in post-independence Ireland' (2004: 2). On the topic of the relatively weak role of class in Irish politics also see Mair (1992).

3 In addition to Whyte (1974) and Carty (1983) see discussions in: Sinnott (1978), Laver (1986a, b), Laver *et al.* (1987), Laver (1987), Sinnott (1987), Marsh and Sinnott (1990), Marsh and Sinnott (1993), Sinnott (1995, Chapter 7), Marsh and Sinnott (1999), Garry *et al.* (2003).

4 Currently, there are no data available for the 1973 election.

5   For a robust defence of the 'Goldthorpe' approach rather than the social grades approach in electoral analysis see, for example, Heath *et al.* (1985: 13–16).

6   A recent study of voting behaviour in Britain (Clarke *et al.*, 2004) has downplayed the importance of the distinction between the social grades approach to measuring class and the Goldthorpe approach, essentially arguing that there is a similar amount of variation in voting behaviour explained by both approaches.

7   The contrasting class bases of Fianna Fáil and Labour are borne out by the levels of support for each of these two parties among voters with differing levels of education. Our 2002 data show that Fianna Fáil attracts the support of 49 percent of those with primary school education or less and 51 percent of those with only a junior certificate qualification. In contrast, it attracts 37–38 percent of the votes of those with leaving certificate or third-level diplomas or certificates and only 25 percent of the votes of those with a university degree. What is striking about the Labour vote is its strength among those with a university degree. Labour attracts 11 percent of the overall vote but 19 percent of those who are university educated.

8   The qualifier 'broadly' is necessary because, as we have seen, the factor analysis produced two socio-economic attitudinal dimensions where one had been expected and also showed that the left–right self-placement item did not load on either of these factors. Given this outcome, we use two scales in this area – self placement on a tax cut/increase and spending more/less scale and self-placement on the standard left–right scale. The distributions of opinion on all 24 items used to identify the six attitudinal dimensions in Table 3.4 are presented in full in Appendix 1.

9   This question was asked in only half of all interviews.

10 It should be borne in mind that these responses date from mid-2002, i.e. well before the recent major progress on the decommissioning of IRA weapons.

11 There is also the possibility that for some voters there is little or no value content to their left–right perceptions and they simply regard certain parties as 'left' because that is how those parties are described in the media. In further work we intend to explore exactly what it is that Irish voters mean by the terms 'left' and 'right'.

12 The liberalism-conservatism scale is based on factor scores and shows, for example, that Fine Gael receives 30 percent support among the one-third with high scores on the scale while receiving only 18 percent among the one-third with the lowest scores.

13 In the interests of space, the tables for the tax/spend issue and the European integration issue are not shown but may be requested from the authors.

4

The extent and meaning of party attachment

The idea that people have strong predispositions to vote for particular parties should not sound unfamiliar to most observers of Irish elections. A widely held view is that the legacy of the civil war is a set of strong party attachments held by a large section of the population – attachments that were passed down through the generations. The question of whether someone 'is' Fianna Fáil or Fine Gael, or whether their family was Fianna Fáil or Fine Gael, makes sense in Ireland, although placing one's family might be easier than placing oneself, as there is a perception that such attachments are less widespread today. The nature of such attachment has been little explored in academic analyses of Irish electoral behaviour. While there is a substantial literature on Irish electoral behaviour, this has depended for the most part on commercial opinion polls carried out at election time. They generally do not measure identification. Use has also been made of comparative surveys, like Eurobarometer, that measure identification, but rarely coincide with actual elections. The 2002 election survey facilitates an extensive consideration of the value of this concept for explaining the behaviour of Irish voters and the outcomes of Irish elections.

The most common explanation of electoral stability involves the idea that voters have a predisposition to favour one party and this tends to insulate individual voters from competition between the parties. Over time, voters tend to vote for 'their' party and to resist enticements from others. Thus, parties are, to a large extent, protected from apparently adverse electoral circumstances; they can depend on the support of 'their' core voters no matter how bad things seem to be. This notion of voters having enduring partisan predispositions arose from electoral research carried out by a team from the University of Michigan into US voting behaviour in the 1950s. Earlier studies had assumed that voters made up their mind afresh at each election on the basis of what happened during the official election campaign, but the Michigan team discovered that most people seemed to make up their mind much earlier. Indeed, reported voting histories were remarkably stable and, in so far as voters did decide afresh each time, they were clearly disposed in most cases to do what they did last time, and the time before. This 'predisposition' was described by Campbell *et al.* as party identification, a psychological attachment to a party which serves not only to define an individual's relationship to political society (Campbell *et al.*, 1960; Miller and Shanks, 1996 for a recent restatement), but also provides an informational filter which helps the individual to deal with the constant stream of information about politics. Like other identities, party identification is something acquired quite early in life and, while it may not be set in stone, it would normally be expected to become more stable as the voter gets older, reinforced by the act of voting for the same party. The roots of party identity typically lie in the family and the network of social relations which define the young adult experience, so we would expect to see party identification being passed on from one generation to another, providing a stable anchor to electoral behaviour over a long period of time.

This theory of party identification has been the basis of intensive research in the USA, some of it critical.[1] A major objection has been that party identification may be not the 'unmoved mover' proposed by the Michigan School. In other words, one's party identification may be unstable rather than stable; rather than remaining constant over time it may in fact change as a result of how parties actually perform. Fiorina (1981) argued that predispositions consisted of a running tally of evaluations of parties built up over a long period. Hence, predispositions derived from policy outcomes and governmental performance and so could change even in adulthood. Even so, evaluations themselves are filtered via partisanship, a point argued consistently by Warren Miller (1976) and reaffirmed by Bartels (2002).

Exported to Europe, this party identification explanation of stability underwent some adaptation with more emphasis being placed on the way in which political divisions were underpinned by clear social structures, most often those of religion and class (Lipset and Rokkan, 1967). In many cases political identities were inculcated and reinforced by a dense network of social relationships. Yet in key ways, the explanation remains unchanged (but see Richardson, 1991). Voters have a stable predisposition to vote in a particular way. This predisposition is learned and, once acquired, serves to reinforce itself by screening out information that might weaken it.

The predisposition of an identifier to vote for a particular party should manifest itself as a tendency, not a certainty. Under the circumstances of a particular election voters may vote for another party's candidate, but the expectation would be that this is a temporary deviation and that, at subsequent elections, the voter's behaviour will, more often than not, be consistent with his or her identification. This separation of vote (behaviour) and identity (psychological orientation) allows for short-term change.

This is not simply an important question for those interested in Ireland, but has a wider relevance for students of electoral behaviour. The concept of party identification has, perhaps, a special value in the USA as the social structural foundations of parties have generally been seen to be weak, and the multilevel character of the electoral decision (that is, the congressional and presidential level), as well as the existence of primaries, provide a context in which party can provide a particularly useful cue for voters and in which voter registration itself gives a formal basis for the concept of party identification. As shown in Chapter 3, Irish party competition lacks the sort of strong ideological or sociological underpinning typical of most other European countries. When we add to this the use of a preferential vote electoral system that separates candidate from party, at least in the larger parties, it means that the Irish context resembles the US context in some significant respects. If party identification proves to be a useful concept anywhere in Europe, Ireland would seem to be a prime candidate.

Carty (1983) argued that party identification was very strong in Ireland and that, in the absence of social structural underpinning for the parties and ideological differences between them (explored in Chapter 3), party identification provides the only plausible account of the stability of Irish party support. Carty was relying on data from the 1960s, and while the argument still holds true, in principle, it remains to be seen how strong the contemporary evidence is to support it. Writing in the 1980s, Marsh suggested there were strong grounds for thinking that identification with parties was weakening and that the electorate was becoming dealigned (1985a: especially 193–7). There has been more recent evidence of such dealignment, as we will see (Mair, 1987; Schmitt and Holmberg, 1995; Sinnott, 1998; Dalton, 2000; Mair and Marsh, 2004). While party identification may once have provided an anchor, that anchor may be much less secure today.

This chapter examines the strength and spread of party identification and how it relates to the vote: can it be separated from the behaviour it purports to explain, empirically as well as conceptually? Party attachment, a more common term in Europe, is used interchangeably with identification here. The argument that a voter is predisposed to vote for one party might be taken to imply that such a voter has no regard for any other party. How exclusive are the terms in which identifiers see the party world: is it in black and white terms or are there shades of grey? Finally, the chapter looks at the roots of party attachment, and voting behaviour in the family to assess the degree to which partisanship is 'inherited'.

Measuring party attachment

Any measure of party attachment should do several things. First, it should tap some kind of psychological orientation rather than behaviour. Second, it should not force almost all voters, or almost no voters, to claim an identity. Third, it should provide some indication of how strong is each respondent's identification. And finally, the instrument should permit some comparison with the situation in other countries and at other times in Ireland, if that is possible. The classic measure of party identification was a set of questions:

- Generally speaking, do you usually think of yourself as Party A, Party B or what?
- [If so] Would you call yourself a strong [supporter of Party], or not so strong?
- [If not] Do you think of yourself as closer to the Party A or Party B?

This wording is not easily adapted to a multi-party system. Moreover, this wording has been criticised for leading respondents to provide an identity, and to provide only one identity. In theory, at least, voters could have multiple identities (van der Eijk and Niemoller, 1983). This wording has been used in Ireland, but on only a few occasions, between 1976 and 1982 (Marsh 1985a: 194). The measure employed here is more appropriate to Ireland, is also employed by the first two waves of the Comparative Study of Electoral Systems (CSES) project now in progress, and is comparable in many respects to the question asked by the Eurobarometer between 1978 and 1994 (Sinnott, 1998).

Like the traditional question it has several parts:

- Do you usually think of yourself as close to any political party?
- [If so] Which party is that?
- [If so] Do you feel very close to this party, somewhat close, or not very close?
- [If not] Do you feel yourself a little closer to one of the political parties than the others?
- [If so] Which party is that?

This overcomes some of the criticisms of the classic wording and its variants although the removal of the 'generally speaking' preamble might be expected to lead to responses more closely linked to current

Table 4.1 Party attachment in Ireland in 2002 (%)

	Electors	Voters
Close	25.5	27.8
Very close	8.1	9.3
Somewhat close	13.7	14.6
Not very close	2.0	1.9
DK	1.8	2.0
Closer to one party than the others	25.2	25.7
Not close at all	49.3	46.5
Total	100	100
N	2663	1983

vote. While use of the term 'close' has also been criticised for confusing identity with affect, or liking (Katz, 1985), the time series already available for this question outweighs such considerations. The responses can be seen in Table 4.1. Attachment in Ireland is far from universal, but just over 50 percent of the electorate, and a slightly larger proportion of voters, have some degree of party attachment as measured in this way. When we look at the strength of this attachment it is evident that it is quite weak, with half of those who have some attachment feeling no more than a little closer to their party than any other. Most of those who feel 'close' describe themselves as 'somewhat close'. (Almost nobody who claims to be 'close' admits that they are 'not very close', perhaps unsurprisingly, as it might be considered something of a contradiction.) In view of the small numbers reporting that they are 'not very close' to a party, in the analysis that follows these will normally be combined with those who are 'somewhat close'.

Data gathered by the Comparative Study of Electoral Systems project (CSES) allows us to put these figures in context. The range across some 15 countries (the older EU countries plus Australia, New Zealand, Canada and the USA) is considerable, ranging from 85 percent with some attachment in Sweden and Norway, to just over 50 percent in Ireland and Denmark.[2] On the basis of these numbers, party identification in Ireland can make a much weaker contribution to political stability now than it might elsewhere. Even if everyone with some degree of attachment to a party did vote for that party, the other half of the electorate could still be responsible for huge changes, if it were so minded. These unattached votes may be very stable in their behaviour, but on this evidence we cannot ascribe that stability to anything like party identification. The relative weakness of attachment in Ireland is

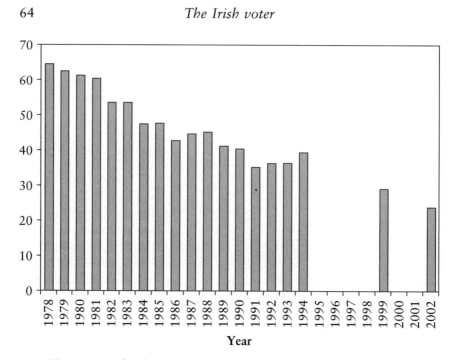

Figure 4.1 The decline of party attachment in Ireland since 1978

Sources: Eurobarometers 1978–94; European Election Study 1999; and Irish
Election Study 2002. One 1978 and one 1981 Eurobarometer excluded
due to very different question wording
Notes: 2002 response categories are 'Very close', 'Somewhat close' and 'Not
very close'; those not knowing how close they are have been are excluded;
otherwise, all measurements are based on all respondents

almost certainly not of long standing. Figure 4.1 shows the decline
since 1978 in the percentage of those who have some party attachment:
that is, those saying they are close to a party – the first of the two questions above. As has been pointed out before (Sinnott, 1995; Mair and
Marsh, 2004) attachment declined in the 1980s, particularly between
1981 and 1984, a period that saw three elections, and between 1990
and 1991. The sample on which the bar for 1999 is based was both
much smaller and collected in a different way (a telephone poll), but
the decline indicated by that data seems to be confirmed by the 2002
data.

Party identification and the vote

How does identification differ from vote intention? One of the criticisms
of the concept as applied in Europe has been that it differs insufficiently

from the vote, and is little more than another measure of the same thing. This is part of a much more general criticism which sees measured identification as much less stable than it theoretically should be (Butler and Stokes, 1969; Thomassen, 1976). For a start, how consistently do respondents give a first preference vote to 'their' party? The answer is that most of those with a party attachment do vote for their party, but that there is a distinction between vote and attachment. In fact, 78 percent of voters who declare a partisan attachment vote in accord with it: 88 percent of those 'very close', 84 percent of those 'somewhat close', but just 71 percent of the 'leaners' do so.[3] Respondents who do not follow their partisanship are divided between those who vote for someone else and those who do not vote at all, with both defection and abstention rising as the strength of attachment drops. This link between partisanship and the vote is comparable with that found elsewhere, although in the USA in particular the strong partisans, those 'very close', are more likely to report a consistent vote (see Blais *et al.*, 2001).

As already explained, Irish voters may of course indicate a preference for any number of the candidates standing in a constituency, and parties running several candidates will encourage supporters to give a high preference to all of them. When this is done, it increases a party's chance of using all its support to win seats; when it is not, the result may be suboptimal for the party. Are partisans of a party more likely to give all of their highest preferences to 'their' party's candidates? This is a test of voting consistency not generally applicable as few countries give comparable power to their voters. However, in the USA, where voters choose several levels of government simultaneously, and in mixed member electoral systems like that of Germany, there is the parallel of straight and split-ticket voting (e.g. Beck *et al.*, 1992; Gschwend *et al.*, 2003). The incidence of straight-ticket voting declines elsewhere with the strength of party attachment (Dalton *et al.*, 2000) although characteristics of the candidates themselves and their campaigns are also important (Roscoe, 2003). We would certainly expect partisans to favour all of their party's candidates over those of other parties.

Table 4.2 shows that Irish voters are more likely to do this when their attachment is stronger, and least likely when they have no attachment at all.[4] While 70 percent of those with a strong attachment vote first for all candidates of their party, and 54 percent of those with a moderate attachment do so, this declines to 43 percent of 'leaners' and a mere 34 percent of other voters.[5] (In the case of non-partisans this involves voting a straight ticket for any further candidates if the party of the first preference candidate fields more than one.) While there is little sign that the strength of partisanship makes much difference to

Table 4.2 Pattern of voting by strength of party identification (%)

	Very close	Somewhat/not very close	Leaners	None
Straight ticket	70	54	43	34
Split ticket	19	36	40	66
Defection	11	10	17	na
Total	100	100	100	100
N	147	260	346	521

Notes: cases where partisans had only one candidate of their party to vote for are
excluded, as are those cases where a simulated ballot was not filled in. Among those
with some attachment, all straight and split-ticket voters voted first for 'their' party.
Since the concept of 'defection' is inappropriate for those with no party attachment
that cell is empty.

defection rates, the weaker partisans are much less likely to show
what Gallagher has called 'solidarity' (1978) by following a party line.
'Solidarity' as measured by transfer patterns has certainly declined over
the last twenty years or so (see Gallagher 2003) and this trend ties in
well with the decline in aggregate party attachment. Parties may well
record as many first preference votes, but can no longer expect first
preference voters also to give them second, third and fourth preferences.[6] The importance of partisanship for straight ticket voting can be
emphasised by looking at the proportion of straight-ticket voters who
are partisans. While partisans account for only 46 percent of the voters
(as defined in Table 4.2, but excluding those who do not vote) they
account for 69 percent of all straight ticket voters.

A further aspect of the effect of party attachment on voting can be
observed in the reported vote shifts between 1997 and 2002. We have
seen in Chapter 2 the evidence that many voters change their behaviour from election to election. Does consistent voting across these two
elections increase with the strength of partisanship? Table 4.3 provides
the answer: it does. The big contrasts here are between the leaners
and the unattached, and between leaners and those more attached. A
majority of the unattached switched votes between the two elections.
There is little difference between the behaviour of those who feel very
close and those who feel only somewhat close: in each case about
three-quarters of them were loyal to their party on both occasions. In
the case of the 'leaners', 58 percent were consistent. If we look at the
numbers a different way, they tell us that 64 percent of stable voters
had some attachment to that party; in contrast, almost 60 percent of
unstable voters had no attachment. Even so, this means that 36 percent

Table 4.3   Voting choices in 1997 and 2002 by strength of attachment (%)

	Very close	Somewhat/ not very close	Leaners	None
Loyal to party attachment both times, or to same party if no attachment	78	76	58	41
Against 2002 party attachment at least once, or switched party if no attachment	22	24	42	59
Total	100	100	100	100
N	168	309	405	747

Note: those ineligible to vote in 1997 and don't knows are excluded.

of all voters who did not see themselves as having any form of partisan attachment nevertheless showed a stable voting pattern. This sort of recall data is prone to exaggerate stability, but there seems to be no good reason why it should do so more for partisans than non-partisans – especially as partisanship was measured after items about voting in 1997 and 2002 in the questionnaire.

The key point that these several analyses reinforce is that the measure of party attachment behaves broadly as it should. It is close to the vote, but not identical, and the link with the vote, whether measured by first preferences, lower preferences or voting history, grows weaker as the strength of the attachment wanes. As with straight-ticket voting, partisans account for most stable voters. Sixty-four percent of all stable voters have a sense of partisanship, compared with only 37 percent of those with an unstable voting record. Even so, this means that over a third (36 percent) of all voters who did not see themselves as having any form of partisan attachment, nevertheless, showed a stable voting pattern. Moreover, as we have seen, one-third of those voting a straight ticket also declared no party attachment.

The analysis so far indicates three things. First, that partisanship and vote are not synonymous. Second that, as would be expected, partisans have a more party-centred pattern of vote choice and partisans show more stability over time than non-partisans. Third, that while partisanship can thus be seen as contributing to party voting and stability, it is neither a sufficient condition for it, nor a necessary one. Partisanship contributes to stability, but stability exists to some degree in its absence.

Table 4.4 Party of those with a party attachment,
by strength of attachment (%)

	Very close	Somewhat/not very close	Leaners	Total
FF	53.3	54.3	55.3	54.6
FG	22.8	23.0	17.2	20.0
Greens	3.9	3.0	6.9	5.2
Labour	7.8	8.1	10.3	9.2
PDs	0.8	2.9	4.7	3.5
SF	11.5	7.6	3.4	6.1
Independent/ Others	0	1.1	2.2	1.5
Total	100	100	100	100
N	224	450	684	1358

We now turn from examining the link between attachment and vote to exploring the extent of attachment to different parties. Which parties are best served by partisans? There are two aspects to this question: what is the party preference of partisans, and how strong is this partisanship. Table 4.4 shows the distribution across the parties by strength of partisanship. A majority are Fianna Fáil, with Fine Gael also having a reasonable share, although underrepresented among leaners. This might be expected to provide the major party with a head start in any election, once it can mobilise that core support. The larger parties also have an advantage over the smaller ones in having a higher proportion of partisans who are strong in their attachment, although Sinn Féin (SF) outdoes both of them in this respect. Labour, the Greens and, in particular, the Progressive Democrats are well behind. The strength of attachment to Sinn Féin by that party's partisans is remarkable. Like the Progressive Democrats and the Greens it has been contesting elections only over the last two decades, but it perhaps illustrates the advantage of 'clearcut, positive symbols' in building a strong party identity (Sinnott 1978: 39).

We have already seen that partisans tend to vote for their parties. Table 4.5 shows the detailed voting preferences of partisans of each party. There is not much to choose between Fianna Fáil, Fine Gael, Labour and Sinn Féin partisans in their tendency to vote for their parties, but Greens and Progressive Democrats are much more likely to defect. Of course, these two parties, and particularly the Progressive Democrats, ran candidates in fewer constituencies than the other parties, but even if we confine the analysis of the smaller parties to those constituencies where each ran at least one candidate, then the tendency

Table 4.5 First preference votes by party attachment (%)

| | Attachment | | | | | | | |
Vote	FF	FG	Greens	Labour	PD	SF	Other	None
FF	81.8	2.7	3.9	5.1	13.1	3.2	15.2	34.3
FG	5.7	79.8	12.2	6.6	16.4	3.3	6.5	23.2
Green	1.1	0.8	65.4	0.0	5.2	0.0	0.0	3.7
Lab	1.6	6.6	1.5	78.9	6.5	0.0	0.0	13.1
PD	2.0	4.0	0.0	0.0	48.6	0.0	0.0	4.9
SF	2.2	0.4	5.5	0.0	5.7	87.8	0.0	5.6
Ind/Oth	5.7	5.7	11.5	9.5	4.6	5.7	78.3	15.3
Total	100	100	100	100	100	100	100	100
N	602	220	56	75	31	48	10	795

of partisans of Greens and Progressive Democrats to vote for their party rises, to 69 percent in the case of the Greens, to 70 percent in the case of the Progressive Democrats and to 91 percent in the case of Sinn Féin. The weaker levels of consistency that are shown by partisans of the Progressive Democrats and Greens is largely due to the weaker partisanship in those parties.

Partisans and other parties

In a critique that questioned the capacity of party identification to offer us much of a guide to the future, Crewe pointed out that the concept might conflate some very different types of partisans (Crewe, 1976: see also Garry, 2007). The classic partisan would have a very black and white view of the political world in which their own party was good and the others were bad. Weaker partisans would like their own party a little less while also disliking the other parties a little less. This pattern would be mirrored in the views of partisans of the other party. Crewe suggested that some might be partisan because they disliked the altern- ative and not because they liked their own party very much. He sug- gested the term 'negative partisans' for those who followed this pattern, and advanced several variations on the same theme. The significance of this is that, particularly in a multi-party system, changes in partisan- ship could easily come about because a third party also offered a home for those people. The key point is whether partisanship indicates loyalty or convenience. If the former, it should be more durable. Of course in a multi-party system, the black and white model also seems more problematic. Are *all* other parties viewed in equally unfavourable terms?

Van der Eijk and Niemoller (1983), writing about the Netherlands, suggested the answer to this was no, a conclusion also drawn for the USA
by Weisberg (1980). Weisberg also pointed out that the degree of warmth
between some parties undermined the notion of identification because
many voters have warm feelings about more than one.

We found very few Irish voters who feel close to more than one party.
While 25 percent of respondents provided the name of a party to
which they felt close, only 2 percent felt close to more than one, and
only 0.2 percent close to more than two. This is not to say that partisanship is generally exclusive. It is still worth examining the views of
partisans about the other parties. Do they have black and white views?
Are there significant numbers who are *against* one party rather than *for*
another? The argument has certainly been made that Fine Gael has
gathered significant support because it is *not* Fianna Fáil. Members of
the Fine Gael party themselves report that a strong motive for joining
the party was a desire to fight Fianna Fáil (Gallagher and Marsh, 2002:
74) and if that is true of members, it may also be true of mere partisans.
If such partisanship is widespread it implies the potential exists for
greater instability as change can come about from a much wider variety of sources, not simply because of what one party does, but because
of what any of the parties might do. It is also important to know how
close partisans (and voters) of each party are to one another. Even if
they like only one party and dislike all the others the degree to which
they like and dislike may vary, and this may make people more or less
likely to change parties in response to short-term influences.

In Figure 4.2 voters are separated according to their degree of attachment to Fine Gael or Fianna Fáil, if any. (These two parties still attract
the support of three out of every four partisans.) This gives nine groups,
ranging from strong Fine Gael attachment, through moderate Fine Gael
attachment, weak attachment, no attachment, but voted Fine Gael, and
so on up to strong Fianna Fáil attachment. The middle point comprises
those with no attachment towards either party who also did not vote
for either party. For each group four values are displayed: the evaluation
of Fine Gael, the evaluation of Fianna Fáil, the evaluation of the next
best party and the average evaluation of all other parties excluding
Fianna Fáil and Fine Gael. Evaluations were made using a thermometer
scale where 50 is the neutral point, above that is increasingly warm
and below that increasingly cold.[7] The figure shows that Fianna Fáil
and Fine Gael partisans each like their own party and do not like the
other. This is particularly true of Fianna Fáil partisans, even Fianna
Fáil voters, who almost uniformly have a poor view of Fine Gael.[8] In
general the typical evaluation of other parties follows the same pattern.

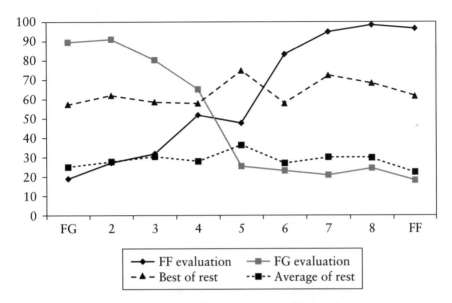

Figure 4.2   Evaluations of parties on a 0–100 scale by party
attachment: Fine Gael to Fianna Fáil only

Thus, Fianna Fáil supporters see Fine Gael as a typical 'other' party, and Fine Gael supporters have the same view of Fianna Fáil. However, in the case of both sets of supporters there is a range of views about other parties and those in each set see at least one other party in at least lukewarm terms. This suggests that, at least as far as Fianna Fáil and Fine Gael supporters are concerned, support is not exclusive. In general, supporters, and partisan supporters in particular, like their own party and do not like the main alternative, but each group does seem to hold at least one other party in some regard. This is generally no truer of those who simply vote Fianna Fáil or Fine Gael than of those who vote for either of these parties and who claim a stronger attachment.

A more general evaluation of their own and each of the other parties by those with an attachment to each party is shown in Figure 4.3. This simply gives the average thermometer rating for each party for those attached to Fianna Fáil, the Progressive Democrats, Fine Gael and so on. This confirms, for a wider set of parties, the more detailed pattern described above: partisans like their own party and tend to dislike most, and in some cases all, other parties. Not all other parties are disliked. Sinn Féin partisans have some warmth for Fianna Fáil, and Progressive Democrat partisans also like Fianna Fáil, their coalition partners; Greens and Labour also have some mutual regard, but in the

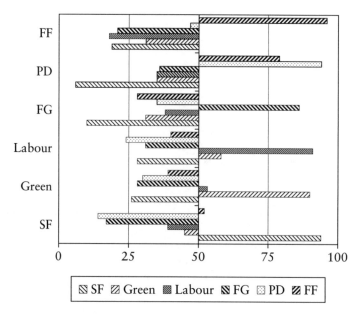

Figure 4.3 Partisans' views of other parties

aggregate Fianna Fáil and Fine Gael display no warmth towards any party even if Fianna Fáil partisans are pretty neutral about the Progressive Democrats. Surprisingly, perhaps, in view of their tradition of alliance, Fine Gael and Labour do not show the same degree of mutual warmth, but this could be a function of the absence of any alliance in the 2002 campaign. The typical partisan indeed has warm feelings (i.e. a score above 50) towards two and three parties. The fact that different people within the same party like a different group of parties makes the aggregate picture appear more exclusive than is really is. While the overall pattern might not be very well defined it is evident that partisans do not see the party system in black and white terms. There are several shades of grey with respect to other parties, but they do tend to have very warm feelings towards their own party. Overall, partisanship seems to be positive rather than negative.

Partisanship and the family

Party identification theory identifies the intergenerational transmission of partisanship as key to the stability of party systems. This may be supplemented, or even replaced, by strong social networks. The absence

Table 4.6 Father's and mother's vote when respondent
was growing up (%)

	Father	Mother
FF	40	40
FG	18	18
Labour	6	4
PDs	*	*
SF	2	1
Others	1	1
Voted for different parties	2	3
Don't know / no response	27	32
Did not vote	1	3
Total	100	100
N	1983	1983

Notes: voters only; * indicates less than 0.5 percent but more than zero.

of strong links between social institutions and political parties in Ireland, in contrast to much of Europe, suggests that the family has a significant role in socialisation and anecdotal evidence, as well as scattered survey evidence, would certainly support an argument that the family has been a strong influence (Carty, 1983, chapter 4; Sinnott, 1995: 148–9; Gallagher and Marsh, 2002: chapter 4). Respondents were asked about the voting behaviour of their parents when they were growing up. While about a third did not know,[9] or reported that their parents did not vote, a majority indicated that their parents usually voted for Fianna Fáil or Fine Gael with small numbers mentioning other parties, some of them long extinct. Remarkably few opted for the 'different parties' option (see Table 4.6).

Knowledge of parental voting habits is not a prerequisite for the transmission of predispositions to support a party. Cues given by parents may be more subtle and absorbed almost unconsciously in some cases, but it would be surprising if intergenerational transmission was widespread in the absence of any recall. The evidence here indicates that there is a basis for transmission in the fact that the majority can recall parental vote. Even among our youngest respondents, those born after 1981, 64 percent can report parental voting habits. This is comparable to the 76 percent of secondary school students who knew parental habits in the early 1970s: (see Carty, 1983: 81, n47).

If recall of parental voting habits is the first step towards transmission of partisanship we still need to see how far partisanship then

Table 4.7 Family transmission of partisanship

Party attachment	Mother and father voted for party	Father only voted for party	Mother only voted for party	Neither parent voted for party
% FF partisans	52 (N=634)	35 (N=176)	28 (N=152)	15 (N=1021)
% FG partisans	38 (N=270)	28 (N=104)	25 (N=121)	5 (N=1488)
% Labour partisans	19 (N=55)	21 (N=57)	14 (N=23)	4 (N=1848)

Notes: voters only; entries indicate percentage of cell respondents who are Fianna Fáil, FG or Labour partisans; cell totals in brackets.

follows any parental lead. A comparison of parental voting habits with each respondent's partisanship gives clear evidence of transmission. While there are many respondents with no attachment, the strength and direction of attachment tends to follow parental voting. Table 4.7 shows the respondent's partisanship broken down by the respondent's recall of their mother's and father's votes. Fifty-two percent of those with a Fianna Fáil mother and father have a Fianna Fáil partisanship, a number that falls to 35 percent if a mother is not Fianna Fáil, 28 percent if a father is not Fianna Fáil and only 15 percent if neither parent is Fianna Fáil. A uniformly Fianna Fáil family is thus more than three times as likely as a non-FF family to produce a Fianna Fáil partisan. This ratio is even greater for Labour and even more so for Fine Gael where a uniformly Fine Gael family is eight times as likely as a non-FG family to produce a Fine Gael partisan. Overall, 71 percent of Fianna Fáil partisans report at least one parent with a Fianna Fáil voting habit. The pattern is broadly similar for Fine Gael, where 68 percent of all partisans can point to a parent who voted Fine Gael. For Labour, partisanship is much more common where *either* parent typically voted Labour, but only 27 percent of Labour partisans come from a Labour voting family. The roots of Labour partisanship would appear to lie elsewhere.

Family loyalties are also evident in the respondent's voting behaviour (see Table 4.8). The patterns here are similar to those for partisanship in some respects. People are much more likely to vote for a particular party if both of their parents did so and, to a lesser degree, if only one parent did so, either mother or father. It is evident that transmission rates in most groups are similar for partisanship and for vote, but the incidence of voting for Fianna Fáil among respondents from non-Fianna

Table 4.8 Family transmission of vote choice

Vote	Mother and father voted for party	Father only voted for party	Mother only voted for party	Neither parent voted for party
% FF voters	57 (N=634)	42 (N=176)	35 (N=152)	26 (N=1021)
% FG voters	51 (N=270)	35 (N=104)	30 (N=121)	14 (N=1488)
% Labour voters	24 (N=55)	21 (N=57)	14 (N=23)	9 (N=1848)

Notes: voters only; entries indicate percentage of those in each cell who are Fianna Fáil, FG or Labour voters; cell totals in brackets.

Fáil families is much higher than is the incidence of partisanship. Hence, the ratio of Fianna Fáil voters from uniformly Fianna Fáil families to the incidence of Fianna Fáil voters from non-FF families is only about two to one; and the corresponding ratio is only about four to one among those from Fine Gael and Labour families. Parental tradition has a weaker impact on vote choice than it does on partisanship. Sixty-three percent of Fianna Fáil voters could recall a Fianna Fáil parent, 48 percent of Fine Gael voters recalled a Fine Gael parent and only 18 percent of Labour voters could recall a Labour voting parent. Thus, while parental loyalties translate quite well into the voting patterns of offspring, it is only a bare majority of the voters for one of these three well-established parties who may have 'inherited' their party, and, bearing in mind that only three-quarters of all voters supported one of the three, this means a minority of voters overall vote as their parents did.

The numbers in Table 4.8 can be contrasted with the results of a 1969 study reported by Carty (1983) which found 78 percent of those whose father (the only parent for which data was available) was Fianna Fáil voting for Fianna Fáil, and correspondingly 65 percent voting Fine Gael and 53 percent Labour.[10] These are much higher than for 2002, where numbers are 61 percent, 48 percent and 25 percent. Sinnott, using data from 1990, reported numbers of 68 percent, 53 percent and 30 percent respectively for Fianna Fáil, Fine Gael and Labour transmission, somewhat closer to 2002 rates (1995: 149). Just as identification has declined, so has intergenerational transmission of the vote although there has been little decline over the past decade.

This evidence on the political affiliations of the family is consistent with the view that partisanship is generally rooted in childhood socialisation and, therefore, both separate from, and antecedent to, current vote. The argument that parents inculcate in their children a predisposition to vote for a particular party is certainly consistent with this evidence, even if it is clear that this does not seem to be the case for a significant number of voters. It makes sense to see this effect as one that engenders partisanship in the offspring, but it may also create a predisposition that does not show up in our partisanship questions. For instance, children of a Fianna Fáil father tend to vote Fianna Fáil even where they are not partisans, and the same is true of children of Fine Gael parents. It could be that this is simply due to a shared outlook and set of interests by parents and children and that a family tradition of support for a party is not tapped by the partisanship question used here.

We explore the relative impact of family voting and partisanship on the vote in Table 4.9. This analysis excludes non-voters and those whose vote choice is unknown. Cell entries show the percentage of cases in each cell where the respondent voted for that party as opposed to voting for a different one. (Note that the Ns here are seven times as large as the number of respondents, as we have stacked the data matrix by seven parties, including Independents/others.) It can be seen that where attachment and family traditions are in accord on the main diagonal of the table, 81 percent vote for the party when they are positive and only 6 percent when they are negative: that is, neither attachment nor family tradition. When only one positive factor is present, the influence of attachment on vote is much stronger than the influence of family tradition: 73 percent as against 28 percent. This means that both tradition and partisanship exercise separate influences. Partisanship seems the stronger direct influence but, as we have already seen, tradition may be seen in significant part to account for partisanship, at least in the largest parties.

Table 4.9 Family vote traditions, party attachment and vote choice (%)

| | | Party attachment | | |
		Attached to party	Not attached to party	All
Parental traditions	Parent voted for party	81 (N=659)	28 (N=1,054)	49 (N=1,713)
	Parent did not vote for party	73 (N=473)	6 (N=12,919)	9 (N=13,392)
	All	77 (N=1,132)	8 (N=13,973)	14 (N=15,105)

Notes: voters only; the data had been stacked for this analysis according to the seven vote options in Table 6 and so the N is seven times as large as the number of respondents.

These numbers are not unvarying across parties, a feature shown in previous tables. For Fianna Fáil, when parental traditions and partisanship coincide positively, 82 percent vote Fianna Fáil as opposed to only 22 percent when both are negative. Corresponding numbers for Fine Gael and Labour are 79 percent and 10 percent, and 70 percent and 6 percent. (The numbers are too small to permit separate analyses of the other parties.) While each party had much the same success in 2002 in translating favourable predispositions into votes, Fianna Fáil – the clear winner in the election – clearly did much better at translating non-favourable predispositions into votes than the other two parties.

It remains to be seen how far such patterns persist across elections, but generally these results are consistent with the argument that family voting tradition and partisanship are linked – most plausibly, the former gives rise to the latter – but also that vote tradition has a significant impact even when not channelled through partisanship. In other words, voting – and stable voting – may come not simply from partisanship as measured by our party attachment questions, but also via a family tradition of support for a party that is not picked up by those questions. It seems unlikely that this is simply a problem with the question although evidence suggests that in the USA more people respond to the classic party identification measure than to this one (Blais *et al.*, 2001). It may also be due to the changing political climate in Ireland as party competition has intensified and politicians have been subject to much more intense public scrutiny that in the past. These days, perhaps, some voters do not admit to feeling close to a party, even if they always tend to vote for it.

Conclusion

In many respects the concept of party identification makes sense in the Irish context. We see most identifiers belonging to the long-established parties, particularly Fianna Fáil (the most stable of them), and identification is separate from the vote. Partisans are more likely to vote in a particular way, but are not certain to do so; and voting with the identified party declines with declining strength of partisanship. Straight-ticket voting and consistent voting between 1997 and 2002 also declines as partisanship weakens. We also see the roots of partisanship in the family, as we would expect. Most partisans have at least one parent who usually supported their party. It is hard to disentangle the separate impact of familial support and current partisanship on the vote although each has a sizeable effect taken alone, as we have seen. Yet, just as a large proportion of voters report no partisanship, so also does a sizeable proportion report not knowing whether parents usually supported a particular party. While family socialisation obviously plays a significant part in current partisanship and voting habits, there are many voters whose political preferences cannot be accounted for in this way.

Partisans in general have a positive basis for their attachment. They like their own party a lot and do not like other parties, or certainly like them a lot less than they do their own. There is little evidence of attachment being negative, stemming from a dislike of alternatives rather than the attraction of a particular party and this suggests partisanship is more likely to provide a stable support base for those parties who have many partisans. However, partisans are not exclusive in their affections and attachment is quite consistent with warm feelings towards more than one party. This may reflect some ideological affinity (SF and Fianna Fáil, and Labour and Greens perhaps) as well as current alliances (PDs and Fianna Fáil).

Having discussed the causes and consequences of partisanship at some length it must be emphasised that on the evidence of the party attachment question the Irish electorate is now significantly dealigned. A majority of voters are open to persuasion according to the balance of short-term forces. If these were evenly balanced, Fianna Fáil would win most elections, since that party has a disproportionately large share of partisans, and we would see few Independents elected to the Dáil. Beyond that, nothing much would change. In fact, Fianna Fáil did very well among partisans and non-partisans in 2002. Although in relative terms short-term influences seemed to favour Independents and work against Fianna Fáil, in absolute terms Fianna Fáil won a large plurality of the vote among both partisans and non-partisans, but since we have no point of comparison it is not possible to say that Fianna Fáil, or any other party, did 'well' or 'poorly' this time among the non-partisans. What we would have expected is that Fianna Fáil, as the party winning the election, and increasing its vote over 1997 and 1992, did better among its own partisans than did Fine Gael but, as we have seen, the differences here are relatively small.

While the concept of attachment is, therefore, helpful in examining voting patterns, this exploration of party identification in Ireland cannot provide a baseline against which we can judge the 2002 election. By examining partisanship we might hope to provide an indication of what an election would look like if all the short-term factors were to be neutral in their effects – providing what Stokes called a 'normal' election (Stokes, 1966). This is not really possible, first, because a substantial proportion of the electorate do not have a standing decision to vote for any particular party, and second, because we have insufficient information about what 'normally' happens in Irish elections. At least half of the electorate has a bias towards a party but, for half of these, it is only a slight one. If we are looking for stronger predispositions we are talking about only a quarter of electors. It is apparent that this situation was different in the past. Even 25 years ago we might have found that most voters had some attachment, as we know that half had a strong one (see Figure 4.1), but no longer. The anchor is now loose. Short-term factors therefore have an increasing potential to make a big impact on Irish elections.

Notes

1 A recent set of review articles in *Political Behavior* 24 (2, 3) 2002.
2 Authors' calculations using CSES wave 1: see www.umich.edu/~cses.
3 In the case of the small number of respondents who said they were close to more than one party we have taken the first mentioned party as 'their' party.
4 Analysis here is restricted to those giving their first preference to a candidate with at least one running mate.
5 About half of the split-ticket voters do, however, vote at some point for all 'their' party's candidates even if not in sequence. In all, 82 percent of those 'close' vote for all such candidates, 75 percent of those who are 'somewhat close' and 64 percent of leaners while 33 percent of those with no affiliation do so.
6 Actually, there are relatively few instances where a party fielded four candidates and few instances even of three. Only Fianna Fáil provides enough instances of 2, 3 and 4 candidates to allow comparisons. It appears that a majority of strong identifiers are likely to show solidarity, however, many candidates are standing. There is some decline in the solidarity of moderate identifiers and leaners as the number of candidates increases to 4, but the number of cases here is too small to show significant differences.
7 'I'd like to ask you how you feel about some Irish politicians, using what we call the "feeling thermometer". The feeling thermometer works like this: If you have a *favourable feeling* (a warm feeling) towards a POLITICIAN you should place him/her somewhere between 50 and 100 degrees; if you have an *unfavourable feeling* (a cold feeling) towards a POLITICIAN you should place him/her somewhere between 0 and 50 degrees; if you *don't feel particularly warm or cold* (have no feeling towards the politician at all) then you should place him/her at 50 degrees; where would you place these Irish politicians? And where would you place each of the following PARTIES; and where would you place these CANDIDATES who ran in your constituency in the general election in May?'
8 There is a striking contrast here between Fine Gael and Fianna Fáil voters as Fine Gael voters do not have any particular distaste for FF. How far

this is typical, and how far due to the particularly dismal performance of Fine Gael in the 2002 campaign and election is not known at this time.

9 This was the first option on the showcard, an ordering that should minimise the chance that respondents would invent a memory. The 30 percent who don't know is much the same as that found by Larsen in 1969: see Carty, 1983: 82.

10 It is not clear whether the question asked was about father's typical vote or something stronger, although the Ns suggest the former.

5

Credit and blame for the 'Celtic Tiger'

Political debate, both in Dáil Éireann and in the media, often focuses on policy issues. In the run-up to an election, political parties put a lot of resources into producing election manifestos that outline what they will do if elected to government office (Garry and Mansergh, 1999). But does any of this effort matter? Are the vote decisions of Irish people influenced by policy issues? Certainly, some are sceptical about the role of policy issues in Irish elections. P. J. Mara, Fianna Fáil Director of Elections in 2002, claimed that, contrary to the notions of many journalists, elections in Ireland were not really about issues at all. Another senior party adviser, Labour's Fergus Finlay argued that Irish parties do not occupy distinct positions on a policy dimension. In Ireland, he says, there is not so much a policy dimension as 'a policy dot' with all parties identically positioned.[1] In a critique of the spatial metaphor in electoral analysis, Donald Stokes (1963: 372–3) observed that many important issues in elections concern goals on which the vast majority of voters agreed (for example, the need for a prosperous economy or the need for virtue in government).[2] The electoral dispute over such 'valence' issues is largely about which party, or leader, could best achieve them in the future, or should get credit or blame for having, or not having, done so in the past. The argument has also been made that voters know too little about politics to make coherent decisions about credit and blame.

However, as another American political scientist, V. O. Key, responded, voters know quite enough to judge whether things they cared about were getting better or getting worse. In a sense, elections let voters play the 'rational god of vengeance and reward' (Key, 1966). From this point of view, voters reject bad governments and support the not so bad ones. It would appear that Irish voters have played the role of a very vengeful god. Between 1969 and 2002, no government was returned to office. While Fianna Fáil did succeed in staying in office after the 1989 and 1992 general elections, their coalition partners differed; being first the Progressive Democrats and then Labour (and the Progressive Democrats again in 1997 and 2002).

So far, we have been concerned with long-term influences on Irish voting behaviour. We have learned that the roots of stability in Irish party preferences lie more in general attachments to parties (for the most part transmitted down through the family) than in social cleavages, values or ideologies. In this chapter, and the next, we shift gears somewhat and look at short-term mechanisms that influence how people vote. The main emphasis in these chapters is not fundamental policy disagreements, but general evaluations of the relative competence of parties, and their leaders, to govern effectively. In this chapter, we look at the issues that dominated the 2002 election, and at voters' judgements on the performance of the outgoing government. We see that while the record of the outgoing government was a mixed one it was in credit on the big issues. The government's record of having delivered higher employment and lower taxes outweighed the debit column of criticisms of the health services, the cost of living, housing and crime.

Election concerns in 2002

The main theme of the election campaign, both the official one in April and May 2002, and the informal one of the previous two years, was the imbalance between the objective success of the economy and citizens' dissatisfaction with the quality of public services and infrastructure. During the government's term of office, there had been unprecedentedly high rates of growth and record low levels of unemployment. However, many voters perceived a decline in the quality of public services in many areas, or at least felt that they had not lived up to people's expectations.

Over the five years in which the Fianna Fáil-Progressive Democrat coalition was in power, the performance of the economy reached levels never experienced before in the history of the state. Over the second half of the 1990s the Irish economy grew very quickly. Between 1997 and 2002, the Central Statistical Office (CSO, 2003) reported year-on-year increases in GDP of about 10 percent (and increases in GNP of about 9 percent). The strong growth in the economy had a positive impact on job creation. Unemployment – a problem that had plagued Irish governments from the late 1970s – fell from 10 percent in 1997 to just 4 percent in 2002. As part of the social partnership agreements and in exchange for low wage increases, the government introduced a series of reforms to the tax system. These not only involved the reduction of tax rates (the standard rate of tax was reduced from 26 percent to 20 percent and the higher rate from 48 percent to 42 percent), but also the widening of tax bands. Not only did these reforms stimulate job creation and demand in the economy, but also over this period interest rates fell to very low levels. At the end of May 1997 the one-month inter-bank interest rate stood at 6.2 percent. By the end of April 2002 it was 3.3 percent. (Department of Finance monthly reports, www.finance.gov.ie/publications/). This decline means that those who had mortgages and loans have more money in their pockets than they had when interest rates were higher. Falling interest rates also mean that the cost of (borrowing) money falls and this encourages investment in industry, which stimulates further economic growth. Finally, low interest rates had an impact on house prices. The average price of both new and second-hand houses in Ireland almost doubled over the five-year period, with increases in house prices exceeding 100 percent in the Dublin area (CSO, 2003: 342).

In terms of headline economic indicators, pressures from strong growth as well as from external factors (such as high oil prices and low interest rates) were contributing to rising prices. The annual percentage change in the consumer price index increased from 1.5 percent in 1996/7 to 4.6 percent in 2001/02, having peaked at 5.6 percent in 1999/0). The improved performance was a double-edged sword in that it led to increased demands on, and expectations of, the quality of public services such as health and transport (in particular, roads and rail). The state of the health service concerned many voters, and to a far greater extent in 2002 (39 percent saw it as a crucial issue) than in 1997 (when less than 10 percent did so) (Garry *et al.*, 2003: Table 6.4). In the government's defence, €7 billion were spent on health; as a proportion of the national economy spending had increased from 6.6 percent of GNP in 1997 to 7.3 percent in 2001 (CSO, 2003: 143, 191) and in the months prior to the election the government published its strategy for reforming the health service. However, as a proportion of GNP, spending on health in 2002 was slightly less than it had been in 1983 (7.8 percent of GNP) (CSO, 1986). Given the public spending cutbacks of the late 1980s, it might be suggested that there is substantial lost ground that needs to be made up before people will feel that they have a health service adequate to deal with their needs.

Increased demand on the transport infrastructure was also evident with overcrowding on trains and traffic jams on motorways and in the centres of large towns and cities. Iarnrod Éireann (Irish Rail) embarked on a process of upgrading the rail network and eventually the construction of a lightrail system for Dublin began. Spending on roads was also increasing. However, for some people all this was taking a very long time.

Concerns about crime are a feature of many election campaigns and 2002 was no exception. Fianna Fáil had promised a 'zero-tolerance' law and order policy at the 1997 election and this promise proved a hostage to fortune as the crime level showed no sign of declining. While statistics produced by An Garda Síochána showed a drop in the number of reported crimes, the detection rate showed no improvement between 1997 and 2002 (CJO, 2001: 103; CSO, 2003: 124). A problem for political parties is that, even if crime rates are falling, enough high-profile cases can still give the public an impression that nobody is safe in their homes or on the streets. Right at the start of the campaign the issue of crime was pushed to the forefront of people's minds, as two gardaí were killed by so-called joy-riders. Fianna Fáil promised a lot more gardaí if elected, a recognition that not enough was currently being done.

The backdrop for the election was an imbalance between private affluence and public squalor. For the government parties, the strategy was to highlight their effectiveness in providing economic growth and ask the electorate to let them finish the job. The Fianna Fáil slogan exemplified this approach: 'A lot done – more to do.' Fianna Fáil's own research suggested that although voters were concerned about spending on health and infrastructure, they were more concerned that the next government should not be reckless with the government finances and, as a result, damage future economic prospects. Fianna Fáil thus sought to portray itself as the party of fiscal responsibility.

The opposition parties argued that the government had not done enough and that it had mismanaged the wealth created by the economy. Sinn Féin, in particular, argued that the benefits of wealth had simply gone to the rich. Fine Gael and Labour also criticised the government for failing to deliver better services on health, crime and education. These criticisms had been highlighted well in advance of the election. At the end of 2000, Fine Gael launched a campaign intended to highlight the slow movement in areas such as transport, education and health: 'the Celtic Snail'. However, the campaign was negatively evaluated by the media and, since many members of the party considered it ill-judged, it proved the catalyst in the move to replace John Bruton with Michael Noonan as leader of the party.

The promises that the various parties made during the election campaign depended on future growth in the economy. All of the main parties sought to convince the electorate that they had the best plans for providing major investment in health, education and infrastructure, while at the same time maintaining the low-tax regime and keeping the public finances stable. The parties put forward different plans as to how they would pay for their promises. Fianna Fáil suggested a National Development Finance Agency to raise money for capital spending, while Fine Gael's plans relied on well-managed growth. What was generally missing from the parties' proposals was any clear recognition that the economy was far less strong than it had been. In the year before the election, evidence of a slowdown in the economy began to emerge. In 2001, growth in GDP fell to 5.7 percent (and in GNP to 4.6 percent). While the press gave a lot of attention to this topic, the parties resisted any temptation to make much of it (see Brandenburg and Hayden, 2003; Brandenburg, 2005). The government parties hardly wanted to damage their own reputation as economic managers, while the main opposition parties did not want to undermine their promises of better services that rested on the assumption of continued economic success.

Punishment and reward

There is now an extensive body of research on the link between government performance, particularly in economic affairs, and voting behaviour. Initial findings stressed the link between economic indicators and the vote and sought to demonstrate that the electorate operated a system of reward and punishment in which governments presiding over good times were returned and those who did not were ejected (Tufte, 1978). Later work argued that it was more plausible to see voters using the economy as a basis for assessing competence: good times would lead voters to judge that an incumbent party was worth supporting, while bad times would lead voters to look elsewhere (Duch and Stevenson, 2008). Voters' assessments may also be nuanced and asymmetric, with voters rejecting a failing government, but being slow to reward a good one (Bloom and Price, 1975). However, when this asymmetric relationship has been examined, particularly where data on individuals have been used, the findings have been mixed (Stevenson, 2002: 46).

While there is a link between election results and economics, the strength and nature of this relationship varies. Not only do electors respond to different economic indicators at different times (unemployment at one time and inflation at another), but also the link between economic factors and vote is stronger in some countries than others. One reason for this is the difference between political systems. It is easier in some political systems than in others to identify responsibility and thus apportion blame. In a very influential piece of research, Powell and Whitten (1993; see also Palmer and Whitten, 2000) demonstrated that elections are more likely to follow the reward–punishment model in countries where responsibility is most easily allocated to a single party. However, where responsibility is divided (because of coalition government, minority government, strong parliamentary committees or a decentralised federal structure), it is harder for voters to identify who is to blame. With coalition governments, for example, the voters must decide whether responsibility should be distributed equally between the parties or whether one party is more responsible than the others. Other important factors include the length of time a government has been in office and how open an economy is to outside influence.

The key point is that a reward–punishment model (or a competence signalling model) requires voters not simply to evaluate the performance of the economy, but also to apportion credit and blame as appropriate. A further element may also be important. Voters may need an alternative (for example, Sanders and Carey, 2002; Anderson, 2000). In the classic two-party system this is easy. Discontented voters can support the opposition. But in a multi-party system things are less clear-cut and a vote against the government may not do much to effect a replacement if there is no alternative government in waiting. V. O. Key argued that voters required little special information to know when times were good and when they were bad. Even so, this raises the question of how they know. General sources of information are the media, as well as their own experiences and the experiences of people they talk to.

Irish voters' evaluations of the government are not limited to the economic realm. The health service has been a major item in the media for a long time, both in terms of the policy debate (the details of which some voters may not follow) and people's stories of waiting lists, two-tier services and hospital ward closures. Many who may have had no need of the service themselves have family members or friends with more direct experience. From this it is easy to see how a voter with little interest in politics can come to an evaluation of the state of the health services. The same is true of other issues such as housing and transport, where voters can easily form an evaluation about how well things are working. This is not to say that all such evaluations are necessarily 'objective' and, as we will see, not everyone shares the same viewpoint. However, it is reasonable to assume that if we ask voters to assess whether things have been getting better or worse in relation to housing or transport they will have some basis for their evaluation. Research has suggested that perceptions of economic performance are influenced by information levels, group interests, personal economic circumstances and partisanship in ways which vary over time, implying that aggregated perceptions are not unbiased measures (Dalmer *et al.*, 2000). Importantly, people's long-term attachments to political parties present a problem for the reward–punishment model. The story that people vote against the government because they see it as doing badly is less convincing if it turns out that this perception stems directly from life-long commitment to an opposition party. We shall keep partisanship in mind and return to it.

In other Irish elections the evaluation of the government's performance on economic matters has been seen to play a role in shaping voting. In the 1997 election, for example, the Rainbow coalition and Fianna Fáil could each claim credit for economic growth, since both had been in government since the previous election. In 2002 the opposition also could argue that the economic boom was not of the government's making, but was due to a combination of favourable circumstances in the world economy, while the government could also point to the slowing of the world economy as a reason why growth would be much slower in 2002 than in earlier years. Differential responsibility within the government was also an issue with the small Progressive Democrat party seeking to highlight their contribution on issues where performance may generally be seen to be good – economic growth, cutting taxes and increasing employment, for instance, and disassociating themselves from less popular proposals such as building a new national sports stadium. The importance of an alternative government also exercised the main opposition parties, with Fine Gael seeking an alliance with Labour and the Greens and those parties preferring to keep their options open. With the polls overstating the Fianna Fáil vote and understating support for the opposition parties, voters might well have perceived that there was no plausible alternative government to the Fianna Fáil-PD government.

Perceptions of performance

The general perception was that the Fianna Fáil-Progressive Democrat government had been a good one. Opinion poll evidence shows that public satisfaction with the performance of the government recorded average levels of 58 percent over its five years in office; these levels were maintained over its last eighteen months in office (see Figure 5.1). While there were troughs, the government was always able to bounce back. These levels of satisfaction were remarkably high, given an average satisfaction level of 42 percent since 1977, and just 38 percent

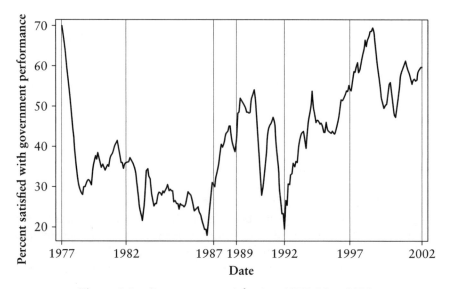

Figure 5.1   Government satisfaction 1977–May 2002

Source: IMS/Lansdowne and MRBI polls

before the 1997 election. Thus, we might imagine that voters would have fairly positive evaluations of how well the government performed on a range of important policy themes.

Our examination of the role played by policy issues begins in a very general way. Respondents were asked, '*in general* how good or bad a job do you think the government has done over the last five years . . .' The responses to this question show a positive appraisal of the government: 13 percent said it had done a 'very good job', 68 percent a 'good job', 12 percent a 'bad job' and 4 percent a 'very bad job' (a further 2 percent were undecided). Given these circumstances, it is hardly surprising that the government was returned to office. However, it is significant that electoral support for the government (46 percent) was not nearly as high as the proportion of people who thought the government had done a good job (81 percent). Clearly, many who thought the government had done well voted for opposition parties.

Given the record itself and the substance of the campaign, it is important to know how perceptions of the economy and other policy issues, such as the health services, feed into this overall assessment. It is also important to know whether any of these perceptions were decisive in determining overall assessment. We begin to address these questions by focusing on the salience of issues for the voters (i.e. the relative

Table 5.1   Major problems facing the 1997–2002 government

	Percentage mentioning issue	Balance major issue	Balance overall record	Percentage supporting government
Health	20	−8	+60	43
Jobs/unemployment	15	+73	+73	49
Crime/drugs	12	−7	+67	49
Economy	11	+69	+78	48
NI	7	+83	+65	47
Inflation	6	−28	+57	56
Immigration	6	−12	+59	51
Other	27	+8	+48	39
Total	104	+28	61	45

Note: voters only.

importance of different issues). First, respondents identified the most important issue the government had to deal with in the last five years; they were then asked whether or not the government's record on this issue was a good one.

There is little agreement on what was the most important issue. The four most commonly cited policy areas were health, jobs and unemployment, crime and drugs, and the management of the economy (see Table 5.1). In addition, at least 1 in 20 voters cited Northern Ireland, inflation and immigration. Smaller numbers mentioned the European Union (including the Nice Treaty and the common currency), housing, roads and traffic, and honesty/political corruption. Just 1 in 100 mentioned inequality.

The impact of issues on the vote may be bound up with the government's performance. The second column of Table 5.1 shows the balance of opinion (positive *minus* negative) on each of the issues mentioned. In general, for the issue people identified as the most important one, many more people said the government had done well than poorly. This is especially so for those who mentioned the economy, in general, and jobs/unemployment, in particular. Given the role played by the government in the Northern Ireland peace process it is not surprising that people saw the government's performance on this issue in a very positive light. People who were concerned about health and crime/drugs tended to be somewhat critical of the government's performance. Only with respect to a few issues, each mentioned as important by small proportions of voters, was there a negative perception of performance: inflation, the environment, honesty in government, immigration and its consequences, and inequality.

The third column shows the balance of evaluations of the government's record as whole. It is clear that almost all groups – regardless of the issue mentioned – approved the overall performance of the government. Only those concerned with equality were, on balance, critical. It is interesting that voters, who were relatively critical of the government's record on a particular issue, approved of the government's overall record. It may well be that when answering the more general question, the performance of the economy had a greater influence on respondents than issues like crime and health. We explore this in more detail below.

There is a school of thought that argues that party competition consists of each party trying to emphasise those issues on which they are strong (Budge and Farlie, 1983).[3] The final column shows the extent of electoral support for the two government parties in each issue group and there is little sign that an emphasis on particular issues hurt or harmed the government very much. In general, most of the issues of more widespread concern seem to have helped the government marginally. The main exception is health, as the percentage of people mentioning this issue, who voted for the government, is slightly less than overall electoral support for the government (43 percent and 46 percent, respectively). If health rather than economic management issues had been more widely salient, the government would have done less well. The government would have done very badly if inequality had been the main issue (24 percent); but inequality would have to move a very long way up the agenda to make much difference. As we see from the 'Other' row, those citing issues off the main agenda were more critical of the government and less likely to vote for it (39 percent).

As well as focusing on issues that were salient to them, we asked voters to evaluate the government's record on selected major issues. The evidence suggests that there is a strong relationship between voters' evaluations of the government's record on these issues and vote choice (see Table 5.2). Those assessing government performance as very good were almost three times as likely to vote for Fianna Fáil as were those seeing it as very bad (the Progressive Democrat pattern is less clear cut, perhaps because of smaller numbers). In contrast, the main opposition parties did much better among voters who saw the government as failing to deal with the major problems. While support for Fine Gael is strongest among those who judge government

Table 5.2   Vote by evaluation of government's record on major problems facing the 1997–2002 government (%)

	Very good	Good job	Bad job	Very bad	Don't know	Total
FF	67	45	29	22	32	42
FG	13	21	27	30	30	22
Green	2	3	6	6	4	4
Lab	3	9	15	21	12	11
PD	4	4	5	1	1	4
SF	5	6	6	9	14	7
Ind	6	9	11	8	8	9
Others	1	2	2	4	0	2
Total	100	100	100	100	100	100
N	228	931	424	163	70	1816

performance as 'very bad', this group accounts for less than a tenth of the number of voters.

Earlier we noted that the reward–punishment model involves not simply evaluating the government's performance, but also apportioning credit and blame as appropriate and the identification of a credible alternative. To take account of these factors we asked our respondents a series of four questions. First we asked whether, in a given policy area, things had got better or worse over the last five years (the lifetime of the Fianna Fáil-PD government). We asked this question in relation to a number of issues, including those that pre-election polls had indicated were salient to voters as well as those which had been salient in the past (i.e. the economy in general, the health services, housing, transport, crime and the cost of living as well as unemployment and the levels of taxation).[4] We then asked people whether they thought the improvement/decline was due mainly to the policies of the government (or due to other factors). The point here was to find out about the attribution of responsibility for success or failure (is it really the government who should be rewarded for the success or blamed for the failure?). The next question asked people to say which of the two parties in government, if any, was mainly responsible: was it both parties equally, mainly Fianna Fáil or mainly the Progressive Democrats. Finally, we asked whether any other party (and if so which one(s)) would do a better job. In other words, on the issue in question was there a credible alternative to the outgoing government?

While people's evaluations of economic issues were broadly positive (with the exception of the cost of living), their evaluations of other

Table 5.3　Policy evaluations (%)

	Worse	Same	Better	Better–worse
Economy	10	8	82	+72
Unemployment	22	11	67	+45
Tax	35	13	52	+17
Housing	41	13	46	+5
Health	51	22	27	−25
Crime	86	9	5	−81
Transport	93	4	3	−90
Cost of living	97	2	1	−96

Note: voters only.

issues, in particular crime and transport, were negative (see Table 5.3). This is a mixed record, and perhaps gave rise to the sort of campaign we saw in 2002; a campaign that revolved around the perceived competence (or otherwise) of parties to solve the problems generated by a growing economy.

When we compare these particular evaluations to the overall evaluation of the government (in Table 5.2) it appears that the only issues that directly influence overall assessment are health, the economy and housing. Simple correlations (ranging from 0 to 1, with 1 being strong and 0 weak) summarising the relationship between each of them and the summary overall evaluation are 0.28 for health, 0.22 for the economy and 0.21 for housing. One reason why the association between issue evaluations and assessment of the government might be low is that voters do not hold the government to be responsible for some matters. The evidence suggests that there is considerable disparity in the degree to which voters attribute credit/blame to the government and that this can vary in some areas according to the evaluation (see Table 5.4).

Decisions regarding taxation are directly the responsibility of a government (allowing for some EU constraints) and almost all voters hold the government responsible for them. Other issues are only partially amenable to government decisions. The government is more likely to receive credit/blame for the state of the economy and health services than for crime and transport.[5]

Judgements also vary somewhat according to whether voters evaluate the government's performance as either good or bad (columns 2

Table 5.4 Attribution of responsibility to government policies (%)

	Attribute responsibility to government policies	Attribute responsibility to government policies record good	Attribute responsibility to government policies record bad
Tax	89	95	85
Health	81	89	80
Housing	74	81	71
Economy	65	64	72
Unemployment	65	69	64
Cost of living	64	41	65
Transport	50	86	49
Crime	47	79	45

Note: voters only.

and 3, respectively). In general, this pattern is one that works in the government's favour. The percentage of voters crediting the government for improvements in a particular area tends to be greater than the percentage of those blaming them for a worsening situation. There are few very big differences, but where these exist (crime and transport) the number of cases in the 'better' category is very low (see Table 5.3). However, when it comes to the economy the reverse is the case. Voters who think the state of the economy has declined are more likely to blame the government than those who think it has improved are to give it credit (Table 5.4). However, only 10 percent thought the economy was worse off. Housing is an interesting case because evaluations are more evenly balanced (Table 5.3). Those giving positive evaluations are 10 percentage points more likely to attribute responsibility to the government than are those with negative evaluations (Table 5.4).

Given the arguments and evidence put forward in Chapter 4, there must be a suspicion that partisanship will influence some voters either to point the finger of blame at the government or to clap their hands in approval. We examined the link between evaluation and attribution on the health issue for two different groups of partisans: those attached to a government party and those attached to an opposition party. We found that government partisans were a lot more likely to attribute credit to the government than blame. Over 90 percent of those who thought the health service was getting better attributed this to the government, but

Table 5.5   Attribution, evaluation and partisanship

	Percentage attributing performance to govt policy (FF partisan)	Percentage attributing performance to govt policy (Non-govt partisan)	Percentage attributing performance to govt policy (All)
Health much worse	63	83	82
Health worse	68	89	78
Health same	72	90	76
Health better	94	83	88
Health much better	100	*	97

Notes: voters only; * indicates that there are too few cases; minimum elsewhere is 39.

only two-thirds of those who thought it was getting worse blamed the government. In contrast, opposition partisans made no such distinction, with over 80 percent attributing responsibility to government, whatever their evaluation. This shows how partisanship can play a filtering role, allowing favoured parties to gain credit and evade blame to a greater extent than would be expected among non-partisans. It also highlights how complex the link can be between performance and electoral support (Marsh and Tilley, 2006; Rudolph, 2003).

The outgoing government was a two-party coalition. Do people attribute responsibility to the government as a whole or do they hold one party more responsible than the other? Examining the third part of the credit and blame questions, we see that neither Fianna Fáil nor the Progressive Democrats emerge as having the lion's share of responsibility (see Table 5.6). Most voters saw both government parties as sharing the credit or blame. Those who did distinguish one from the other tended to emphasise the role of Fianna Fáil. The one exception is tax, where voters saw the Progressive Democrats as more important. This is an interesting result given the size of the Progressive Democrats relative to Fianna Fáil. The Progressive Democrats' campaign sought to highlight their contribution to the government. (One slogan was: 'Look what we could do with 4 [TDs], think what we could do with 8'.) These results indicate that they had some success and that, in the case of tax, they have developed a relatively high profile. Significantly, it is among those who see tax as declining that their profile is highest,

Table 5.6 Attribution of responsibility within government (%)

	Attribute responsibility to both parties equally	Attribute particular responsibility to FF	Attribute particular responsibility to Progressive Democrats
Tax	81	8	10
Health	83	14	3
Economy	83	14	3
Unemployment	88	8	4
Housing	90	8	2
Crime	89	9	2
Cost of living	92	6	1
Transport	92	7	1

Note: voters only.

with 16 percent of those who thought tax was falling crediting the Progressive Democrats.

Finally, we come to the question of whether or not voters felt there was a credible alternative to the government. Voters were asked if they thought any other party could do better. Despite the fact that the opposition parties won 54 percent of the vote, most voters thought that they would not have done better. Only a minority of those who attributed responsibility to the government said some other party could perform better (see Table 5.7).[6] While the government looked best on economic policy, what the evidence highlights is the weak position of the opposition (column 1). For the eight policy issues, sizeable majorities believe that no other party could have done a better job than the governing parties. This is even the case where voters have been critical of the government's performance on issues such as health, transport and crime.

Separate sets of percentages are displayed according to whether people's evaluations were positive or negative in that issue area. As we might expect, the unwillingness of voters to regard any other party as being able to do better is even more apparent when we look at those who think things had improved. That said, about 15 percent of those who think things had improved still put more faith in an alternative. When the evaluation is negative there is more opportunity for opposition parties to convince people that they would do a better job. This is indeed the case, but even on issues about which people tended to be

Table 5.7 Perceptions that another party would do better (%)

	No other party could handle issue better (All)	No other party could handle issue better (Positive evaluations)	No other party could handle issue better (Negative evaluations)
Economy	86	87	56
Tax	80	85	67
Unemployment	79	84	62
Housing	71	87	47
Health	67	86	50
Crime	67	82	62
Cost of living	67	*	66
Transport	62	85	60

Notes: voters only; includes only those crediting/blaming government policies;
* indicates that there are too few cases; minimum elsewhere is 47.

dissatisfied with the government's performance, there was no instance in which an opposition party was seen as a credible alternative by a majority of voters. Despite being critical of the government on crime, the cost of living and transport, more than 60 percent believed that no other party could do better than the government. At best, about half of the voters regarded the opposition as a whole as a credible alternative on housing and health.

As to which opposition party would do better, the distribution of responses reflected each party's overall popularity. Fine Gael's lead over the other opposition parties was clearest on the economy and crime (also Sinn Féin's best issue). That said, there are some interesting deviations. Labour had a marginal lead over Fine Gael on housing and health. The Greens were the most popular alternative on transport: 16 percent of respondents who blamed the government for poor performance on transport thought the Greens would do better.

It is also worth noting that the differences between columns 2 and 3 are generally sharper than in Table 5.4. This suggests that evaluation is linked much more closely to the attractiveness of alternatives than it is to attribution of responsibility. On health and housing, where opinion is reasonably well divided in terms of evaluation, the difference between the two columns is over 30 percent, compared with differences on attribution of only about 10 percent.

The aggregate picture

Putting all this together, it is apparent that the government was in good shape in terms of underlying voter evaluations. Voters judged the government positively in several areas, particularly the economic ones, and gave credit for policies in those fields. Where evaluations were negative, there was more uncertainly about responsibility and few thought anyone else would do better. Hence, while there were areas in which the opposition parties might have hoped voters would take it out on the government for performing poorly, their own lack of credibility inhibited many voters from doing so.

As suggested above, issues are most likely to damage the government if evaluations are negative; the government gets the blame and the opposition is seen as a better alternative. However, when we take into account the proportion of voters falling into each category, we see that the expected negative impact on the government is generally small (see Table 5.8). For instance, health was the issue for which 51 percent of evaluations were negative. Of those voters seeing a decline in health services, 80 percent blamed the government. This implies that 41 percent of voters had negative evaluations of the health services *and* blamed the government. Of these only half saw the opposition as a better alternative. Taken together, this implies that 20 percent of those who had a negative evaluation of the health services blamed the government for this state of affairs, and believed that the opposition would do a better job (0.51 * 0.80 * 0.50). By this crude calculation, health could cost the government the support of 20 percent of voters. However, 27 percent of voters thought the health service had improved and, of these, 89 percent credited the government. This means that 24 percent of voters thought the health service had improved and that this was due to the government. Of those who think it has improved, 86 percent believed that no other party would have done better. This implies that 21 percent of voters thought the health service had improved, that this was due to the government and that no other party would do better (0.27 * 0.89 * 0.86). Taking both calculations together, this suggests that the net effect of health, an issue most evaluated negatively, gave a one-percentage point bonus to the government.

We make similar calculations for the other issue areas (see Table 5.8). While the economy, unemployment, tax and even housing were obviously net vote winners, crime, transport and the cost of living were net losers. Overall, the gains outweigh the losses; the average net gain to the government across these eight issues was almost nine percentage points. This represents the expected gains and losses according to the

Table 5.8 Assumed positive and negative effects on the
government vote (%)

	Negative effects	Positive effects	Net effects
Economy	−3	45	+42
Unemployment	−5	38	+33
Tax	−10	34	+24
Housing	−15	33	+18
Health	−20	21	+1
Crime	−15	3	−12
Transport	−18	2	−16
Cost of living	−21	0	−21

Notes: voters only; effects calculated by multiplying proportions evaluating
negatively/positively, blaming/crediting the government and seeing/not seeing
an alternative.

simple reward and punishment model outlined earlier and takes all
reports of evaluations, attributions and credible alternatives at face
value. The average figure indicates that, across the issue areas defined
and explored here, the government came out well ahead of the opposition. These results highlight the importance of taking account not just
of voters' evaluations, but also of who they credit/blame, and of their
assessments of alternatives. Earlier, when the focus was on evaluations
(see Table 5.3), the government performed poorly across the eight issue
areas (the average evaluation is −19). However, the government deficit
becomes a surplus once we factor in blame/credit and some assessment
of alternatives.

The position of the government is even better if we examine each
voter's views across the range of issues. We score '1' for each set of
considerations that should help the government: issue evaluated positively, the government credited and no party seen as likely to improve
on. A score of '−1' is given for each set of considerations that should
act against the government: issue evaluated negatively, the government
blamed and another party seen as likely to do better. We allocated a
score of '0' for the remainder. When we aggregate across these issues,
most voters have a positive score (56 percent of voters), while a quarter
have a negative score (24 percent) and a fifth (20 percent) give no
advantage to either the government or the opposition. That is, there
are more issues that voters evaluate positively, where they give credit to
government policy and where they do not see any party as likely to

improve on, than issues they view negatively, blame the government for and where they see an alternative party as potentially better. This considerable lead goes some way toward explaining why the government was returned, but raises the question of why the government did not do a lot better. It is to this direct relationship between evaluation and vote that we now turn.

Vote choice and performance assessments

To examine the importance of issues to voters' decisions, we begin by focusing our attention on the relationship between net evaluations and party support. Above, we noted that support for the government is not as strong as the net evaluations might lead us to expect and that those who evaluate government performance as 'good' are not particularly likely to vote for the government parties. Is it just evaluations that matter, or does attribution and assessment of the opposition come into play? In examining this question we assume that all issues are equal, but, as we have already seen, some are more salient than others. For instance, voters are much more likely to mention health, crime and housing as important issues than transport, tax or cost of living.

We start by looking at the net weight of assessments and its impact on the vote (see Table 5.9; we group the scores as otherwise there would be too few cases in many columns). As we would expect, there is a strong relationship between Fianna Fáil support and the summary issue scores, with the party winning many votes from those scoring positively and almost no votes from those scoring negatively. However, the same cannot be said of the Progressive Democrats. There is little difference in Progressive Democrat support between those with a moderately negative score and those with a strongly positive score. When it comes to the opposition parties, Labour and Fine Gael are, to a large degree, the mirror image of Fianna Fáil. Support for both parties increases as voters' assessments grow more negative. Sinn Féin supporters are particularly numerous in the most discontented column. The independent vote is stronger at mild levels of dissatisfaction, in contrast to the vote for other non-government parties or candidates, which is strongest when voters are most dissatisfied.

A major limitation of this analysis is that partisanship may have a huge influence on one of the factors used to explain the result: the credibility of an alternative to the governing parties. For instance, those with negative assessments on health, who blame the government and see another party as better are unlikely to vote for the government: only 13 percent of voters do so. However, regardless of evaluation and

Table 5.9 Net issues assessment scores and the vote (%)

Vote	−8/−4	−3/−1	0	+1/+3	+4/+8
FF	2	9	33	56	72
FG	45	37	22	16	11
Green	10	6	5	2	1
Lab	21	20	14	6	3
PD	0	4	5	4	6
SF	15	7	5	7	2
Ind/others	7	16	16	9	5
Total	100	100	100	100	100
N	106	335	322	831	243

Notes: zero category also includes missing data cases; scores calculated from combinations of evaluation, attribution and preferable alternatives with pro-government scoring 1, anti-government scoring −1 and the rest zero.

attribution, only 19 percent of those who see another party as better vote for the government. This suggests that the perception that another party would do better is strongly associated with voting against the government. The problem with the 'alternative party' element of the question is that it may be driven by vote and partisanship, rather than making an independent contribution to these. To get a more realistic idea of the impact of the different issues on vote we, therefore, look at evaluation and attribution alone.[7]

We explore this by examining the relationship between evaluation and vote among voters who attribute responsibility for each issue to government policies (see Table 5.10). There is a clear relationship between evaluation and the Fianna Fáil vote on all issues, although this relationship varies in strength. On the economy, the difference between the tendency to vote for Fianna Fáil of those with positive and negative evaluations is 39 percentage points; on tax it is only 11 percentage points. Health and housing provide the other two strong associations. Earlier we saw that these were the three issues most strongly correlated to general evaluations of the government record. The biggest surprise here is perhaps crime, an issue with a high public salience, which attracted considerable media attention and a lot of coverage during the campaign, but an issue that is related only weakly to the vote. As numbers are small it is harder to see any particular impact of evaluations on the Progressive Democrat vote. Earlier, it was noted that voters regarded the Progressive Democrats as more responsible for changes in the tax

Table 5.10 Issue evaluations and the vote among those who attribute responsibility for performance on that issue to the government (%)

	Economy		Health		Housing		Crime		Unemployment		Cost of living		Tax		Transport	
	−	+	−	+	−	+	−	+	−	+	−	+	−	+	−	+
FF	19	55	25	58	29	55	36	43	33	52	36	60	33	46	35	43
FG	29	16	27	19	24	21	28	24	35	17	25	0	30	20	30	21
Grn	3	2	6	1	7	1	3	2	2	3	5	0	4	5	4	7
Lab	21	7	16	5	17	5	13	10	8	9	12	40	7	10	13	2
PD	1	4	3	5	4	3	2	8	2	6	3	0	5	4	3	9
SF	8	5	8	5	9	6	7	7	8	6	8	0	9	4	7	5
Ind/Other	18	9	14	7	13	8	11	5	12	8	11	0	11	10	11	13
Total	100	100	100	100	100	100	100	100	100	100	100	100	100	100	100	100
N	108	973	690	454	472	684	667	65	206	785	1023	5	431	832	740	40

situation than Fianna Fáil. However, voters' evaluations of the tax issue are not associated with support for this party. If we look only at constituencies where the Progressive Democrats ran candidates the picture is much the same, with no evidence that favourable economic or tax evaluations helped the party, though there are some signs of benefit from perceptions of falling unemployment.

The issues that benefit the opposition parties vary from party to party. Support for Fine Gael is related to voters' negative evaluations of the general economy and unemployment. Negative valuations of the general economy are also strongly linked to support for Labour, as are poor evaluations of health and housing. Green support is linked to negative evaluations on housing and health. Those blaming the government for poor performance on housing are seven times as likely to vote Green as those who credit the government for a good performance. Support for Independents is linked to the economy and health. This suggests that issues such as health and housing might have influenced the choice between Fianna Fáil and Labour/Greens/Independents, while economic evaluations had an effect on the choice between Fianna Fáil and Fine Gael/Independents. Other issue evaluations did not have much impact on the result at all.[8]

It would be wrong to see these assessments as entirely independent of one another. There is a tendency for people with negative assessments in one area to have negative assessments in other areas and vice versa. In part, this may be due to underlying differences in partisanship, but it may also be due to different personal experiences. Untangling this would be outside the scope of this chapter, although we attempt do so in the concluding section of this book. Even so, it is evident that there are considerable differences across areas. The most important areas as regards the vote seem to be health, housing and the economy, with the latter summarising some of the other economic perceptions.

Perceptions of local circumstances

So far, all the evaluations discussed are of 'national issues' – the national economy the national health service and so on. We now investigate the role of sub-national, or local, issues. In particular, our focus is on peoples' perceptions of their own local economy relative to the national economy. The question we are interested in is whether people reward a government for doing well on the national economy or their local economy, if they distinguish between the two at all matters more (on the USA see Nadeau and Niemi, 1995).

Table 5.11   Vote by perceptions of local–national relativities (%)

	Local economy relative to national economy		
	Worse	Same	Better
FF	39	41	43
FG	24	24	14
Green	2	3	8
Lab	9	11	11
PD	3	4	7
SF	7	6	6
Ind	16	9	10
Total	100	100	100
N	462	1026	334

Note: voters only.

Most Irish people saw little difference in their local economies over the last five years. Fifty-nine percent of voters said things were much the same, as opposed to 22 percent who thought things had got better and 19 percent who thought they had got worse. There is surprisingly little association with voting behaviour (see Table 5.11). Looking across the rows from 'worse' to 'better', the Fianna Fáil vote goes up 5 percentage points while Fine Gael's vote goes down 10 percentage points. For Fine Gael the important distinction is between those who think the local economy is not better (in other words, 'worse' or 'the same') and those who think it is 'better'. Fine Gael did badly among voters who thought their area had done well, but failed to pick up additional support among voters who thought their areas were deprived relative to the national economy. The Labour vote is steady across all three categories. The Greens did better in areas seen as well off relative to the rest. Independents did much better in 'deprived areas', picking up votes that the established parties could not win. There may be some spurious effects here. The Greens and the Progressive Democrats are parties with a predominantly middle-class vote and do better in well-off areas. This does not account for the strength of Independents in 'deprived' areas, or for the sharp difference between Fianna Fáil and Fine Gael.

These comparisons of the local area with the national economy may depend on voters' perceptions of the national economy. Those who

Table 5.12 Government support by perceptions of national
conditions and local–national relativities

| | Local economy in comparison to the national | | |
National economy	Worse	Same	Better
Worse	21	30	27
	(68)	(85)	(20)
Same	38	32	40
	(26)	(106)	(11)
Better	41	44	50
	(400)	(910)	(315)

Notes: voters only; cell entries are percentage voting for government parties and cell numbers are in brackets.

thought the national economy was getting worse were more likely than those who thought it was getting better to see their area as worse-off than the rest of the country. However, the differences are quite small. Thirty-six percent of those who thought the national economy was getting worse thought that their area was worse off, while 25 percent of those who thought the national economy was improving thought their area was worse off. The relationship between these two evaluations is weak (a correlation of just 0.08).

When we examine the degree of government support by national and relative local perceptions it is evident that national considerations predominate (see Table 5.12). For a given perception of the local situation (columns), support for the government increases by between 14 and 23 percentage points as perceptions of the national economy change from 'worse' to 'better'. If we control for perceptions of the national economy (rows), the increase in support for the government as perceptions of local economy change from 'worse' to 'better' is at most 9 percentage points. From the point of view of government support, the perception of relative local well-being is unimportant once perceptions of national circumstances are taken into account. On the one hand, where voters see the local area as lagging behind a vibrant national economy, the government vote of 41 percent was only 4 percent less than the national average. On the other hand, when the local economy as well as the national economy were seen as improving, support for the government was only 5 percent ahead of the national average.

Conclusions

The unprecedented performance of the economy over the previous five years meant that the 2002 election was fought on rough terrain for the opposition parties. Unemployment fell to a previously undreamed-of low rate, direct taxes were cut and inflation, though rising, still left a real annual income increase in most people's pockets. If we accept that elections will broadly follow a pattern whereby the government will suffer in bad times, but flourish in good ones, the outlook for the outgoing government was good. However, even in good times, there is a tendency for the government to have to pay for the what Nannestead and Paldam (2002) called the 'cost of ruling'.

There were various downsides to the government record that the opposition could seek to exploit and there was always the hope that the electorate would ignore the good things and concentrate on the bad ones. Certainly it is true that pre-election polls highlighted things like housing and the health service as election issues, rather than growth rates and low unemployment. We outlined here a simple model under which voters would punish the government if they evaluated a state of affairs as being poor, blamed government policies for the decline and thought someone else would do better (and would reward a government where a situation had improved as a result of government policy and thought no other party could have done better). On this reckoning the government was in pretty good shape, as even though many evaluations were negative, these were mitigated by the fact that blame was often not laid at the government's door and that the opposition parties did not constitute a preferable alternative. Far fewer voters considered the opposition would do better than actually voted for opposition parties. For most voters there were more positives than negatives, and while all those with a positive assessment did not necessarily go on to vote for the government it is easy on this evidence, to understand why the government did so well.

For a more detailed analysis of the importance of different issues we discounted the last part of our model – a preferable alternative – judging that it was too closely bound up with partisanship, and instead concentrated on the evaluations of those who attributed responsibility for an area to government policies. Of course, it is clear that the attribution of blame is also bound up with a tendency to vote for a government or opposition party for other reasons, but we argue that this was a necessary part of how credit is taken and blame avoided in the political process. In particular, voters gave the government the benefit of the doubt in some areas. Whether that was because many Fianna Fáil voters are strongly partisan, or whether it stemmed from factors specific to the 2002 election, we do not know. What is clear is that on most issues evaluations are linked to vote, but on some of the issues where the government might have been damaged severely by a strong link, the association was a weak one. This is so in relation to the cost of living, transport and, particularly, crime. Voters may well have cared about crime and certainly most perceived the struggle against rising crime as unsuccessful but, even where they blamed the government, voters did not flock to the opposition as an alternative. The biggest effects, judged one by one, were on the economy, health and housing. When we take into account the degree to which all these assessments are interrelated, these three still significantly affect vote choice, although the effect of assessments of unemployment is almost certainly obscured by the impact of the economy as a whole. The improved state of the economy undoubtedly helped the government – although the positive effects for the Progressive Democrats are not clear – and rising levels of concern about health and housing seem to have benefited the opposition significantly, though not Fine Gael. Fine Gael support is linked particularly strongly to perceptions of the economy. We might surmise that the general health of the economy (as perceived then) hurt Fine Gael most, particularly as that party was relatively unsuccessful at picking up support on the other salient issues.

Given the importance of Independents in the 2002 election, and the generally perceived importance of local matters in Irish elections, we would have expected to find that the relative performance of the local economy was a strong influence on the vote, but that did not turn out to be the case. National perceptions were much more powerful, although there are indications that perceptions of purely local economies do matter. Again, we saw some evidence here of Fine Gael's weakness in its failure to capitalise when the local economy was seen to be under-performing, and it seems possible that the high levels of Green support where the economy was doing well were at Fine Gael's expense. Independents did best where the local area was missing out, again, perhaps taking votes that Fine Gael would have hoped to win.

The central conclusion that must follow from this analysis is that issues of competence apparently move Irish voters. The party system does not lend itself to articulating major policy debates, because the major parties lack strong ideological or even social identities, but its adversarial nature does allow and encourage voters to play the significant role of assessing governments on performance, and the evidence here suggests that, while the government parties were not seen as successful in all they did, they were perceived overall to have done a decent job by the great majority of voters. That their vote majority was not greater must in part be due to the stabilising features of Irish politics, notably party predispositions. Support is 'sticky', and short-term considerations will not be sufficient to move large numbers of voters away from habitual behaviours.

Notes

1 An interview with John Garry and Lucy Mansergh for Garry and Mansergh (1999).
2 Stokes observed, on the matter of corruption, that 'if we are to speak of a dimension at all, both parties and all voters were located at a single point: the position of virtue in government' (1963: 372).
3 This strength is not stable. Fianna Fáil is now seen as more capable on NI whereas in the 1980s under Haughey it was less capable (e.g. MRBI/3510/87 in January 1987 and IMS J.452, February 1982; athough Fianna Fáil led in May 1981 (IMS J.4880)). FF's reputation in being best able to manage the economy has also risen following the economic success over which it presided. In 1997, the outgoing 'Rainbow' coalition had a slight edge in this respect (IMS 29 May 1997: CMC/SOS/Id J.7S–317). It has been suggested that parties 'own' particular issues (Petrocik, 1996), but this strength is not stable.
4 Housing, transport and taxes were mentioned by 4, 3 and 1 percent respectively as the most important issue the government had had to deal with.
5 These attributions are in many cases very similar to those of British voters in 1997 (Heath *et al.*, 2001: table 3.11).
6 We asked whether anyone else could do better. It could be that many think others could do as well and, if so, we are underestimating confidence in opposition parties.
7 Of course these may not be completely independent of partisanship either. See Wlezien *et al.*, 1997.
8 Of course any assessment of how much difference any issue could have made is a product not simply of the strength of the relationships we see in this table – the differences in percentages across pairs of evaluations – but also of the distribution of cases across each set of evaluations and the counterfactual we consider in assessing impact. So if we say: how would the outcome have been different if everyone had evaluated the economy positively, we can calculate the increase in, for instance, the Fianna Fáil vote that would come from reallocating all those cases where evaluation was not positive. How much this increases the notional Fianna Fáil vote is a function of how many extra cases this involves and how big the difference is between those who see the economy positively and those view it negatively. The difference is quite large. However, since almost four out of five voters see things positively already, assuming that all do so cannot

make that much difference. If the counterfactual is that everyone is not positive there would be a much larger movement in the other direction. Using non-positive evaluations as the counterfactual suggests the big effects in 2002 came from the economy, with health and housing next. Unemployment and tax were also important but the rest were not important at all.

6

Leaders and their parties

The previous chapter concluded that the balance of issues favoured the governing parties in 2002. While the voters saw some black marks on the government's record, most either did not hold it to be culpable or, where they did blame it, did not weigh such items heavily in their voting calculations. For most observers and commentators, the leadership issue also favoured the governing parties. On the government side, the Taoiseach, Bertie Ahern, and the Tánaiste, Mary Harney, leaders of Fianna Fáil and the Progressive Democrats respectively, were seen by most observers as electoral assets, while for Fine Gael, Michael Noonan appeared to be a particular liability. Noonan had engineered the removal of the previous leader, John Bruton, less than a year before the election, at a time when the party's opinion poll ratings seemed stuck in the low 20s and following an advertising campaign designed around the theme of the 'Celtic Snail' and intended to highlight the government's shortcomings. This provoked less anger at the government than laughter at Fine Gael. However, his record as minister for health in the 1994–97 coalition government soon attracted media attention. An RTÉ documentary highlighted his clumsy handling of compensation claims on behalf of women who had become infected with Hepatitis C by contaminated blood dispensed through the health service before he became minister. Noonan felt it necessary to make a public apology for his role in the affair at the party's annual conference in the spring of 2002. In contrast, Fianna Fáil felt it was appropriate to built their campaign around Ahern, who traversed the country in a high-speed cavalcade, stopping only to press the flesh and deliver photo opportunities.

There is no doubt that the media find it convenient to personalise parties and political competition, but the question of how far voters respond to such efforts remains open. Fine Gael's inability, since 1982, to win an election has seen first Alan Dukes, then John Bruton and most recently Michael Noonan replaced in the hope of finding a leader who would repeat the successes of Garret FitzGerald in the early 1980s.

Labour's Ruairi Quinn, also stood down in the wake of a very disappointing result. Both Fine Gael and Labour each won their highest vote ever under leaders now in retirement. The failure of their sucessors may indicate personal shortcomings, but may also suggest that the sources of electoral weakness (and strength) lie elsewhere. Moreover, while Mary Harney's popularity was seen to contribute significantly to her party's electoral success in winning eight seats, that party still secured the support of only 1 out of every 25 voters. The exchange rate between personal popularity and electoral support is not necessarily a generous one.

In Ireland there certainly seems ample potential for a leader to have a considerable impact. First of all, the electorate does appear to be open to competition: the long-term influences of political values, social cleavages, family traditions and even party attachments are relatively weak. Indeed, as we have seen, party attachment is weaker in Ireland than almost anywhere else in the western world. Second, parties focus a lot of attention in the campaigns on leaders, particularly when they feel they have an electoral asset. Most campaigns, and 2002 was no exception, feature a 'Great Debate' between the rival leaders. In 2002, this featured Ahern against Noonan, balanced by 'big' interviews with other party leaders. Television and radio bring leaders into every household with viewing figures for such debates around 600,000. They are well-known names and many voters who might have little other knowledge of political affairs could well use their evaluations of leaders in deciding how to vote. Eighty-six percent of voters were able to identify Trevor Sargent as leader of the Green Party from a list of four alternatives and he received less media coverge than any of the other leaders. Party leaders might be expected to matter more when they are seen as candidates for the highest office. Moreover, governments are identified firmly with the Taoiseach of the day.

Yet there are counter-arguments. Campaigns also feature extensive face-to-face contacts between candidates, party activists and voters. Moreover, if elections really are about a choice of Taoiseach, it seems odd that so many voters now give their support to a minor party or an independent. There are also reasonable questions to ask about how clearly voters distinguish between leaders and parties, and the direction of any cause and effect with respect to popularity. The argument that leaders matter implies an effect from leaders to parties. Yet Irish parties are, for the most part, long established and permanent, while leaders are relatively ephemeral. It seems likely that perception of a party leader will be coloured significantly by partisanship. Ahern is the Fianna Fáil leader, not a political leader who was recruited by Fianna Fáil.

In some countries leaders build their own parties – institutions that are little more than vehicles designed to transport the leader into high office. In the late 1980s the Progressive Democrats under Dessie O'Malley may have been one such party, but this remains exceptional. Of course, leaders may transform their parties, as Blair claims to have done in the UK and perhaps FitzGerald did in Ireland, but this was not a feature of the election in 2002. Almost any leader of Fianna Fáil will have a reasonable level of popularity. In general, we would expect approval of parties to influence approval of leaders. Yet it must also be accepted that some leaders may change the way many voters see their parties. Ahern, it is often argued, makes Fianna Fáil more widely acceptable, and those who do not give Fianna Fáil a first preference are less hostile to the party than they once were, allowing it to win more lower preference votes; Dick Spring may have done the same for Labour in 1992. Many would feel Noonan's unpopularity may have dragged down his party in 2002. These may be relatively marginal effects, but marginal effects may still be critical in some circumstances.

Much of the literature on leaders deals with alternative candidates for executive office (presidency, or prime ministership) where there is a simple either/or choice. The critical question is not so much whether a candidate is liked, or deemed capable, but whether he or she is liked *better than the other candidate*. In a multi-party system the question of leader evaluations is much more complicated because there are more than two of them, but it may still be reduced to the question of who is preferred to all others, and by how much. A very simple model of a leader-driven voter would expect a voter to support the party of the leader they prefer. If this does not provide for a clear choice, perhaps because two or more leaders are ranked equally, then voters will fall back on a secondary criterion.

The scholarly literature on the electoral impact of leaders gives little support to those who see leaders as crucial to success and failure. A recent study (Curtice, 2003) looking at the importance of leader evaluations to party success in over 100 parties across more than two dozen countries concluded that, in parliamentary systems, 'voters still make judgements about the collective merits of the parties as a whole rather than their leaders in particular' (Curtice, 2003). Even in two-party systems electoral effects are generally modest (Curtice and Holmberg, 2005). However, other studies, using a variety of methods, have also found what they see as important effects: see, for example, Jenssen and Aalberg, 2006; Costa Lobo, 2006 and Evans and Anderson, 2005; Clark and Stewart, 1995; Stewart and Clark, 1992.

Rather than simply measuring popularity, some studies have tried to pin down the nature of leader evaluations. They ask: What is it that voters like about leaders? What traits are appreciated most? Is it simply the perception of competence, or are leaders valued for being caring, or trustworthy, for being close to the people, or being, in one sense or other, superior to them? An early study, which found very significant leadership effects, argued that the most important characteristic was competence (Bean and Mughan, 1989; Bean, 1993), a finding that operates across different political contexts.

A recent collection of papers on six different countries sought to ascertain the importance of leaders' personalities. The point is less to find out if it matters whether voters like leaders than whether it matters what voters think about them. The message conveyed by this collection was summed up in the editor's comment that 'personality factors determine election outcomes far less often than is usually, indeed almost universally, supposed' (King, 2002, conclusion p. 220). This is because even where such characteristics may have swayed votes they did not sway enough to be decisive. This collection tried to identify leader effects by isolating personal characteristics (general popularity) from their views on the issues of the day and a host of other factors that are seen as causally prior to leader evaluations. We have already made the point that factors which some might see as causally prior, such as party attachment, might plausibly follow rather than precede leader evaluations. If so, leaders might be more important than many studies conclude.

There has been little work on the Irish case. The most extensive analysis was done on the 1987 election, using IMS and MRBI poll data (Laver *et al.*, 1987). This was an election which pitted Haughey against FitzGerald and O'Malley, all significant figures in the historical electoral landscape. The authors concluded that parties and leaders were assessed independently and that liking a leader, and even ascribing favourable attributes to that leader, did not necessarily lead to voting for the leader's party. A popular leader, O'Malley did not generate a huge vote for his party, while Haughey, a leader generally unappreciated outside his own party, nonetheless won the election and became Taoiseach. A later piece of research examined poll data over time, asking how far the popularity of leaders and their parties rose and fell as one, and whether leaders or parties seemed to be the primary determinant of change. Results were mixed, being stronger for Fianna Fáil than for Fine Gael (Harrison and Marsh, 1994). Further tests failed to establish causal ordering. However, if a causal path from leader to party is assumed, the impact of the former is quite strong. A 10 point rise in leader popularity could move the party's popularity up 2 point in the case of Fianna Fáil and Fine Gael, though only marginally (0.3 percent) in the case of Labour (Harrison and Marsh 1994: 377–9).

Popularity in 2002

Figure 6.1 shows the pattern of leader popularity for the leaders of the three largest parties from 1977 to the eve of the 2002 election. This figure is based on all commericial polls over the period. The question asked in all these polls is something like: 'Would you say you are satisfied or dissatisfied with the way Mr Noonan is doing his job as leader of Fine Gael?' and 'Would you say you are satisfied or dissatisfied with the way Mr Ahern is doing his job as Taoiseach?' Options are 'satisfied', 'not satisfied' or dissatisfied and 'no opinion'. The graph shows the percentage expressing satisfaction. What is clear is that between late 1997 and 2002 Ahern established a very clear lead over the Fine Gael (Bruton, then Noonan) and Labour (Quinn) party leaders. The Fianna Fáil/FG gap was much greater than at any previous election and certainly very much greater than in 1997, when the gap was quite small. Ahern's ratings had improved and those of his rivals had declined. The graph also makes clear the considerable popularity of Garret FitzGerald from 1977

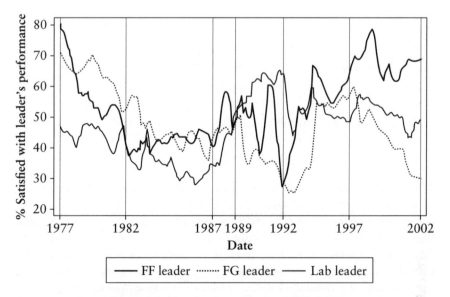

Figure 6.1   Leaders' popularity 1977–2002

Source: IMS, MRBI and Lansdowne polls

until the mid-1980s, and of Dick Spring in the early 1990s. If leadership does matter to voters, and particularly those voters conscious that they might be voting to select a Taoiseach, 2002 should show that Ahern was a big vote winner for Fianna Fáil. Given the outcome, a clear win for the government parties and a firm majority, Ahern's popularity (and Noonan's unpopularity) may not have proved decisive, but it may have been very significant in terms of party support.

The poll questions on which this graph is based are far from ideal. The object of the question is not so much the individual as the job they are doing in a particular context. Arguably, a respondent could think a leader is doing a good job if the party is doing well, which would bias any conclusions about the link between 'satisfaction' and support. This would also mean that expressing satisfaction would not necessarily imply that a respondent liked a leader. Many might feel, for instance, that Gerry Adams had done a good job as leader of Sinn Féin without wishing ever to vote for him or his party. In place of this approach the design of the election study questions followed a path well trodden by other election studies. Respondents were asked a number of questions about the party leaders. First there was a thermometer question in which respondents were asked to rate each leader on a 0–100 scale:

> I'd now like to ask you how you feel about some Irish politicians, using what we call the 'feeling thermometer'. The feeling thermometer works like this: [Interviewer Show Card]
>
> If you have a *favourable feeling* (a warm feeling) towards a POLITICIAN you should place him/her somewhere between 50 and 100 degrees;
>
> If you have an *unfavourable feeling* (a cold feeling) towards a POLITICIAN, you should place him/her somewhere between 0 and 50 degrees; and
>
> If you *don't feel particularly warm or cold* (have no feeling towards the politician at all) then you should place him/her at 50 degrees.
>
> Where would you place these Irish politicians?

This question has the advantage that it can be repeated for each party as well as for other politicians, so that answers can be compared across leaders and between parties and their leaders. A second set of questions was asked only about the Fianna Fáil, Fine Gael and Labour leaders. Respondents were asked to rate each of these leaders in terms of honesty, being in touch with ordinary people and being good at running the country (see questions Q43, Q44 as Q45 in Appendix IV).

We use these to assess how far different leaders were liked or disliked for different reasons, and which ones seem most important for approval and most important when it comes to the vote. A third set of questions asked whether any leader (and before that, any party) represented the respondent's views:

> Would you say that any of the parties in Ireland represents your views reasonably well? If so, which ones?

> Regardless of how you feel about the parties, would you say that any of the individual party leaders at the election in May of this year represented your views reasonably well? If so, which ones?

One concern about the data should be raised at this point. All post-election studies are somewhat handicapped by having to make the assumption that the views expressed by people in the surveys are those they would have held on polling day. This is particularly problematic in the case of leaders. When leaders are assessed *after* an election the outcome of the election is known and individual assessments may well be tainted by success and failure. Moreover, both Noonan and Quinn had announced their intention to step down from leadership by the time the survey was completed. This effect may be seen in the answers to a particular question that asked people who would make the best Taoiseach, Bertie Ahern or Michael Noonan. There was a huge majority for Ahern, 84 to 12 with 5 percent giving no answer. However, the same question had been asked in the exit poll carried out for RTÉ by Lansdowne Market Research and in that poll the gap, although very significant, was much smaller, 64 to 23 and 13 percent seeing no difference or having no opinion. The alternative measures used here do not refer to a particular office and instead deal with how warm a respondent feels towards particular politicians. These seems less affected by the resignations as we will see.

Figure 6.2 shows the distribution of leader evaluations. Remember that 50 is the mid-point on the thermometer scale: above 50 denotes warm feelings and below 50 cold ones. The box identifies the locations of the middle 50 percent of respondents, with the bottom line denoting the low end and the top line the high end of that group. Fifty percent rated Ahern at between 51 and 80 on the scale. Ahern, then, was liked by almost three-quarters of all respondents. Harney was the second most popular leader with almost half of all respondents giving her a score above 50. Noonan was liked by less than a quarter of respondents. The same was true of Sargent, but the shorter box, when compared with Noonan's, indicates that fewer people felt negative towards him. Adams also attracted a lot of negative evaluations but, in contrast to Noonan, had rather more people who feel positive about him. These results are very much in line with poll evaluations: just prior to the

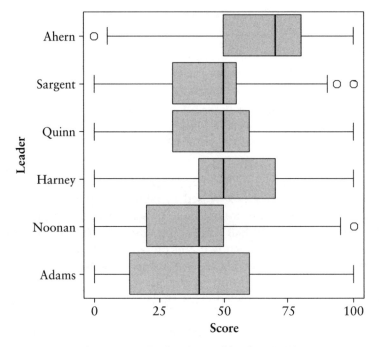

Figure 6.2　Evaluations of leaders 2002

Note: voters only

election 68 percent were satisfied with Ahern, 51 percent with Quinn and 30 percent with Noonan (Millward Brown/IMS/*Sunday Independent*, 12 May 2002), while 59 percent approved Harney, 50 approved Adams, and 39 percent approved Sargent. A very high proportion, 45 percent, were uncertain about Sargent and this again we see in the fact that 30 percent accorded him a score of 50 – the neutral position.

If these figures make it very clear that Ahern was popular and Noonan was not, they alone cannot tell us how these evaluations are related. For instance, is it the case that those who liked Noonan did not like Ahern, and who was it that liked Harney? If her popularity was no more than the appreciation of Fianna Fáil supporters for a secure alliance with their party, such evaluations can hardly be expected to translate into first preference votes. What we want to know is how far each leader's set of supporters is shared with the set of support for other leaders. Table 6.1 shows this. The first row shows the percentage of voters who liked each leader, that is, who gave them a warm score of over 50. It reinforces the picture given by Figure 6.2, but is more exact. It highlights the popularity of Ahern and Mary Harney and the

Table 6.1 Levels of individual and shared support for party leaders

	Ahern	Noonan	Sargent	Quinn	Harney	Adams
% who like leader	70	19	25	27	46	29
% who like only that leader	15	2	1	1	1	2
% of those liking each column leader who like row leader:						
Ahern	100	62	68	69	85	76
Noonan	16	100	29	33	24	22
Sargent	23	37	100	41	27	30
Quinn	26	49	47	100	35	33
Harney	56	59	54	60	100	46
Adams	31	34	37	36	29	100

Notes: voters only; 'like' means a score of over 50 on the 1–100 thermometer scale.

profound lack of sympathy for the Fine Gael leader. The second row gives the percentage of voters who liked just one particular leader. Ahern is again on his own here, with 15 percent of voters liking only him, while no other leader commanded the unrivalled support of more than 2 percent. This does not mean voters might not have a clear preference; only that most voters do have some sympthy for more than one leader.

The remaining rows indicate how far support is shared. Essentially, supporters of most other leaders also liked Ahern. This is particularly true of those who liked Harney (85 percent also liked Ahern), but is also true of Noonan (62 percent also liked Ahern) and Adams (76 percent). Interestingly, more of those who liked the Labour leader, Quinn, liked Harney than liked Noonan, and more of Noonan's supporters liked Harney move than Quinn. All of this suggests that the government had a lot going for it when it came to leadership. The two governing parties had the two most popular leaders; the main opposition party had the most unpopular one. Moreover, Ahern and Harney tended to be more popular among those who supported Labour or Fine Gael leaders than were Fine Gael and Labour leaders respectively. In general, a pattern of dislikes would be the mirror image of this table, except that Sargent would seem more popular, as the large number of people who were indifferent to him would then appear as 'not dislike' rather than 'not like'.

Table 6.2 Percentage saying leader represents views

	Ahern	Noonan	Sargent	Quinn	Harney	Adams	None
% saying leader represented their views particularly well	39	8	4	5	8	4	38
Average score for that leader	8.0	6.2	6.9	6.4	7.3	7.8	NA

Note: voters only.

When it comes to 'representing views', the pattern is much the same (see Table 6.2). A large minority thought no leader represented them well, but an equally large minority thought Ahern did so. Other leaders got little approval with Noonan's support being no greater than Harney's. This question does not force the respondent to choose a particular leader and we might assume that those specifying 'no leader' think relatively little of any of them, and probably do not think that any one leader is better than another. In fact, the average score, on a 0–10 scale, given by this group to their most favoured leader is 7.5 which is below the mean of 7.9 and the median of 8, so the majority of voters give their best leader a higher score. Even so, those who think Noonan, Sargent, Quinn or even Harney represents their views well still give those leaders a lower score than those who favour Ahern. Only the small group favouring Adams comes close to matching Ahern's supporters in the strength of their approval. There is obviously a fair match between voters' overall evaluations and a consideration of there being a leader who does represent their views well, but clearly there is also a difference between the two assessments, which may be something more than just error associated with such measures. Leaders seen as representing views average 7.5 on the evaluation scale; those who do not average only 4.3. This raises the issue of what people look for in a leader.

What matters in a leader?

While it is clear that some leaders were rated more highly than others, we also sought to find out what it was that voters liked and did not like about each leader. We asked about three things: honesty, being in touch with ordinary people and being capable of running the country. The last of these has been considered the most important in previous research, as we have seen above, and it could be argued that this is what should matter most. Yet being in touch with ordinary people could also be considered vital in a representative democracy. Not all leaders, even popular ones, might be considered strong in this respect. Honesty was included as a criterion because the activities of tribunals of inquiry into past misdoings of politicians was a potentially significant election issue although, as we saw in Chapter 5, few voters rated this as such.

Figure 6.3 shows the results. Again, we display a box plot where the box indicates the range of the middle 50 percent of responses. Ahern was well ahead on all criteria. Quinn and Noonan came closest to Ahern on honesty, and furthest behind on capacity to run the country. Almost three-quarters of all voters thought Ahern was in touch with ordinary people, and more still felt he had the capacity to run the country. His median rating on both of the last two was 8 on the 0–10-point

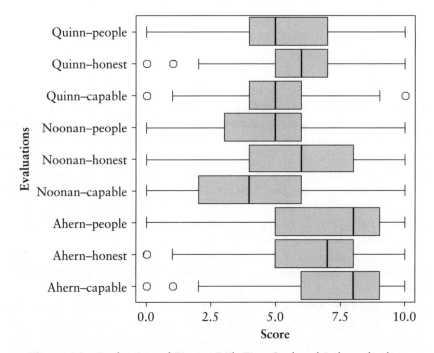

Figure 6.3 Evaluation of Fianna Fáil, Fine Gael and Labour leaders
on several characteristics

scale. Given Ahern's huge popularity relative to that of Quinn and Noonan, we might expect that perceptions of honesty will get less weight in people's overall perceptions than being in touch or capable. This seems to be the case. The simple correlations between overall evaluations of leaders and each of these criteria are 0.45 for honesty, 0.55 for being in touch and 0.66 for capacity to run the country.[1] These are themselves interrelated so these correlation coeffcents are not necessarily a good guide to their relative imprortance. When this interrelationship is allowed for, the coefficients are 0.07, 0.12 and 0.53, indicating the very much greater impact made by the capability criterion.[2] The exception to this is the Fianna Fáil leader, for whom honesty correlates much more closely with his overall evaluation. Those who thought Ahern was more honest liked him a lot more. Those who did not trust him evaluated him more negatively, whatever they might have thought of his other attributes. Had the opposition been able to persuade more people that Ahern's character was more dubious, they might have damaged him, but they were unable to do so.

Leaders and the vote

How are evaluations of party leaders linked to voting behaviour? We initially examined for each party the percentage of those giving its leader a particular evaluation who also vote for the party. The percentage voting Fianna Fáil increases steadily as Ahern's evaluations get better. At the lowest point almost nobody votes Fianna Fáil, with only around 10 percent of those rating Ahern below 40 supporting his party. Thereafter, there is a considerable rise to a figure in excess of 80 percent for those rating him between 91 and 100. The pattern is almost exactly the same for Noonan and Fine Gael. The relationship between vote and evaluation is also there for the smaller parties, but approval does not translate into electoral suport so well for these. This is particularly so for Harney and the Progressive Democrats. Only a little over 20 percent of those rating her between 91 and 100 on the 0–100 scale vote Progressive Democrat.

On this reading, we might suggest that if any leader had been more popular, their party would have won more votes. Noonan supporters were as likely to vote Fine Gael as Ahern's were to vote Fianna Fáil. The problem for Fine Gael is that there were so few of them. However, the ability to transform leader support into party support does vary across parties. There are several reasons why this might be so. The first may be that those who like leaders of small parties may like those of large parties more: there are perhaps fewer voters who give their highest evaluation to, for instance, Harney. The second is that bigger parties are bigger for all sorts of other reasons. Fianna Fáil gets votes even from people who do not like Ahern, while the small parties get almost no votes at all from people who do not like their leader. To answer these questions we need to first examine who voters like best, and second, to bring in some more general evaluations of party.

Ahern is the overwhelming favourite, with two-thirds of all voters rating him most highly. The next best is Harney, well behind with 25 percent. Noonan and Quinn each get only 13 percent, behind Sargent with 14 and Adams with 16 percent. These add up to more than 100, indicating that for some voters there is a tie for first place. In fact, only 74 percent of voters manifest a clear first choice, with another 18 percent placing two candidates equally and another 5 percent placing three equally in first place. Ties are associated with lower scores. Top single leaders have an average score of 80 on the thermometer scale, paired top candidates a score of 72 and so on downwards. Where 6 are given the same score it is really a question of 'a plague on all your houses' since the average is only 46, but that aside, the average is always positive (in the sense that it is over 50 on the 0–100 scale).

Table 6.3 shows the apparent impact of the most favoured leader on voting behaviour. Fianna Fáil and Fine Gael each do very well among those who prefer their leader, although each gets a fair amount of support even among those who do not. In the smaller parties the differences between the two groups is much greater: those who prefer the Green leader are more than 9 times as likely to vote Green as those who do not. In Sinn Féin the equivalent respondents are 23 times as likely. However, as the bottom line of the table makes clear, many parties get much, even most, of their support from voters who do not prefer that

Table 6.3 Percentage voting for party of most favoured leader

	FF	FG	Green	Labour	PD	SF	All
Voting for party when leader most favoured	61	56	18	30	8	23	41
Voting for party when leader not most favoured	14	17	2	6	2	1	6
Party's voters for whom leader is top	89	32	60	44	64	77	67

Notes: voters only; Independent and 'other' voters excluded.

party's leader. Most remarkably, however, only 32 percent of Fine Gael voters rated Noonan as the best leader, which means more than two-thirds can be said to have voted for Fine Gael despite its leader. Much the same is true of Labour, where less than half of Labour voters rated Quinn as best. Overall, voters were more than six times as likely to support a party whose leader they prefered as not to support it, but almost a third of voters still gave their first preference to a party other than that whose leader was perceived to be best.[3]

It is still apparent here that the smaller parties are less able to translate their leader's popularity into votes than are the larger parties. Almost 62 percent of Ahern supporters voted Fianna Fáil compared with only 8 percent of Harney supporters voting Progressive Democrat, and even only 18 percent of Sargent supporters voting Green. If we look only at those voters who have a single preference with respect to leader (that is, the 74 percent mentioned above), where one is rated above all others, we can see how far this failure to translate popularity into votes is due to the fact that many voters have no single preference. In fact, we see that the small party weakness is not all down to this: the percentages voting for Fianna Fáil, Fine Gael, Green, Labour, Progressive Democrats and Sinn Féin respectively, once they see that party's leader as the single best of the set, are 68, 78, 31, 55, 12 and 42.

What this seems to suggest is that leaders are not the sole, or perhaps not even the most important factor. Other influences have been discussed in earlier chapters and for a more accurate assessment of the importance of leaders for votes we would have to take account of these – we do so in Chapter 9 – but here we contrast the importance of leaders and their parties, using the party evaluations collected along with the leader evaluations. These are the outcome of many factors and so provide a simple way to assess the impact of leaders relative to other influences. It is clear that leader and party evaluations are not the same thing. The average correlation between the two sets of evaluations is 0.72, ranging from 0.80 for Fianna Fáil to 0.59 for Fine Gael.[4]

Table 6.4 shows the average difference between the two sets of evaluations by party. Noonan-FG is the exceptional one here, with Noonan running significantly behind his party. Quinn and Sargent also run behind, while Adams, Harney and Ahern (just) run ahead of their parties. The majority of voters tend to perceive a small difference for most leader-party pairs and half of all voters see a Noonan-FG difference of more than 20 points. (For Harney, half see a difference of more than 10 points, but typically this is in the other direction.) When we look at vote by the differences we see that those who value party more than leader tend to vote for that party in greater numbers than those who

Table 6.4   Difference between leader and party evaluations, by party

	Leader evaluation minus party evaluation
Ahern–FF	+1
Noonan–FG	−13
Sargent–Green	−6
Quinn–Labour	−3
Harney–PD	+4
Adams–SF	+5
All	−1

Note: voters only.

rank leader higher. Fifty-four percent of those who rank the party more highly than they rank Ahern vote Fianna Fáil, but only 26 percent of those who favour Ahern himself over the party do so. In the case of Fine Gael and Noonan the comparable figures are 28 percent and 13 percent, and a fairly similar order of difference is characteristic of the other parties.

While this is suggestive, we also need to look at which parties people like best, just as we did with leaders. Again, we use a set of thermometer scores and calculate which party is liked. Slightly more people have a favourite party than have a favourite leader: 76 percent as opposed to 73 percent. Some voters rank one party and its leader top. We would expect them to vote for that party. Others rank another party and its leader top. We would expect them to vote for *that* party. Most interesting are those whose favourite party and leader diverge. How do such voters behave? Do they follow the party, or follow the leader? Those who argue that leaders are a prime determinant of party support would expect many, if not most, voters to follow the leader; those who think leaders are relatively unimportant would expect voters to follow the party. This is an acid test of the 'leaders matter' argument. When evaluations of the two coincide we cannot be sure which of the two is more important, whether leader evaluations pass on to parties or vice versa. This holds both when neither party nor leader is rated highly, and when both are seen as strong. Only when the two are not aligned can we see clearly the separate impact of each.

We explore this in Table 6.5. Each row shows the percentage of the vote going to the party in each of four groups: those who rate neither party nor leader most highly, those who rate the leader best, but not the party, those who rate the party as best, but not the leader, and

Table 6.5 Voting behaviour according to ratings of leaders
and parties, by party

	Neither best	Best leader, not best party	Best party, not best leader	Best party and leader	Percent of party's vote coming from best leader only
Ahern–FF	6	8	43	73	1
Noonan–FG	9	14	64	68	*
Sargent–Green	*	3	14	25	2
Quinn–Labour	3	7	39	48	2
Harney–PD	1	3	6	16	7
Adams–SF	1	3	18	40	*
All	3	6	37	57	1

Notes: voters only; 'Best' includes cases where more than one leader or party is in joint first place in terms of evaluations; * indicates less than 0.5 but not zero.

those who rate both most highly. The most significant aspect of this table is the contrast between columns 2 and 3. Only 6 percent vote for the party that they see as having the best leader if they do not also rate that party as best, whereas 37 percent vote for the best party even when they do not feel it has the best leader. For almost all parties the difference is quite striking, with a ratio of 5:1 or 6:1 characteristic of all but the Progressive Democrats. Leadership does seem to matter more when the party is seen as the best one as well, pushing Fianna Fáil voting up from 43 percent to 73 and Harney from 6 to 16. The two elements of leadership and party evaluations seem to add up to more than the simple sum of their parts, which raises the suspicion that there is something else, perhaps a stronger attachment to party, that is manifested by the perception that both party and leader are better than anything else on offer. However, as it stands, leadership alone seems to have made little difference to the votes won by most parties. The final column shows the contribution made to each party's vote by those who rated the leader as the best, but did not rate the party similarly. On average, this amounts to a little over 1 percent with only Harney's contribution to the Progressive Democrats much higher at almost 7 percent. Given that the party won only 4 percent of the vote, this could have added only about 0.3 percent to the Progressive Democrat vote share.

Taking into account the fact that there are ties in both leader and party ratings and limiting analysis only to those cases where there are

Table 6.6   Voting by leader characteristics

	% voting for party with best leader on row criterion 1 but not on row criterion 2	% voting for party with with best leader on row criterion 2 but not on row criterion 1
Capable vs in touch	39	15
Capable vs honest	27	17
Honest vs in touch	23	20

Notes: voters only; 'Best' includes cases where more than one leader or party is in first place in terms of evaluations.

no ties does not alter the findings. Overall, just 6 percent vote for a party which has the best leader, but which is not evaluated as the best party, while 66 percent vote for the party which is evaluated as the best party, even when it does not have the best leader. Seventy-eight percent vote for the party which is best on both counts and just 3 percent vote for the party best on neither count.

We have seen that the overall evaluations are related more to a leader's capability than to being 'in touch', or 'honest'. Does this also apply to the impact of such evaluations on the vote? It would appear so. The simplest way to look at this is to compare the impact of each pair of attributes on the vote, using the same strategy used for comparing parties and leader. We, thus, look at those for whom, for instance, Ahern is most capable, but not most honest; or most honest, but not most capable. Table 6.6 shows the results. These should be seen as suggestive as cell numbers are in some cases below 40, but they indicate that capability outweighs being in touch and honesty, with little evident difference between the last two. In each case almost nobody votes for a leader not top on either crierion, and between 40 and 50 percent vote for the leader best on both. However, when the leader is not perceived as being the most capable, being top on honesty and being in touch nets less than 20 percent voting for that leader's party.

These results may, of course, be tied up with Ahern's popularity and his experience as a Taoiseach, something no other candidate had (although both Quinn and Noonan had been senior ministers in the 1994–97 coalition government). However, it does tie in to at least some previous research which stressed the importance of capability above all things (Bean and Mughan, 1989). How someone gets to be perceived as capable is another matter, particularly in the absence of experience.

Conclusions

Fine Gael ousted its leader, John Bruton, in January 2001 in the hope of improving its electoral fortunes, just as it had done when replacing Alan Dukes with Bruton eleven years before. After the 2002 election Fine Gael (again) and Labour each changed its leader, with Enda Kenny replacing Michael Noonan and Pat Rabbitte replacing Ruairi Quinn. It was widely perceived that the incumbent parties had the edge in the leadership battle in 2002 and we have seen that the perception was correct. Ahern's popularity was extraordinarily widespread, with almost three-quarters of all voters evaluating him positively, and Mary Harney too was assessed more favourably than any opposition leader. In the contest between Ahern and the main opposition leaders, Noonan and Quinn, Ahern won, whether the criterion for a good leader was honesty, being 'in touch' with ordinary people, capacity to govern, or more generally, representing people's views. Yet the conclusion that this provided the government with a huge electoral advantage may be less well founded. In 1997, the gap between Fianna Fáil and Fine Gael leaders seems to have been a small one, yet Fianna Fáil won almost 40 percent of the vote and Fine Gael only 27 percent. This time the gap was very considerable, but the Fianna Fáil vote rose by only 2 percent, while the Fine Gael vote fell by 5 percent. It is unlikely that the gap between the two major alternative candidates for Taoieach is ever likely to be greater. This in itself suggests that if leadership does matter, it does not matter much. It may well make a difference at the margin, but this was not an election whose outcome turned on marginal effects.

The assessement of leader effects is difficult because of the real possibility that voters' assessments of leaders affect evaluations of parties, and evaluations of parties also affect those of leaders. We have sought to explore the effects of leader evaluations on the vote here by examining the behaviour of those for whom leader and party evaluations were inconsistent. We found that in such cases the party evaluations were much more significant. Moreover, the contribution made to each party's vote by the votes of those apparently attracted by its leader rather than by the party is very small, being no more than 1 percent of each party's vote. It would be unwise to conclude that leader effects were quite this tiny because of the possibility that for some people – and we have no way of knowing how many – party evaluations were improved (or lessened) by a particular leader. To get a more reliable estimate of how important leaders were requires a more sophisticated multivariate analysis in which a number of possible influences on the vote are assessed at the same time. This will be done in Chapter 9. Before that we shift our focus from the top of the party down to the grass roots, looking first, in Chapter 7, at the campaign in the constituencies, led by the parties' candidates, and then, in Chapter 8, exploring in more depth the assumption that 'party' is important for many voters. Votes, after all, are formally cast for individual candidates, not for parties nor for leaders.

Notes

1 As in Chapter 4, Table 4.9 these calculations are made on a 'stacked' data set in which the unit of analysis is a respondent's evaluation of a leader.
2 These are standardised regression coefficients from a multiple regression of overall evaluations on these several criteria. Contrasting these assessements to the assessment of leaders who represent a respondent well, there is a again a stronger link between representation and capability and than between representation and honesty or being in touch.
3 Of course, almost 10 percent voted Independent, or for a small party whose leader is not mentioned here. This figure of 33 percent applies to those who voted for parties. If we added in Independents the percentage would rise to 40 percent.
4 These seem fairly typical in comparative perspective although the correlation for Fine Gael is on the low side: see Curtice and Holmberg, 2005.

7

Grass-roots campaigning

Observers have identified several new trends in election campaigning. The increased role of marketing experts in campaigning, the greater degree of central control and national focus, and the downgrading of labour intensive campaigning activities have received much attention (Norris, 2002). In particular, there is an increase in the central control of campaigning, making full use of the latest media and professional assistance and decreasing use – often through necessity – of local party workers. Campaigns are now typically described by analysts as sophisticated PR operations, directing professionally constructed messages straight to the voter, allowing minimal opportunities for distortion by 'untrustworthy' intermediaries such as journalists and party workers. This is not to say that everything takes place in the political capital. In fact, great attention is given to constructing a local element – not least through leaders' appearances at carefully chosen sites – but this is centrally directed and controlled. The campaign itself is not decentralised.

In line with these international trends, election campaigning in Ireland has, in some ways, also become more centralised and professionalised. As late as 1970, Chubb observed that the 'small and comparatively underdeveloped' resources of central offices left candidates dependent on their own efforts (Chubb, 1970). Generous funding from the public purse, which some parties have been able to supplement with considerable private donations, has provided central organisations with far more resources. Campaigns are much more professional, making widespread use of marketing and PR skills and information. In 2002, Fianna Fáil's campaign provided a fine illustration of early planning, using focus groups, as well as local and national polls, to develop an effective set of campaign themes and a well-staffed publicity operation to ensure that the media itself stayed 'on message' during the campaign. Fine Gael's did not, and a late change of leadership contributed to a badly planned and ill-focused effort that certainly did not help the party maximise its opportunities (see Collins, 2003).

Yet, in important ways Irish election campaigning does buck the international trends. The local element of campaigning in Ireland plays a key role – many would say it plays *the* key role. Parties may put much effort into deciding which particular candidates should run in each constituency, but they do so within severe local constraints. Candidate selection has been a matter for the local party organisation and central party controls are largely indirect (Galligan, 1999, 2003). For the most part, the candidates themselves increasingly fund their own campaigns, and they decide how closely they will work with the party. Most candidates cooperate with the central party, but some candidates may distance themselves if their local constituency priorities clash with the priorities of the national party. These local campaigns generally take the very old-fashioned form of door-to-door canvassing, supplemented by a presence at school gates, supermarkets, railway stations and shopping centres. Candidates will also put up many posters and will seek publicity in the local press and, increasingly as the broadcast media market becomes decentralised, on local radio.

When a party fields more than one candidate in a constituency the national party must manage the inevitable competition between those candidates so that each works to the advantage and not to the disadvantage of the party. This is typically done chiefly by 'bailiwicking', dividing the constituency into territories and getting the candidates to make agreements about who can campaign in each area. There are some areas exclusive to each candidate – usually their 'home' areas – and others where there is a free-for-all. There is also some attempt at 'vote management', whereby party supporters in an area are asked to support one particular candidate, so as to obtain a reasonably even distribution of the vote across the candidate slate.[1] This maximises the chances of winning seats (see Gallagher 2003 for a full explanation). These strategies have different degrees of success. Every election gives rise to complaints to national party headquarters about canvassing agreements being broken and a few stories of altercations between the workers for rival candidates from the *same* party. Likewise, at every general election there are instances of seats being lost that would have been secured by more effective vote management.

There are thus at least two campaigns, the national and the local.[2] However, to date, most academic analysis has focused on 'national' aspects rather than 'local' aspects of campaigning. In particular, analysts have focused on parties' production of national election manifestos, parties' promotion of their national party leaders and parties' attempts to influence, if not control, the election agenda in the national media (see Collins, 2003; Brandenburg and Hayden, 2003). These are obviously very important aspects of any Irish election. However, we focus here on the much understudied area of local election campaigning in Ireland, and in particular on the old-style door-to-door constituency campaigning. In doing so we ask how extensive it is and how much it actually matters. Furthermore, we also explore the role of individual candidates in this process. In doing so, we return to the theme of the importance of parties relative to candidates that we introduced in Chapters 1 and 2.

A lot of international evidence suggests that local campaigning matters. The impact was shown by experimental data in Britain more than 30 years ago (Bochel and Denver, 1971) and some recent US studies have served to underline the importance of this aspect of campaigning for turnout in what are usually seen as television dominated elections (Gerber and Green, 2000; Green *et al.*, 2003; Gerber *et al.*, 2003). A succession of UK studies underlined the importance of the local campaign for party vote shares. These used a variety of methods. Surveys of party agents or candidates in constituencies provide measures of general campaign activity (e.g. Denver and Hands, 1997; Denver *et al.*, 2002, 2004). Surveys of party members have provided measures of the incidence of grass-roots contact (e.g. Whiteley and Seyd, 2003). Campaigning has also been measured more indirectly by the use of local campaign expenditure (e.g. Pattie *et al.*, 1995). There have been a few individual level analyses using election study data to explore the link between contact and voting (Butler and Stokes, 1969; Whiteley and Seyd, 2003; Johnston and Pattie, 2003; Pattie and Johnston, 2003; see also Karp *et al.*, forthcoming, for a comparative analysis). Denver *et al.* (2004) report strong correlations between these several measures.

In general the conclusions from these analyses have underlined the argument that local campaigns matter in terms of vote share, with the individual level analyses giving added weight to the aggregate data analyses by showing that local campaigning works by mobilising or reinforcing the predispositions of those contacted directly. There is also evidence from the USA on the impact of personal contact on vote choice (Kramer, 1970; Huckfeldt and Sprague, 1992; Wielhouwer and Lockerbie, 1994; Krassa, 1988; Wielhouwer, 1999; Beck *et al.*, 2002; Wielhouwer, 2003). The studies mentioned largely reject the argument that local campaigning is irrelevant, but do not all agree on how much and in what ways campaigns matter.

While anecdotes are common, good evidence on the electoral value of local campaigns in Ireland is harder to find. Gallagher and Marsh (2002) examined the impact of Fine Gael member activity on the Fine Gael vote, and Benoit and Marsh (2003, 2004, 2006) have assessed the impact of local campaign expenditure on candidate and party success. However, there has been little work on the importance of individual contacts for the vote and no work on its importance for the party share of the vote. For reasons we have already set out, local campaign effects should be found in Ireland if they can be found anywhere. Personal appeals provide a means of getting through the perceptual screen that many voters might put up to avoid political information from the media. Moreover, candidates themselves can make the most personal of appeals, asking for a vote for themselves as an individual – an individual the voter will probably have met on other occasions prior to the campaign.

Local campaigning in 2002

The experiences of the candidates have been well documented in the now well-established series of *How Ireland Voted* books dating back to 1987, each of which contains a number of accounts by candidates themselves of their experiences during the general election campaign. In all cases they emphasise the importance of the canvass. One Fianna Fáil candidate sees it as 'by far the best method of making direct contact with the individual voters' (Fleming *et al.*, 2003: 60). A Fine Gael candidate explains that 'every single house in the constituency had to be canvassed by a member of my campaign team, or myself' (Fleming *et al.*, 2003: 62). Even so, a well-resourced Sinn Féin candidate complained that 'some [canvassers] found that, as has been the case in other recent elections, more often than not people were not at home, so a second canvass was required midway through the election campaign' (Fleming *et al.*, 2003: 81).

A Labour candidate, recognising the problems of the door-to-door campaign at a time when a very high proportion of voters are in the labour force, explained the need for 'a very early morning start at commuter railway stations, bus queues, traffic congestion points, school drop-off points and early morning shopping or breakfast stop cafes'. She still found voters who complained that 'they saw few candidates actually coming door to door looking for votes' (Fleming *et al.*, 2003: 68). Not surprisingly, candidates realise they must make rational use of their scarce resources. A candidate from the Greens expressed regret that 'as a small party, a full door to door canvass in a three-week election campaign period was not going to be possible' and so his team 'canvassed more intensively areas where we already polled well' (Fleming *et al.*, 2003: 76). This sort of targeting must be expected, even in relatively small constituencies.

Candidates will typically distribute leaflets extolling their achievements and, where it seems helpful, the achievements of their party as part of their canvass. They ensure that their names and photographs are displayed prominently through extensive use of posters hung on lamp-posts and on telegraph poles. One independent candidate (Liam Twomey, Waterford) explained how his team postered the road that would be used by a television team coming to make an election programme on his constituency, in order to build the impression that he was a 'credible candidate'. There will be party posters, some bearing the names of the local candidates, but these are usually supplemented by personal candidate posters that may or may not carry the party name conspicuously and may or may not mention any running mates. Advertisements in local papers were less widespread in the 2002 election, as candidates had to confine their spending within legal limits. Most of the reported expenditure went on posters and leaflets.

The attentiveness of the voters

Before looking at the effect that the campaign may have had on the vote we must ask how much it was actually noticed by the voters. Were they, in fact, contacted by a candidate or by those working on behalf of a candidate, and did they see posters or read leaflets? Respondents to our survey were asked whether or not a candidate or party worker had called at their home during the campaign. Table 7.1 shows that over half of all voters reported that a candidate did call at the house, and over half also reported contact by a party worker.[3] In a further question, respondents were asked if they had personally been contacted by a party or candidate seeking their vote and 56 percent reported that they had. This raises the level of overall contact even higher, as 4 percent of these did not report any contact with the home. This is a much higher figure than we find elsewhere. A comparative study of general elections in eight countries emphasises how atypical is the Irish case. Twenty-three percent reported contact in New Zealand, 18 percent in Portugal, 13 percent in Germany and less than 10 percent in Bulgaria, France, Hungary and Poland.[4] Karp *et al.* (2003: Figure 1) showed the Irish experience was equally remarkable in the context of a European Parliament election campaign.

Most contact is in person. Very few voters are telephoned. That medium seems to be used much more extensively in Britain and the USA, particularly to identify party supporters: so-called 'voter identification' (e.g. Denver and Hands, 2002). Its lack of use in Ireland may indicate that parties already have this information, but it may also

Table 7.1 The extent of the local campaign: household contact

Number of parties who called	Visit by a party's candidate(s) (%)	Visit by party workers (%)	Party worker or candidate phoned (%)	Visit or phone by workers or candidates (%)
None	49	47	96	24
1	28	22	2	25
2	16	15	*	25
3	5	9	*	16
4 or more	1	7	0	10

Notes: voters only; Independents treated as a single group.

underline the importance placed by parties and voters on face-to-face contact. A few voters were lucky enough to have several candidates knocking on their door, but contact by one candidate is the norm. The figures for each particular type of contact are individually quite high, but even more striking is the total proportion of people who are contacted (or rather whose home is contacted) by the candidates or party workers in person or by phone. This reveals that 76 percent report some kind of contact, with the median household contacted in one way or another by two separate parties. When the fact that not all respondents would have necessarily known that their household had been contacted, or would have recalled correctly, is taken into account the real level of contact may be even higher (see Bochel and Denver, 1971).

Which parties were most active? As we might expect, the larger parties were able to make a more extensive effort. Of course, they fielded more candidates, although the 138 Independents were the largest group of candidates. Candidates are supported by canvassers from their party as well as by personal supporters (Gallagher and Marsh, 2002). Fianna Fáil's supposed potential advantage in terms of members[5] did not translate into the same sort of dominance in terms of door-to-door coverage that we might have expected. Its activity was not much greater than that on behalf of Fine Gael. Independents are by far the least active as a group, but this set of candidates contains a huge range. Some Independents canvass heavily, some hardly at all. When it comes to the smaller parties Sinn Féin has more resources to put into canvassing than do Progressive Democrats or the Greens. The small parties did not run candidates everywhere, so the extent to which they cover their potential electorate is greater than these figures suggest. Moreover, if analysis is limited to the voters from the target

Table 7.2   The extent of the local campaign: household
contact by parties (%)

Contacting Party	Share of candidates	Visit by candidates	Visit by party workers	Visit or phone by workers or candidates
FF	23	32	34	55
FG	18	25	26	44
Greens	4	2	5	5
Labour	10	13	16	24
PD	7	8	8	7
SF	8	9	14	17
Ind/others	30	12	17	22
Total	100	101	120	174

Notes: voters only; columns 2, 3 and 4 do not total 100 because while not all respondents were contacted, some of those contacted were contacted by several parties.

constituencies of the smaller parties, the coverage achieved by some smaller parties comes quite close to that of the larger parties. Sinn Féin ran candidates in almost three-quarters of all constituencies, but activity would have been low in most of them. In the 10 or so where it had a serious chance, it reached the homes of 35 percent of voters. In contrast, using the same criterion, Greens and Progressive Democrats only reached 18 percent – a confirmation of the relative scale of Sinn Féin's machine.[6]

Many voters were contacted by more than one party. Table 7.3 shows, for each group of voters (by first preference), the extent of contact from each of the seven parties (treating Independents/Others as a single group). Analysis is confined in each case to those voters who were in constituencies where such a candidate was standing. Thus 65 percent of all Fianna Fáil voters were contacted by their party. Corresponding numbers for Fine Gael, Sinn Féin and Independents were 64 percent, 60 percent and 57 percent. The numbers are smaller for Labour (50 percent), Progressive Democrats (35 percent) and Greens (30 percent). Each of these figures is the highest in each column. In other words, each party is more likely to contact those who eventually vote for it than it is to contact those who vote for some other party. This is most marked for those parties who do the least canvassing. Greens are more than four times as likely to contact Green voters than they are to contact Progressive Democrat or Independent voters.

Table 7.3 Contact with each party's voters

| | Percentage of each party's voters with a contact from | | | | | | |
Vote:	FF	FG	Green	Lab	PD	SF	Ind
FF	65	42	4	26	12	17	20
FG	54	64	5	20	20	13	18
Green	39	31	30	13	10	11	20
Lab	39	28	7	50	12	12	17
PD	45	33	7	11	35	6	6
SF	39	37	7	21	9	60	13
Ind	54	43	4	24	15	23	57
All	56	44	6	26	15	19	21

Notes: voters only; each column calculated only on the basis on constituencies where the column party ran a candidate; 'others' excluded; 25 percent of those voting for 'others' were contacted by such a candidate.

However, not all contact is with each party's 'own'. In fact, most contact is with unsympathetic voters. For the smaller parties only 20–30 percent of contacts were with 'their own' voters. This figure rises to 33 percent for Fine Gael and 49 percent for Fianna Fáil, perhaps a low figure given its vote. If these numbers indicate that parties may spend much of their time canvassing those who give first preference votes to someone else, this does not mean that their time is wasted. In fact, such a strategy makes good sense from the perspective of the parties because of the operation of the single transferable vote. Giving a preference to a candidate, even if it is a lower one, can make the difference between success and failure. Candidates who won no second or third preferences would find it hard to get elected, as few make the quota on the first count.

We might expect overall levels of canvassing to vary locally with resources in addition to considerations of political strategy. The two largest parties report relatively low levels of membership in Dublin, so activity should be lower there. However, we might also expect levels to vary with the costs of canvassing, and these costs are higher where housing density is lower. In fact, over the country as a whole there is relatively little variation, but the proportion of voters in Dublin City and County reporting contact (68 and 71 percent, respectively) is about 10 percentage points lower than elsewhere, despite the fact that there are generally more parties running in Dublin.

Voters were also asked what sort of attention they paid to the campaign: what sorts of communication they noticed. What is clear is that,

Table 7.4 Voters' attentiveness to the campaign

	%
Looked at candidate's campaign posters	82
Read election leaflets put in letter box, given in street etc.	67
Saw information about parties and candidates on the internet	5
Attended public meetings related to the election	4
Looked at advertisements for parties and candidates in the newspapers	1

Note: voters only.

in addition to the direct contacts already mentioned, voters read leaflets, noticed posters and saw election advertisements in the press, but that very few attended meetings or used the internet (Table 7.4).[7] The number seeing press advertisements may be lower than it might have been in previous elections since there were fewer such advertisements this time, but posters are clearly visible to almost all voters, and leaflets also seem to be looked at by most people.

Effects of the campaign

Campaigns can have three main objectives. First, campaigners may set out to firm up their potential support, in order to ensure that they will realise all of that potential on election day. Second, they seek to convert those leaning towards another party. Finally, they will seek to encourage all supporters to actually vote on election day. The last of these may be very significant, but it will be examined in a later chapter.

This leaves confirmation and conversion. This is perhaps a continuum rather than a dichotomy: in the PR–STV system it is possible that a voter will give some level of preference for a party at some point on the ballot paper and so campaigners will seek to increase the likelihood of a high preference. Even if they cannot secure a first preference they will ask for a vote of some kind. Hence, in exploring the apparent effects of campaigning it is particularly important to consider effects on both first preferences and lower preferences.

There was little sign in the aggregate level opinion poll data that the campaign changed many minds when it came to party choice. Looking simply at the change between the first and last poll carried out by each of the main organisations, the picture is one of considerable stability. In the MRBI polls Fine Gael dropped 2 percent and Independents rose by a similar margin; IMS polls showed rising Fianna Fáil and Sinn Féin

support, with Fine Gael falling to a similar degree. Fianna Fáil support
was overestimated and Fine Gael underestimated in these polls by a
rather large margin (McElroy and Marsh, 2003: 162). Even so, the
average change over the couple of weeks between first and last polls
was less than two percentage points. If sampling error is ignored, and
these shifts were well within the limits of sampling error, the observed
movement may mean that no more than 3 percent (TNS/MRBI), or
5 percent (Millward Brown/IMS), of voters should have changed their
minds. This should not be surprising. The election came at the end of a
five-year term of office and was flagged well in advance, so we would
not have expected to see a lot of movement during a three-week campaign. TNS/MRBI's adjusted poll figures, taking into account the error
between poll findings and likely outcomes, put Fianna Fáil on 42 percent – well before the campaign started and this was the eventual
result. This, it is worth emphasising, does not mean the campaign did
not matter. It may well have mattered a great deal at the level of the
individual making up his or her mind, and it may have mattered a lot
for particular candidates, but there is no evidence that the campaign
had a big impact on the party share of seats. Party efforts either can-
celled out one another, or served only to cement the loyalties of those
already leaning in their direction.

It could well be that many voters made their final decision during the
campaign, but that these final decisions did not alter the result signalled
in earlier opinion polls. Sixty-nine percent of those who voted reported
that they made up their mind which party to vote for before the campaign, with another 12 percent deciding in the first week, 12 percent in
the next two weeks, and a final 5 percent on the day itself (2 percent
did not know).[8] This indicates a slightly later decision than is typical in
Britain, but earlier than is typical in Australia (where voting is compul-
sory) and the USA (where, of course, the campaign is much longer)
(McAllister, 2002: 28). It is reasonable to be sceptical about whether
people know when they decided but this at least suggests that there is
nothing odd about Ireland in this respect.[9]

The ideal tool for exploring the impact of campaigning on individuals is information on each respondent's voting intention before and
after contact was made. In the absence of this, as is the case here, there
cannot be definitive evidence on the impact of the canvass on the vote.
An association between local contact and vote will not distinguish
between the situation that occurs when a contact actually persuades
voters to support a particular party and that in which a party is simply
being efficient at keeping in touch with its most likely supporters. We
must ask whether a correlation between contact and vote is evidence

that a party is good at convincing voters, or simply evidence that it has been efficient in concentrating its resources on those most likely to support it anyway.

There is certainly an association between contact and vote. This can be seen if we compare the voting behaviour of those contacted by a party with the behaviour of those who are not contacted. As several parties might have called it is necessary to distinguish those who were contacted by one particular party from those who were not, and those contacted by another party from those who were not. This makes a fourfold distinction for each party–voter association. Taking Fianna Fáil as illustrative, there are:

1   voters not contacted by Fianna Fáil who were contacted by another party;
2   voters not contacted by any party;
3   voters contacted by Fianna Fáil and at least one other party; and finally
4   voters contacted only by Fianna Fáil.

It is necessary to compare the proportion of Fianna Fáil support within each of these four groups when considering the effectiveness of campaigning in convincing voters. Table 7.5 does this, using both contact with a candidate from the party and contact with party workers. It should be recalled that the unit for calling is, in every case, the house, not the individual. This can be expected to weaken – in the sense of underestimating – any relationship we might find.

'No contact' can be taken as the benchmark, and indeed the distribution of party support in that column comes very close to the national distribution of party support. There are several significant features of this table. First, any contact with a particular party is associated with higher levels of voting for that party, and contact with some other party but not with the first party is associated with lower levels of support. Moreover, monopoly contact is particularly effective. For Fianna Fáil candidates, contact increases support by 8 percentage points, from 37 to 45 percent, when it is competitive, and 24 points, from 37 to 61 percent, when Fianna Fáil makes the only contact. When some other party makes the only contact, support is depressed by 14 percentage points, down from 37 to 23 percent. A second significant feature is that while this pattern holds for all parties, contact has a stronger 'impact' in the case of the smaller ones. Candidate contact increases Labour support by a factor of 2 and a monopoly of contact by a factor of almost 4. Sinn Féin support increased by a factor of 4, and a monopoly of contact by a factor of 11!

Table 7.5 Association between type of contact and first preference vote

	Contact only by a party other than the row party	No contact at all	Contact by row party and at least one other	Contact only by row party
FF cand	23	37	45	61
wkrs	30	38	40	52
FG cand	10	20	30	45
wkrs	13	22	26	31
Green cand	3	5	27	*
wkrs	3	4	19	*
Lab cand	5	12	26	45
wkrs	7	12	13	23
PD cand	5	9	16	*
wkrs	5	9	20	*
SF cand	3	6	27	65
wkrs	6	6	13	28
Rest cand	5	10	20	41
wkrs	7	8	26	21

Notes: each cell contains only voters from constituencies where row party ran a candidate; cell entries in each row show percentage of each group voting for row party; smallest cell n is 20; * indicates that cells have too few cases for analysis.

A third point is that in almost all cases the 'impact' of *workers* calling is much less than that of a *candidate*, either negatively or positively. For instance, Fianna Fáil contact increases support by only 2 points when it is competitive and 14 percentage points when its party workers party make the only contact. Fianna Fáil support is depressed by just 8 percentage points when some other party's workers are the sole contact. The range here is just 22 points compared with 38 points for candidate contact. Overall, contact is associated quite strongly with vote, a monopoly of contact is associated even more strongly and a visit by candidates of a party is associated more strongly with a vote for that party than a visit by party workers.

Contact is associated not simply with first preferences but with lower preferences too. Table 7.6 replicates Table 7.5, but defines support not as a first preference vote but as a second preference for a party other than that of the first preference candidate. In effect it is a second *party* preference. The sample for each row of Table 7.6 thus excludes those who have already cast a first preference for that party. We have shown

Table 7.6 Association between type of contact and second party voted for

	Contact only by a party other than the row party	No contact at all	Contact by row party and at least one other	Contact only by row party
FF cand	13	16	21	12
wkrs	15	16	18	9
FG cand	13	15	18	23
wkrs	14	14	19	26
Green cand	6	6	9	*
wkrs	6	8	9	*
Lab cand	13	15	24	26
wkrs	14	14	23	16
PD cand	10	10	24	*
wkrs	8	13	18	*
SF cand	6	5	13	10
wkrs	3	7	13	10
Ind/O/ cand	13	14	29	13
wkrs	14	13	18	34

Notes: each cell contains only voters from constituencies where row party ran a candidate; cell entries in each row show percentage of each group voting for row party; smallest cell n is 20; * indicates that cells have too few cases for analysis; in each row, those who gave a first preference to a candidate from that party are excluded.

the analysis in this way to emphasise the association of contact with lower preferences.

The most interesting result here is the existence of clear differences between the second and third columns. These are much smaller than in Table 7.5 but for most parties there is at least a slightly stronger likelihood of support when contact is made than when it is not, whether contact is by candidates or by party workers. The low likelihood of support when parties are the sole contact is surprising at first glance but what this pattern probably indicates is a ceiling effect. Sixty-one percent of those who are contacted only by a Fianna Fáil candidate give that party a first preference. Within this group only 12 percent of those who do not give Fianna Fáil their first preference give the party their second choice. Those in this contact group who intend to support Fianna Fáil clearly tend to do so with a first preference. The broadly similar 'impact' of contact with candidates and with party workers may also be due in part to the fact that first preferences were lower within the group where contact was by party workers alone, so there is less of a ceiling effect. In general, contact by either workers or candidates is linked to support, but that candidate contact is associated with higher levels of party support than contact by party workers.

It would be unwise to infer from this that all candidates and parties need to do is contact more voters directly in order to be guaranteed a seat in the Dáil. As has been pointed out above, the equally reasonable inference from this data is that parties are quite efficient at targeting likely supporters, something parties may not do so well elsewhere (Kramer, 1970; Huckfeldt and Sprague, 1992). And, of course, to the extent that they are efficient, it may appear that contact has an effect that is quite misleading. Some targeting certainly goes on, as the quotation from a Green candidate above demonstrates, but there must be some scepticism about the possible precision of such activity. Personal campaigning on the streets, as opposed to by phone, lends itself easily to targeting areas but not to targeting individuals.

Candidates also know the areas in which they should do well even if they are not so sure about the individuals who support them. Their information comes from the unofficial ballot box tallies carried out at local elections and at previous general elections. Ballot boxes will contain only a few hundred votes at most, in many cases fewer than that. This tells parties clearly where they are strong and where they are weak, and they are better positioned to place particular emphasis where they feel it is most required. The smaller, more socially homogenous parties also have an idea of the sort of people who are most likely to support them and parties also have information on individuals from previous door-to-door canvassing, although this information is surely less precise or reliable. All this knowledge allows parties who have limited resources to target areas, but is less helpful in identifying the individual voters who should be contacted. Moreover, canvassing streets on foot is obviously less precise than canvassing by phone. Because of this there is a chance that parties are more likely to contact supporters than not, particularly if they are well-resourced parties that do not have to limit their canvass to the areas most likely to reward them. For the smaller parties activity is much greater in constituencies where they have a chance to win a seat and this will also tend to strengthen the link between contact and support without necessarily implying that contacts bring additional votes. Ideally, we need to make some allowance for this if we are to estimate more precisely the true impact of contact. It may be that rather than contact determining the likelihood of support it is the likelihood of support that determines contact. Furthermore, there may be some memory bias, with respondents tending to remember contact with parties to which they feel favourable and forgetting the rest. This problem cannot be resolved here but will be considered again in Chapter 9.

Local campaigns and candidate choice

Most voters make decisions about candidates as well as parties, either because they are voting for a candidate rather than a party, or because they have chosen a party that runs more than one candidate. Campaigns are focused on candidates as well as parties. There is a strong link between party contact and party support. What is the situation as regards candidates?

Of respondents who voted, 64 percent said they had decided on their first preference candidate in advance of the start of the official campaign while 69 percent had decided their party. Perhaps there is just a little more uncertainty about a candidate than there is about a party. However, the distinction between picking a party and picking a candidate may be problematic for some respondents. Given that the smaller parties did not run two candidates in many instances, and the questions followed one on another very closely, someone who decided on a party before the campaign would be expected to have decided on the candidate (and vice versa). However, early deciders for Sinn Féin, the Greens and the Progressive Democrats had also decided which candidate they would vote for in only 87, 82 and 80 percent of cases respectively[10] – very similar proportions to those found in the larger parties, where almost 90 percent of those who have decided the party have also decided on the candidate. It is possible that respondents simply meant they did not know who the candidates were.

What is the connection between candidate contact and votes for those particular candidates? Analysis here must be confined to those who were contacted by a candidate in situations where a party ran more than one candidate. In such cases most of those contacted and who voted for a party contacting them, voted for a candidate who contacted them: 86 percent in the case of Labour and 84 percent in the cases of Fianna Fáil and Fine Gael. In other words, only 16 percent of the Fianna Fáil voters who were contacted by a Fianna Fáil candidate gave their first preference to a Fianna Fáil candidate who did not contact them ahead of one who did. The same is true for Fine Gael. Much of this might be attributed to a combination of bailiwicking and vote management as contact will be made typically by the most local Fianna Fáil candidate.[11]

Conclusion

This chapter has examined the campaign in the 2002 general election, paying particular attention to the extent and pattern of personal campaign links. While Irish campaigns show many signs that parties have observed and learned from the style and tactics of parties elsewhere in the world, they are certainly not prime examples of the post-modern era, which some have claimed to see elsewhere. Politicians think that personal contact matters and all parties make considerable efforts to knock on as many doors as possible during the weeks of the official campaign. Despite the glossy posters of party leaders, the extensive use of opinion poll and focus-group research, central management and, sometimes, extensive teams of media watchers and controllers, all seeking to shape the agenda, the essential style of campaigns remains personal, with individual candidates seeking to make an impact and doing so for the most part by the traditional method of meeting the people. Over 80 percent of voters report some kind of party worker or candidate contact.

The big parties, with more candidates and more workers – party members and personal candidate supporters – naturally achieve a wider coverage. Given its supposedly larger organisation it might be expected that Fianna Fáil would do even better than it does, but in fact Fine Gael runs it quite close. There is a strong connection between these direct contacts (at least to the home) and the vote, whether parties or individual candidates are being considered. What is less clear is the process by which this correlation is achieved: does contact produce electoral support, or does (likely) electoral support attract contact? Are parties 'chasing' new voters or 'mobilising' existing ones (Rorschneider, 2002)? The evidence for any answer to this question is necessarily indirect, as the Irish election study lacks a pre-campaign element, but the fact that so many voters report making up their mind *before* the contact was made suggests mobilisation, or reinforcement, may be dominant. Fianna Fáil, Fine Gael and, to a lesser extent, Labour, make contact with a much higher proportion of voters who do not support them and so, at least in theory, may be seen to spend more resources chasing new voters. This difference could stem simply from differences in size, but it could also reflect the fact that Sinn Féin, the Progressive Democrats and the Greens have a more focused appeal. They are 'niche' parties, who have a clearer ideological message and a more homogenous pattern of social support. Arguably, it is this fact, as well as differences in resources, that explains the different pattern of contacts.

This analysis has described the extent of grass-roots campaigning and explored its possible impact on each party's share of the vote. It is very clear that candidates and party workers are involved in an extensive grass-roots campaign. Most voters are contacted; many by more than one party. Elections take place on the airwaves, but they also take place on the doorsteps. There was little aggregate change apparent in party support during the 2002 campaign, but many voters say they decided late and it seems possible that the doorstep campaign was a vital factor for some of those voters. It is very clear that contact is strongly associated with vote: those contacted by Fianna Fáil or by Sinn Féin, for example, are more likely to vote for those parties than are those not contacted. This association could be an artefact of the strategy of concentrating resources in areas where they are more popular, which all parties use. But even if this explains the association found here, the conclusion that contact did not really matter would be unwarranted, and a dangerous one for any would-be politician to draw. Contact could be the mechanism that transforms strong potential support into actual votes. That contact may not simply be at election time. Candidates will typically be known around their districts and will maintain an active presence there, although they will seek to make that final visit in the last few weeks before an election.

The links between support and contact are most pronounced when it comes to candidates. Arguably, individual candidates are more careful of their own resources and so give their personal time where it will be of most use, but it may also be that such personal contacts are especially effective, and effective at winning a vote (at least a lower preference vote) if not a No 1. This raises important questions once again about the relative importance of candidates and parties in campaigns and in vote decisions. This is the central topic of Chapter 8.

Notes

1 Almost a quarter of all voters reported that a party had recommended which of its candidates should get a first preference in the voter's local area. Just over a third, that is about 8 percent of all voters, say they followed this advice, almost all of them supporters of Fianna Fáil or Fine Gael.

2 Indeed, it is often said that there are as many elections in Ireland as there are constituencies.

3 'Called at' means personally, not by phone. This was the topic of a separate question: see below.

4 Authors' analysis of CSES Wave 2, Summer 2003 release: www.umich.edu/ ~cses. The appropriate comparison here is with the 55 percent figure in

the text above as these are responses to the same question; see also Karp *et al.*, forthcoming, figure 1.

5 Fianna Fáil claimed around 40,000 members to 20,000 in Fine Gael, 4,000 in Labour and less than 1,000 in the smaller parties, although a more recent internal study suggested Fianna Fáil membership was closer to 15,000.

6 'Serious' is defined here as a constituency where a party won at least 10 percent of the vote.

7 This last channel may come to be more important in future years. The parties have made some efforts to develop their own websites and party TDs all have standard ones but many challenging candidates also conveyed useful election information in this way.

8 In contrast, only 64 percent decided their candidate before the campaign.

9 Data from a Millward Brown/IMS pre-/post-election panel survey also indicates that the question provides a guide to the stability of vote intention. Of those who had 'definitely' decided how to vote the week before the election (and who did vote), 14 percent did not follow their pre-election party choice, while of those who were not certain, 33 percent apparently changed their mind. These late changes had a negligible impact on the result (McElroy and Marsh, 2003).

10 Moreover, none of these cases are in constituencies where Sinn Féin and PDs ran multiple candidates.

11 In all, only 8 percent report visits by more than one candidate from the same party. Most of these are by two or in a few cases three Fianna Fáil candidates.

8

Parties or candidates?

In most democracies analyses of parliamentary elections focus on the crucial role played by political parties, and most of the analyses of Irish elections have followed suit. As is generally the case elsewhere, Irish parties are central to the democratic process in parliament and each government owes its position to disciplined party voting. In most countries it is assumed that voters at election time choose between the parties on offer: while there may be some element of a 'personal vote' for some candidates, this is generally considered to be a small proportion of each party's overall support. The USA is considered unusual among liberal democracies in the significant personal vote won by congressional candidates. However, conventional wisdom in Ireland sees the personal vote as extremely important. The stability of party support at constituency level and the pattern of largely within-party transfer votes suggests that party is very significant to the voter. As against this, when people are asked about the relative importance of party and candidate in their decision they typically say that the most important factor is the candidate (see Sinnott, 1995). It is critical to our understanding of voting behaviour that we know how important the party label is in structuring the expression of preferences. It makes little sense to look for reasons why a particular voter supported Fianna Fáil, for instance, if that voter was simply supporting a particular Fianna Fáil candidate and would have done so whatever that candidate's party label. The issue also has substantial implications for how we think about Irish electoral democracy.

In Chapter 2 we looked at the patterns of transfers, particularly in situations where a party fields more than one candidate and so allows voters to show what Gallagher (1978) called 'solidarity' – a vote for all a party's candidates in sequence. We saw that, overall, most first preference votes for parties translate into votes for the whole party slate, and the majority of the latter are cast in sequence. Even so, it is clear that a large number of voters for Fianna Fáil or Fine Gael do not vote a classic straight ticket and that a significant number support only some of the candidates of what appears to be 'their' party. This might lead us to conclude that significant numbers of Fianna Fáil and Fine Gael voters and, we can infer, voters who are choosing the single candidate of some other party, are not motivated by party alone (Marsh, 2000). It was also shown in Chapter 2 that while, for some, first and even second party preferences did tend to conform to the pattern we might expect of those choosing a *government*, preferences for government could not be inferred from the way many voters filled in their ballot.

Party is very salient for most voters, but clearly not for all. Indeed, if we take voting a straight ticket as the criterion for being a party-centred voter – quite a strong requirement in the Irish case, particularly where a party fields three or four candidates, we would say that most voters show very clear signs that they choose candidates, not parties. While the evidence we have adduced from the simulated ballots is consistent with previous analysis of aggregate data (e.g. Gallagher, 1978, 2003) and the electronic ballots available from 2002 (Laver, 2004), there are other ways of exploring this question that do not require that we make such a strictly deterministic set of inferences about ballot completion. It could be that a party voter feels a party vote has been cast with the first preference, and in subsequent preferences uses a combination of criteria.

Direct evidence on the importance of the candidates

Asking people more directly about the importance of candidates and parties explores this possibility. Respondents were asked first whether party or candidate was the most important factor in their decision on first preference. Only 38 percent said party, with the majority (62 percent) opting for candidate. A second question posed the counterfactual, asking respondents if they would still have voted for the same candidate had that candidate stood for a different party (46 percent say they would, 37 percent said they would not and the remainder said 'it depends'). There is considerable consistency at the individual level across the two questions, with only 17 percent giving claiming to be candidate-centred on the first question, but saying they would not follow the candidate into a different party, or claiming to be party-centred, but willing to follow the candidate into a different party. The results also look similar in the aggregate in terms of a strong party response, with 37 percent saying they would not follow the candidate who changed party as against 38 percent saying the party (as opposed to candidate) was the major factor in their choice.

However, the strong candidate response is much lower on the second question: 46 percent focus on the candidate in this formulation as opposed to 62 percent in the earlier one. Those who said 'it depends' are drawn almost equally from those who previously gave 'party' and those who gave 'candidate' as the main reason for their first preference vote. Neither response is really inconsistent. 'Party' voters who would nonetheless follow a candidate could well view at least two parties with equal approval. 'Candidate' voters might still see party as a factor sufficient to limit their choice. One respondent explained his first preference vote by saying that his favoured candidate was 'anti-Fianna Fáil'. This underlines the point that both candidate and party factors should be assumed to play a role for any voter, but for some the weighting of the two may be equal, while for others it is very unequal and, as it becomes more unequal, it is reasonable to classify voters as primarily 'party-centred' or as primarily 'candidate-centred'.

Table 8.1 shows a simple index derived from these two questions, and variations in this index across parties. Party is weighted most strongly amongst those who support Green and Sinn Féin candidates and weakest among Fine Gael, Labour and Progressive Democrat voters. Since the analysis in the previous section was based largely on Fianna Fáil and Fine Gael voters, this would seem to imply that the estimates of

Table 8.1 Candidate or party index from direct questions (%)

	Candidate-centred	Mixed	Party-centred	Total
Fianna Fáil	34	37	30	100
Fine Gael	50	30	21	100
Green	15	46	39	100
Labour	36	41	23	100
PD	45	42	14	100
Sinn Féin	24	33	43	100
Ind/others	39	57	3	100
Total	37	38	25	100

Notes: candidate-centred voters are those who report that candidate is the primary factor in their first preference vote and say that if their candidate had run for some other party they would still have voted for him; and party-centred voters are those who say party is the primary factor in their first preference vote and that they would not have voted for him if their candidate had not run for that party; all others are classified as ambivalent or having mixed motives.

the importance of party are certainly not too high. If Greens and Sinn Féin ran more candidates, a higher proportion of voters would express party solidarity. Combining the two measures, we find that 37 percent clearly see themselves as candidate-centred,[1] 25 percent party-centred and 38 percent are not unambiguously of either type.[2] Perhaps the breakdown here indicates less party-centredness than would be expected from voters' behaviour and this may reflect a public unwillingness to appear overtly partisan in a political climate exposed to the wrong-doings of several high-profile politicians.

On the basis of the index, it is clear that voters for the Greens and Sinn Féin claim most often to be party-centred; Fine Gael and the Progressive Democrats' voters are most candidate-centred. This index provides a convenient measure of party- or candidate-centred voting. As has been argued already, some identification of this sort is important in order both to assess the electoral process itself and to understand what lies behind electoral choice. Before much use can be made of this measure, however, it is necessary to examine how well it correlates with other indicators of candidate-centred voting.

To start with, how do candidate-centred voters, so defined, behave when marking their ballot? It must be expected that they will be much less inclined to manifest any party solidarity. Table 8.2 shows the relationship. As expected, those who profess to vote for a candidate are much less likely than those who profess to vote for a party to support the remaining nominees of their favoured candidate's party. More than twice as many 'party' voters as 'candidate' voters show solidarity, and many more also vote for the complete list of their party's candidates. Of course, it is also evident that the more candidate-centred voters may also show solidarity: 29 percent of them do so.

Table 8.2 Patterns of complete and sequential party voting by candidate-centredness of first preference vote (%)

	Motive for first preference vote		
	Candidate-centred	Mixed	Party-centred
Voting for all the candidates in sequence of first preference party	29	48	67
Voting for all the candidates of first preference party	49	64	76

Notes: includes only instances where a party fielded more than one candidate; on candidate-centredness, see Table 8.1.

They pick the best candidates, but they see those as all belonging to the same party. And 67 percent of the more 'party' centred voters do vote a straight ticket.[3] Thus the relationship between reported motive and reported behaviour is a very clear one. Those voters apparently committed to a candidate, but willing to support the full ticket, come close to being what Mair called clientelistic partisans: 'a group of voters who are partisans, but whose commitment to party is mediated by candidate or localistic considerations ... they will vote as partisans *only* if the party nominates a particular candidate or type of candidate' (1987: 73).

Respondents were asked a number of further questions about their choice once they had completed the simulated ballot. One of these was: 'Thinking about the *candidate* you gave your first preference vote to, what was the *main* reason you voted for that particular *candidate* rather than any other *candidate*?' This question was open-ended. The respondents were not prompted with a list of possible answers. The answers can be distinguished according to how important the party, rather than some other aspect of that candidate, was seen to be. Most answers fell into one of four categories, two of which refer to candidates: personal characteristics of the candidate and the fact that the candidate comes from a particular area (shared by the respondent), and two of which refer to the party (candidate's party and the policies). The first set is essentially personal: the voter knows the candidate, the candidate is 'good', the 'best candidate', is 'honest' or 'sincere'. This is not to say that performance does not matter: many see the candidate as a 'good worker', or a 'hard worker', or as someone who has been 'helpful' to the voter. The second set of reasons highlights local representation: the candidate is from the area, or has been good for the area, and has a 'good record' in the area or is a 'good worker' for the area. The third set is essentially partisanship, giving the party of the candidate as the key reason.

Finally, there are 'policy' justifications, citing the views or opinions of the candidate, with environmental and health concerns most often cited.[4] Table 8.3 shows the distribution of these main reasons across the sample. When asked in this undirected fashion, people appear to see candidates in terms of who they are and what they have done rather than their party or policy. Thirty-seven percent of all respondents who gave any reason provided an essentially personal justification and fewer than one in five spontaneously mentioned party. It may be that in some instances a respondent might feel that partisanship would be an inappropriate answer. Anyone voting for one of several Fianna Fáil candidates in a constituency, for instance, might feel the need to

Table 8.3 Main reasons offered for selecting first choice candidate (%)

	Party	Policy	Area	Personal
FF	19	4	31	40
FG	17	5	31	51
Green	29	48	6	16
Lab	21	11	27	35
PD	17	5	15	35
SF	31	18	20	17
Ind	10	30	34	20
Others	8	27	28	12

Notes: cell entries are percentages of each party's voters; the sum of each row may exceed 100 due to multiple responses; up to three main reasons coded for each respondent; 'Other' codes not shown.

explain why they chose *that* Fianna Fáil candidate rather than another. The same could be true of most Fine Gael voters and some of those voting Labour. Yet when analysis is confined to single-candidate parties the pattern is much the same: only 24 percent spontaneously mention party.

Even if this measure underestimates the importance of party, it tallies with the index we have employed. This is shown in Table 8.4. We would expect to see those who claim party to be the predominant motive would also express this when asked the open-ended question. While 'party' is a rare response, this is indeed what we find. While only

Table 8.4 Reasons for first preference by candidate-centredness of first preference vote (%)

	Motive for first preference vote		
	Candidate-centred	Mixed	Party-centred
Personal	48	18	28
Area	37	16	20
Policy	7	7	9
Party	4	9	45

Notes: includes only instances where a party fielded more than one candidate; the sum of each row may exceed 100 due to multiple responses; up to three main reasons coded for each respondent; 'Other' codes not shown; on candidate-centredness, see Table 8.1.

4 percent of those appearing to be more candidate-centred spontaneously mention party, almost half (45 percent) of the party-centred voters do. This increase is at the expense of both area and personal motivations and is further support for the simple measure of candidate-centredness used here, although it also illustrates an inconsistency in some responses that is normal in survey research.

Candidate and party ratings

Asking people their reasons for making any choice is problematic, as people may in reality make decisions without thinking through the sorts of criteria they are asked to consider. They may also be unaware of the way in which certain predispositions may impact on their evaluations of the choices offered. We took another approach to this puzzle by asking respondents to rate parties and candidates on a scale and compare the results. Much electoral research is based on asking people to rate stimuli – leaders, issues, performances and so on – on a number of scales and the most important factors in vote choice are then inferred from the pattern of correlations. We did this in Chapter 6 when looking at leaders. This may be a simple enough exercise where there are only 2 or 3 parties; it is very time-consuming where there may be up to 17, as is the case with candidates. Respondents were asked to rate each of the parties, and each of the candidates from those parties on a thermometer scale (0–100) like those used previously for parties and for leaders. It was feared that most respondents would find independent and minor party candidates particularly difficult to evaluate and so such candidates were excluded from this part of the survey in order to minimise respondent fatigue.[5]

Of interest here are the relative ratings of parties and candidates. It is expected that party-centred voters would rate party above candidate and that candidate-centred voters would rate candidates more highly. A majority of respondents do differentiate between candidate and party, although 58 percent of Sinn Féin voters failed to do so. Table 8.5 shows for each party's voters the average rating of the first preference candidate and the average rating of the party of that candidate.

The average voter rates his first preference *candidate* marginally behind his first preference *party*, but there are considerable variations across parties. In the case of the Greens and Fianna Fáil the average party rating is slightly higher than the average candidate rating whereas in other parties, and particularly in the case of Fine Gael, the candidate is rated more highly. This pattern of party difference is similar to those we have observed above, with party relative to candidate most important

Table 8.5   Candidate and party ratings for respondent's first preference

	Mean rating of first preference candidate	Mean rating of first preference candidate's party	Candidate-party: Mean individual difference
Fianna Fáil	80	81	−1
Fine Gael	79	69	+10
Green	72	75	−2
Labour	76	69	+7
PD	75	69	+6
Sinn Féin	82	77	+4
All	79	76	+3

Table 8.6   Candidate and party ratings and candidate-centredness of first preference vote

	Motive for first preference vote		
	Candidate-centred	Mixed	Party-centred
Candidate	81	77	78
Party	70	76	82
Average difference	+11	+1	−4

Notes: voters only; on candidate-centredness, see Table 8.1.

for Green and Fianna Fáil voters and least important for voters supporting Fine Gael, Progressive Democrat and Labour candidates.[6] Sinn Féin fits less well here.[7] Party is a stronger determinant of lower preferences than it is of first preferences. The candidate's party rates more highly than does the candidate himself when it comes to second preferences, and the party superiority increases further in lower preferences. This can be can be understood in terms of information (Richardson, 1988). Most voters do have good information on their top candidate, but after that they know more about parties than candidates and judge accordingly. This is significant when we remember that, very often, lower preferences did not conform to the pattern expected of party voting; from this we concluded that candidate factors were dominant for many people. Perhaps, while not following strict party lines in the ballots, people, nonetheless, find party a significant cue when judging candidates.

These ratings can be examined in conjunction with the candidate-centredness index developed above. On average, those who are

Table 8.7 Percentage voting for party of most favoured candidate

	FF	FG	Green	Labour	PD	SF
Voting for party when candidate most popular	77	62	24	46	28	40
Voting for party when candidate not most popular	8	4	1	1	1	1
Party's voters for whom candidate is top	92	91	79	91	85	92

Note: voters only; Independent and 'other' voters excluded.

candidate-centred rate their top candidate nine points higher than that candidate's party; for party-centred voters the difference is four points in the opposite direction (see Table 8.6). Again, therefore, we see a relationship between the index measure and alternatives. The correlation here is modest at 0.3 (maximum 1.0), but reasonable given the difference in method between the two measures and it gives some further justification for using this index in subsequent analyses.

When looking at leaders we asked whether knowing which leader was most highly rated told us much about which party the respondent voted for. We found that, in many cases, the link was clear, but not very strong. Here we repeat this analysis using candidate ratings rather than leader ratings. Do respondents vote for the candidate they like most? Table 8.7 suggests that they do. There are still ties in many cases. Even ignoring cases of ties within a party, 23 percent did not single out a particular party's candidates as the best. Overall, including all ties, both within and between parties, 56 percent vote for the candidate they rate most highly. This drops somewhat for Greens and the Progressive Democrats. If we exclude ties the number increases to 89 percent. Very few voters support a party when none of its candidates is most liked. What does this mean? Of course we had already asked people how they voted before we asked them to rate the candidates on offer in their constituency, and we might wonder how some voters still gave us a candidate evaluation that could be seen as being at odds with that vote. Unlike leaders, candidates are on the ballot paper, and voters do choose them. Moreover, while it might seem that the candidate was almost the sole criterion for a particular vote, this would be to ignore the fact that the candidate's party label may be the critical factor in the evaluation of the candidate.

We also repeat the analysis in Chapter 6, where we considered whether respondents would follow a leader or a party in choosing whom to

Table 8.8 The relative importance of party and candidate
ratings for vote choice

	Neither best	Best candidate, not best party	Best party, not best candidate	Best party and candidate	Percent of party's vote coming from best candidate only
FF	2	27	29	86	5
FG	2	38	24	84	24
Green	*	7	4	46	6
Labour	*	21	13	78	23
PD	*	17	4	47	32
SF	*	11	9	71	13
All	1	22	14	79	14

Notes: voters only; * indicates less than 1 but not zero; indepedents excluded.

vote for, this time substituting candidate for leader. Do respondents vote for the best candidate from a party that is not their favourite party, or for a party that is not running their favourite candidate? Table 8.8 shows the results. In the battle between candidate and party, candidate comes off best. Of course when party and candidate are aligned – both being most highly rated – most vote for that party and that candidate. It should be emphasised here that, for most voters, party and candidate were bracketed together: the best party had the best candidate. Relatively few differentiated one from another.[8] However, while 22 percent were willing to vote for a candidate who is not from the most favoured party, only 14 percent voted for their most favoured party when it did not run the best candidate. Relatively few votes come from each of these dissonant categories and the number of cases in each of the dissonant columns can be small for some parties. Even so, 20 percent of all Fine Gael votes seem to stem from candidate rather than party loyalties, while Labour too owed a significant debt to its candidates, as did the Progressive Democrats.

This analysis makes it clear that candidates are a crucial part of any party's electoral appeal, but it does not tell us what it is about the candidates that voters like. The open-ended question suggests that personal factors were very important. There were many references to candidates being good workers, often to their being good workers for the area. In other words, many people stressed a service role for TDs. There are other possible roles. In many countries, the emphasis might be either on performing on a national stage, or simply on representing the

Table 8.9 Rating of preferred candidates on roles of TDs: candidates in first four places only

Preference	Working for the area	Performing on the national stage	Sharing respondents views
1st	7.7	6.8	6.1
2nd	6.7	6.3	5.5
3rd	6.1	5.5	4.8
4th	5.6	5.4	4.3

policy concerns of people like the respondent. We asked each respondent to tell us how important it was that candidates should:

- be good at working for *this* area;
- be good at contributing to national political debate;
- be close to your political views.

Each criterion was rated on a 0–10 point scale. All were considered pretty important, but working for the area was rated, on average, at 9, contributing to national debate at 8.3 and sharing political views at 7.3. While 28 percent of voters thought all equally important, 43 percent saw one factor as most important and almost three-quarters of them thought working for the area was most important, while the remainder divided between the other two roles. We also asked respondents to rate the candidates they had voted for (at least up to four of them) on each of these scales. We show the results in Table 8.9. These rating are weighted by the importance each respondent attached to the role.[9] We excluded the few candidates obtaining less than a fourth preference. We see that working for the area is consistently the highest score, but we also see that lower placed candidates get lower scores than more highly placed candidates on each of the three criteria. However, the fall-off between the first and second candidates is significantly greater with respect to ratings on working for the area, where the difference is 1.0 (7.7 minus 6.7) compared with 0.5 and 0.6 with respect to the other criteria.

Conclusions

While there is a consensus that many Irish electors are strongly candidate-centred, the systematic evidence to support the claim and assess the relative importance of candidate and party has been lacking to date.

We addressed this issue in Chapter 2 by exploring how voters marked their ballots. The typical voter seems to express at least three preferences and these include a vote for at least two parties. There is little pattern in the combinations of first and second party preferences, suggesting little homogeneity in the electorate's perception of their options. It is important to know whether this is because candidates are much more salient than their parties. It was found that a majority of voters behave as if the party of their first preference candidate is a very salient factor in their decision, since the majority go on to vote for all of that party's candidates, many of these doing so in sequence, but some breaking the sequence by supporting a single candidate from some other party. At the same time, only a minority of voters show classical party 'solidarity' by supporting all of the candidates of their first choice party in sequence. Moreover, a significant proportion of voters show no solidarity at all. Instead, they behave as if the party is unimportant by going on to support candidates of other parties rather than the running mates of their first choice. This pattern of behaviour suggests that while parties are salient to many, candidates are more salient for a significant number of voters. Because the simulated ballots can only be used to analyse support for parties running more than one candidate, it is necessary to use other methods to assess candidate-centred voting.

This chapter has built on this preliminary analysis by taking some complementary approaches. This was done first by asking people to say whether the candidate or the candidate's party was most important for them, and then posing the counterfactual question: would the same candidate have been supported had they stood under a different label? The combination of the two questions identified three groups of voters: those more candidate-centred, those more party centred and a third intermediate group. This index was then tested for consistency against the ballot-based measure identified previously and served generally to identify those whose preferences appeared to reflect a differential import-ance of party. Two other measures were examined: an open-ended ques-tion asking about reasons to support a candidate and a set of candidate and party evaluations designed to show whether party or candidate rated most highly. While each might give rise to a different estimate of how much party-centred voting there was in 2002, both served to sustain the simple two-question index, giving substantial justification for its use in subsequent analysis.

All measures also tell much the same story about the relative import-ance of party and candidate in the fortunes of both in 2002. There is a striking contrast between Fianna Fáil and Fine Gael. Voters for can-didates of the former showed more solidarity, and in various ways testified to the importance for them of the Fianna Fáil brand attached to the candidates they supported. Fine Gael candidates, on the other hand, had to make their own way. Fewer Fine Gael voters showed solidarity, and most tended to have a more favourable view of their preferred candidate than of that candidate's party; fewer mentioned party as a reason to support a Fine Gael candidate and more described themselves as candidate-centred. Green and Sinn Féin candidates attract more support on party grounds than do Labour and Progressive Democrat candidates. Labour's image is perhaps not surprising. Like Fine Gael, it had a bad election. However, the Progressive Democrats had a good election and their self-image of being a policy-driven niche party would lead us to expect their label to be more important than it seems to have been.

Irish voters are motivated by a mixture of considerations when marking their ballot. Candidates are important. They have to be, at least to the extent that parties field several candidates, but it is evident that for some voters other attributes of candidates rather than their party affiliation are predominant factors in their choice. For many other voters, candidate considerations are subsidiary, deciding choice within, but not between parties. No firm assessment can be made about how many voters fall into different groups. It depends, like so many things, on the choice of measurement and decisions about cut-off points. The analysis of voting behaviour in Chapter 2 suggests that party carries the most weight for most voters when it comes to first preferences. However, fewer than one in five spontaneously mention party as the reason for their first preference and only a quarter (of voters for candidates other than independents) rate party *over* candidate, even though less than a third rate candidate over party. Our index measure suggests that, for 25 percent of voters, party has primacy. This is certainly an underestimate, given the behaviour of voters. It might be more accurate to add in the mixed group and argue that the breakdown is closer to 60–40 in favour of party.

The further analyses of the rating information for candidates and parties make it clear that candidate plays a very significant role in obtaining support for some parties. Most notably, those who supported a candidate they rated most highly, but who thought there were better parties than that of their candidate, contributed almost a fifth of support for Fine Gael and for Labour, as against only 6 percent for Fianna Fáil. Yet, even in FF, it is candidates who win when party and candidate evaluations diverge. The fact that in the great majority of cases the ratings coincide makes it difficult to know which is the chicken and which is the egg. Candidates may colour party evaluations, but party considerations must also be presumed to colour candidate evaluations. The bases of candidate evaluations depend more on local service work than anything else (see Komito and Gallagher, 2005). Voters tend to say everything is important but, of those who do distinguish, the great majority plump for a capacity to provide a local service. This echoes the emphasis on leaders' capacity to run the government. In both cases, policy representation was less important.

Commenting on the incentives that electoral systems like PR-STV provide for candidates to seek to build individual support, Bowler and Farrell observe that 'while it may make sense to assume that candidates spend time and effort on "pork-barrel" and "constituency service" politics, this is no guarantee that this is the basis for voting behaviour at the level of the electorate' (1991b: 347). This chapter has provided evidence that for many voters the candidate, rather than the party, is the key to their decision on Election Day and that constituency service is a very important factor in that candidate decision. Now, however, it is time to bring together both candidates, parties and other factors and assess more comprehensively what determines the choices of voters. We do this in Chapter 9, looking first at party choice and then, in more detail, at candidate choice.

Notes

1 Opinion polls have commonly asked voters whether they think choosing a prime minister, a set of policies, a set of ministers or a candidate to represent the constituency is most important and on average 40 percent have indicated it is the candidate. This question has been criticised with good reason for its ambiguity (e.g. Mair, 1987: 93) but the conclusions it leads to are not so different to those generated by our measure (see Sinnott, 1995: 169–70).

2 Clear party-centred voters are those who say party is the primary factor in their first preference vote and that if their candidate had not run for that party they would not have voted for him. Clear candidate-centred voters are those for whom candidate is the primary factor in their first preference vote and that if their candidate had run for some other party they would still have voted for him. The rest are classified as ambivalent.

3 This does not appear to be a function of the numbers of candidates standing from their party.

4 Other reasons, given by only 10 percent include a view that the candidate represented particular interests (farmers, workers, business or the elderly), tactical or strategic voting, and vague reference to family factors that are not clearly either personal or party.

5 In fact, over 54 percent of respondents evaluated all candidates, as compared with 91 percent who evaluated all leaders and 95 percent who

evaluated all parties. More than 75 percent evaluated more than half of the candidates.

6 Different voters may use the thermometer scale in different ways despite the instructions they are given: (see Brady, 1985). This can be countered by calculating party and candidate scores for each respondent that are centred on each respondent's mean party and candidate score. However, this standardised measure may be affected by the fact that some parties field more candidates than others. Assuming that the candidates of the favoured party will get a reasonably high rating, this will have the consequence that the difference between the top candidate and the overall candidate mean will then be a function of the number of running mates of the top ranked candidate. For this reason we have used the unstandardised measure here.

7 This superiority of candidate over party in Sinn Féin is surprising and seems counter to the evidence of other measures explored above. However, it should be remembered that only a minority of Sinn Féin supporters distinguished candidate and party and that standard tests of the difference between the two evaluations indicate that there is no significant difference between them.

8 Restricting the analysis to the much smaller number of cases without ties again leaves the pattern unchanged. Overall, just 59 percent vote for a party which has the best candidate but which is not evaluated as being the best party, while only 33 percent vote for a party that is evaluated as best, but does not have the best candidate. Ninety-seven percent vote for the party that is best on both criteria and only one percent for the party best on neither criterion.

9 This was done by transforming the importance scores to run between 0–1 and multiplying the candidate rating score by the importance.

9

Adding it all up

So far, for the most part, we have been examining the potential influences on vote choice one by one in a series of 'bivariate analyses' – bivariate in the sense that the relationship under scrutiny is between the dependent variable (the vote) and one selected independent variable, such as social class, or age or party attachment or whatever. This has been an essential first step, but it is only a first step because, in the real world, relationships are not bivariate: vote choice is a product of an interrelated set of influences; we need to examine the impact of each variable while taking all the other relevant variables into account. In short, our analysis needs to be multivariate. Before embarking on this, we need to outline how we think everything fits together. We do this by adapting the classic 'funnel of causality' framework pioneered by Campbell *et al.*, in *The American Voter* (1960) almost fifty years ago.

The Irish funnel of causality

The argument is that some factors affect the decision to vote for a party earlier and some much later. Party identification, for Campbell *et al.*, was established early in a voter's life, while evaluations based on the campaign itself were made much later. Early factors do not just influence the vote on their own account, they can also colour the perception of later events and stimuli. As we have argued already, partisanship may alter the perception of government competence, perhaps by shifting the blame for poor outcomes, or assigning credit for good ones. Partisanship will also bias the evaluations of a leader. We start with three sets of long-term influences identified in Chapters 3 and 4: social cleavages, values and party attachments. In our analysis we assume that the social cleavages are primary, followed by values and then partisanship. The argument is that social position influences values and these, in turn, influence the sort of party to which a person might become attached. Of course, other stories are plausible: it could be that all three are quite independent of one another, and influence vote choice by themselves. Or it could be that partisanship precedes values, with people acquiring an outlook by virtue of their partisanship, or – more reasonably – that values and partisanship are both acquired through socialisation. To some degree, we can see how reasonable these several interpretations are by what happens in the course of the analysis. If values lead to partisanship, then the impact of values on vote will fall when partisanship is brought into the analysis. If all are independent, the effects of each will not alter when other variables are introduced. Of course, it is still true that such an approach cannot demonstrate definitively that A causes B, but it does enable us to show the impact of A on B given certain assumptions and, unlike much of our previous analysis, it does allow us to take into account the possible impact of C.

We use the following demographic variables: age (dichotomised at the median, 41), class (following the Goldthorpe scale, outlined in Chapter 3), education (dichotomised at the median, pre-leaving certificate only) urban/rural (dichotomised at the median, between villages of 1499 and towns of 1500 or more), and gender (female). These are crude measures but it is best to keep all measures as simple as possible for this part of the analysis. We also use the six value sets from Chapter 3, measured by the factor scores. These are scales showing nationalism, secular/religious values, support for the EU, the environment, more/less egalitiarianism and privatisation. Each of these six value measurements is based on between three and five separate items, as indicated in that analysis.[1] We also have the subjective measure of left-right self-placement. Finally, we add in party attachment and father's typical vote. Attachment here refers to whether the respondent is close to a party. The 'leaners' – those merely closer to one party than another – are treated as non-attached, because we suspect that the attachments of 'leaners' may well be due to short-term factors that follow later in each analysis. Including 'leaners' at this point would thus obscure the real importance of those short-term factors.

The second set of factors comprises the more short-term explanations dealt with in Chapters 5–8: party competence, leaders, candidates and the door-to-door campaigning. There is little to indicate which of these might be seen as causally prior to the others. We introduce them in the following order: competence, leaders, candidates and campaign. Competence comes first, on the basis that the record of the government may well colour evaluations of candidates and leaders, particularly once we have already made some allowance for longer-term party attachment. As argued in Chapter 6, we think it necessary to consider the importance of leaders only in the context of party evaluations, as in Chapter 7. Party evaluations are so powerful that they weaken all other effects, and we want to know *why some people consider a party to be the best one* and how important values, the government's record, and leaders and candidates were in this evaluation. We, therefore, adjusted the measure of leader popularity by regressing the 'top party' variable on it, and taking the residual as our measure. This can be seen as a measure of leader popularity with the priming effect of party 'washed out'.[2] It is almost certainly a conservative measure. It will give us a lower band for leader effects. As we have already said, to the extent that leaders themselves directly influence the thermometer scores of their party, we will be underestimating the true impact of leadership. We take up this concern later, when we sketch out the difference between minimal and maximal effects.

Competence is measured by attributed evaluations on the economy, health, housing and crime. As argued in Chapter 5, only attributed evaluations matter; and other evaluations were excluded for two reasons. First, because they were measured in a drop-off section of the question-naire and the number of cases for analysis are a little smaller. Second, because there was little in Chapter 5 to suggest that these would add much to our explanation of the vote. Campaign effects are measured by whether or not a party – candidate or party worker – made direct contact in some way with the household. Leader effects are measured by whether a leader was most highly rated along with whether the party was most highly rated, as in Chapter 6.

In looking at the reasons for party choice we concentrate mostly on first preference votes, but these, of course, are not the only votes that are important. As we have seen already, almost all voters express a preference for more than one candidate, and most give a preference to more than one party. In the case of the latter group, we look at support for each party as expressed by either a first or second party prefer-ence vote. That is, a vote that may be a second, third, fourth or even fifth preference, but which goes to a second party. Most are second or third preferences and many have an impact on who gets elected. We also look at second preferences and whether they go to a candidate of the same party as the first preference. Parties with many candidates rely on supporters continuing to give preferences to most of their candidates. This strategy allows us to ask how much the straight-ticket voters look like those voters who support the party with only a first preference vote. This can be done only for Fianna Fáil and Fine Gael as there are two few instances to allow us to analyse the other parties in the same way.

Analysis: who voted for who, and why?

The analysis here consists of several sets of multivariate regressions, starting with a regression of the type described above for the Fianna Fáil vote. A vote for Fianna Fáil is contrasted with a vote for any party that is not Fianna Fáil. To stress the point, we are not contrasting Fianna Fáil with Fine Gael, or Fianna Fáil with Sinn Féin, but with all other choices. We have opted for this course of action largely for reasons of simplicity: it makes the exposition of the complex model much easier. However, we are also conscious of the need to compare the reason people vote for Fianna Fáil with the reason they vote for Fine Gael, or Labour or even Independents, and discuss the sets of analysis with a view to highlighting the contrast between them later in this chapter. The regressions use a method for estimating the effects on party support of each variable in which a vote for Fianna Fáil (for instance) is defined as 1 and a vote for anyone else is 0. The tables for the largest three parties are shown below. Those for the smaller parties and for independents are in Appendix IV. The effects that are shown in the tables indicate the ratio between the odds of someone voting for the party (such as Fianna Fáil) and the odds of not doing so.[3] The tables also show the confidence we have in each estimate in the form of the standard error. As a rule of thumb, the estimates need to be at least two standard errors away from 1 in either direction if we are to be at all sure that there is any relationship at all. On the basis of the standard errors, stars are attached to the estimates indicating the degree to which we are sure (one star), very sure (two stars) or very, very sure (three stars) of the existence of a relationship. The bottom row of each table shows how well these various factors account for whether a person voted for the party or not. This is indicated by the McFadden's R^2 coefficient that ranges from 0 to 1. The higher it is, the better the explanation.

Fianna Fáil

Table 9.1 shows the analysis of the Fianna Fáil vote. The first column shows the impact of demographic factors; values are added in column 2 and father's partisanship in column 3, own partisanship in column 5, followed by competence evaluations, campaign effects and finally, leaders. Demographic factors matter little. The odds of those without a leaving certificate voting Fianna Fáil are almost twice that of those with one, but no other factor makes a significant impact. The class/ occupational categories should be considered relative to the omitted (or reference) category, in this case unskilled workers. The odds of skilled workers voting Fianna Fáil are almost 50 percent more that those of unskilled workers doing so. But all other categories are even less likely to do so – although differences are all very small, and not big enough for us to be sure they are not all equally likely to vote Fianna Fáil in reality. As most analyses of Irish politics to date have suggested, Fianna Fáil is a cross-class party. Adding in values makes little impact, but two are significant. Fianna Fáil voters are not environmentalists and see themselves as being on the right, as shown in Chapter 3. We might also have expected a bias towards less secular values, or more nationalist ones.[4] However, partisanship is important, with father's vote having an effect independent of respondent's own partisanship. This falls when own attachment is introduced but remains very significant. Fianna Fáil partisans are 10 times as likely to vote Fianna Fáil as non-partisans; and those whose father normally voted for the party are twice as likely to do so. R^2 now rises from 0.04 to 0.18.

Evaluations of government performance are also significant, pushing the R^2 up further to 0.21. All evaluations except crime are important, each increasing the relative odds of a Fianna Fáil vote by about 20–40 percent and, together, more than doubling the relative odds of a Fianna Fáil vote. The difference in predicted support for the party between those who evaluate improvements in health and the economy as neutral and those who evaluate them both as very good is 26 percentage points – from 42 percent to 68 percent.[5] It is interesting that partisanship now declines in importance. We may see this as indicating a tendency by partisans to evaluate the government more positively, as we might expect, although there is no change in the impact of parental vote. Interestingly education continues to have the same effect. It is thus not the case that the less well educated are more likely to be partisans and, therefore, evaluate the government more positively. The effect is independent of all the other factors. These additional controls also allow us to see religious and anti-environmental values as slight, but significant factors, previously obscured by their relationship with partisanship.

The leader also matters. Support for Ahern translated into votes for the party. Even using our conservative measure, the effect is positive and significant. In the full model, the difference between voters least and most supportive of Ahern – controlling for the party evaluation – is 14 percent. Campaign factors also matter; party contact is a very significant positive factor. The odds of those who were contacted by Fianna Fáil voting for it were twice that of those who were not contacted to vote for the party. This was the conclusion drawn in our chapter on local campaigning. It holds true even when a substantial number of other factors were taken into account.

Table 9.1 Predicting the Fianna Fáil vote

Coefficient	FF	FF	FF	FF	FF	FF	FF	FF 1 or 2	FF Loyal
Under 40	0.98	1.08	1.13	1.09	1.10	1.08	1.07	1.39**	1.52*
	-0.13	-0.15	-0.16	-0.17	-0.17	-0.17	-0.17	-0.23	-0.35
MC	0.90	0.94	0.98	0.90	0.98	0.99	1.00	0.98	0.70
	-0.14	-0.15	-0.17	-0.16	-0.18	-0.18	-0.19	-0.19	-0.18
Self-emp'd	0.83	0.89	0.92	0.91	0.87	0.85	0.81	0.64	0.77
	-0.21	-0.23	-0.25	-0.25	-0.25	-0.24	-0.23	-0.19	-0.33
Farmer	0.95	1.02	1.06	0.96	0.96	0.94	0.95	1.16	0.68
	-0.21	-0.23	-0.25	-0.24	-0.25	-0.25	-0.25	-0.32	-0.24
Skilled	1.33	1.4	1.37	1.45	1.52	1.51	1.61*	2.00**	1.32
	-0.3	-0.32	-0.32	-0.36	-0.39	-0.39	-0.42	-0.57	-0.47
Urban	0.94	1.00	1.02	0.93	0.97	0.98	0.94	1.12	0.98
	-0.12	-0.13	-0.14	-0.13	-0.15	-0.15	-0.14	-0.18	-0.2
More educ	0.58***	0.60***	0.60***	0.61***	0.61***	0.61***	0.64***	0.76	1.08
	-0.08	-0.09	-0.09	-0.10	-0.10	-0.10	-0.11	-0.13	-0.25
Female	1.05	1.09	1.06	1.07	1.10	1.10	1.10	1.11	1.05
	-0.13	-0.14	-0.14	-0.15	-0.16	-0.16	-0.16	-0.17	-0.21
Nationalist		1.08	1.05	0.99	0.96	0.96	0.95	1.03	1.35***
		(0.06)	(0.06)	(0.06)	(0.07)	(0.07)	(0.07)	(0.07)	(0.13)
Secular-rel		1.06	1.03	0.99	0.93	0.92	0.94	0.98	1.09
		-0.06	-0.06	-0.06	-0.06	-0.06	-0.06	-0.07	-0.1
Pro environ		0.90*	0.88**	0.88**	0.88**	0.88*	0.88*	0.85**	1.01
		-0.05	-0.06	-0.06	-0.06	-0.06	-0.06	-0.06	-0.09
Pro EU		1.02	0.99	0.89	0.87*	0.87*	0.87*	1.01	0.93
		-0.07	-0.07	-0.06	-0.07	-0.07	-0.07	-0.08	-0.10

	(1)	(2)	(3)	(4)	(5)	(6)	(7)	(8)	(9)
Pro Buiness	1.00	0.97	1.00	1.00	1.00	1.00	1.00	0.99	0.99
	-0.06	-0.06	-0.06	-0.06	-0.06	-0.06	-0.07	-0.07	-0.09
More/less equal	0.99	1.00	0.95	0.95	0.95	0.95	0.95	0.96	1.31***
	-0.06	-0.06	-0.06	-0.06	-0.06	-0.06	-0.07	-0.07	-0.13
Left-right	1.17***	1.17***	1.13***	1.09**	1.09**	1.09**	1.09**	1.16***	1.10*
	-0.04	-0.04	-0.04	-0.04	-0.04	-0.04	-0.04	-0.05	-0.06
Father FF		3.26***	2.38***	2.22***	2.20***	2.17***	2.17***	2.49***	1.26
		-0.41	-0.32	-0.31	-0.31	-0.31	-0.37	-0.37	-0.26
Attachment			9.45***	7.29***	7.17***	6.77***	7.79***	7.79***	2.36***
			-2.08	-1.65	-1.62	-1.55	-2.54	-2.54	-0.53
Economy				1.37***	1.35***	1.36***	1.38***	1.38***	1.10
				-0.11	-0.10	-0.11	-0.11	-0.11	-0.13
Health				1.25***	1.26***	1.23***	1.38***	1.38***	1.08
				-0.09	-0.09	-0.09	-0.10	-0.10	-0.11
Housing				1.21***	1.21***	1.20***	1.30***	1.30***	0.96
				-0.08	-0.08	-0.08	-0.09	-0.09	-0.09
Crime				1.03	1.02	1.04	1.08	1.08	1.05
				-0.07	-0.07	-0.08	-0.08	-0.08	-0.11
Leader best					1.40*	1.47**	1.39*	1.39*	1.12
					-0.25	-0.26	-0.24	-0.24	-0.37
Party contacted						1.97***	2.54***	2.54***	1.04
						-0.29	-0.40	-0.40	-0.2
Constant	2.17**	0.6	0.32**	0.39*	0.37*	0.36*	0.29**	0.17***	0.32
	-0.76	-0.26	-0.15	-0.19	-0.19	-0.19	-0.15	-0.09	-0.24
Observation	1191	1191	1191	1191	1191	1191	1191	1191	545
R²	0.018	0.036	0.092	0.177	0.214	0.216	0.229	0.258	0.094

Note: cell entries are odds ratio with standard errors underneath; * significant at 05, ** significant at 01, *** significant at 001.

When we look at those who support Fianna Fáil as their first or second party, the impact of the various factors is much the same. Without running through successive models again we cannot be sure that each factor would behave in quite the same way but, in general, column 8 looks like column 7. Moreover, contact matters even more, increasing the relative odds of voting Fianna Fáil first or second by almost two and a half times. The economy, health and housing evaluations are also significant. The particular attraction of Fianna Fáil to skilled manual workers is also more pronounced. This attraction cannot be put down to traditional loyalties, or particular sets of values (at least those discussed here) or some special liking for Ahern. What it means is simply that, once we allow for other factors, the tendency of skilled worker to vote Fianna Fáil becomes increasingly clear.

Finally, what of the Fianna Fáil loyalist, one who votes Fianna Fáil 1 *and* 2? How does such a voter differ from those who defect with their second preference? Apart from the expected impact of partisanship, and the more general party evaluations, there seem to be few explanations. Ahern is not a factor, apparently. However, loyal voters do have slightly different values, are less committed to social equality but more nationalist – not quite the traditional mix associated with classic republicanism. Here at least the nationalist value is significant, differentiating the hardcore loyalist from the passing supporter. Fianna Fáil loyalists are also more likely to see themselves as being on the right. The R^2 is low, so even these factors offer no more than a partial explanation. It is much easier to predict Fianna Fáil supporters in general than it is to separate those who are loyal down the ticket from those who are not. However, in a further analysis, not shown here, we found that the general model in column 8 identified the loyalists more effectively than it did the first preference voter who was not a loyalist.

In general, the multivariate analysis reinforces conclusions drawn earlier in our chapters on the explanations of party support. Fianna Fáil's popularity is hard to pin down. It is broadly based, in sociological and ideological terms. Strong traditional support, a proven record in government, a popular leader and an effective organisation are all significant elements in what has become a hugely successful mix.

Fine Gael

Fine Gael's support is also ill-defined in demographic terms, but there are several significant differences, even if none of these are large: the odds ratios are always between 0.50 and 2.00. As shown in Chapter 3 there is an age gradient in support for Fine Gael and this still holds, with younger voters less likely to support them. There is also a positive link with education once other factors are controlled. The party is weaker in urban areas (the strength among farmers we found in Chapter 3 is not significant once urban-rural is included). Overall, the class profile is almost perfectly flat, with middle class and unskilled working class equally likely (or unlikely) to vote for the party.

Bringing in values makes little difference to the picture, although some demographic associations then fall just short of conventional statistical significance. Essentially, the party appeals more to those with less secular (more religiously conservative), views. Together, demographics and values give us little help in predicting the Fine Gael vote: the R^2 is only 0.036.

Party attachment is much more important, and, together with a father voting Fine Gael, pushes R^2 up to 0.17. Again, father's vote has an independent effect, which drops, but remains important, when respondent's attachment is introduced. Not surprisingly, the relative odds of voting Fine Gael among those who are close to the party are 11 times larger than for those who are not, but among those whose father voted Fine Gael the relative odds are 3 times higher. The factors considered earlier are now even weaker, suggesting that they are themselves associated with party attachment, although urban/rural and education associations remain at much the same level.

Evaluations of the government's performance have little impact on the Fine Gael vote, reinforcing the conclusion drawn in Chapter 5 that the party made little capital out of perceptions of economic mismanagement. Fine Gael voters were less likely to see the government as having done a good job on the economy (or having been responsible for economic progress), but there is little impact of evaluations of health, housing and crime. Using the model in column 5, the difference in predicted support for the party between those who evaluate improvements in health and the economy as neutral and those who evaluate them both as very poor is just 16 percentage points, from 23 percent to 39 percent, with the economy responsible for 14 of those points. It should be also remembered that very few thought the economy was getting much worse. The national campaign simply did not succeed in getting over the desired message that Fine Gael could do a better job in government than the incumbents. Even where voters were critical of the government, many looked elsewhere to express their dissatisfaction.

The leader effect on the Fine Gael vote is not significant, although it is positive. The odds of someone who thought Noonan was the best leader voting Fine Gael are, in effect, no greater than those who did not think so – largely because so many Fine Gael voters did not think he was the best leader. Once we control for other factors that incline

Table 9.2 Predicting the Fine Gael vote

Coefficient	FG	FG	FG	FG	FG	FG	FG	FG 1 or 2	FG Loyal
Under 40	0.72**	0.78	0.73*	0.83	0.83	0.83	0.86	0.67**	0.76
	-0.11	-0.12	-0.12	-0.15	-0.15	-0.15	-0.16	-0.11	-0.25
MC	0.95	0.92	0.81	0.88	0.84	0.86	0.88	1.02	1.18
	-0.18	-0.18	-0.16	-0.19	-0.18	-0.19	-0.19	-0.20	-0.49
Self-emp'd	1.05	0.99	0.86	0.92	0.94	0.94	0.91	1.18	1.28
	-0.31	-0.3	-0.27	-0.31	-0.32	-0.32	-0.31	-0.35	-0.81
Farmer	1.44	1.35	1.11	1.2	1.23	1.24	1.24	1.44	0.85
	-0.35	-0.33	-0.29	-0.33	-0.34	-0.35	-0.35	-0.37	-0.41
Skilled	1.11	1.11	1.30	1.37	1.33	1.34	1.4	1.44	0.49
	-0.29	-0.29	-0.36	-0.39	-0.39	-0.39	-0.42	-0.38	-0.29
Urban	0.54***	0.55***	0.60***	0.61***	0.60***	0.60***	0.59***	0.52***	0.49**
	-0.08	-0.09	-0.10	-0.11	-0.11	-0.11	-0.1	-0.08	-0.17
More educ	1.62***	1.60***	1.59***	1.54**	1.55**	1.54**	1.55**	1.63***	1.15
	-0.27	-0.27	-0.28	-0.29	-0.29	-0.29	-0.3	-0.28	-0.39
Female	1.03	1.07	1.09	1.20	1.19	1.19	1.19	1.18	1.44
	-0.15	-0.16	-0.17	-0.20	-0.20	-0.20	-0.20	-0.17	-0.44
Nationalist		0.91	0.94	1.00	1.00	1.00	0.99	0.90	0.99
		0.06	0.07	0.08	0.08	0.08	0.08	0.06	0.14
Secular-rel		1.14*	1.11	1.09	1.11	1.1	1.09	1.06	0.92
		-0.09	-0.09	-0.09	-0.09	-0.09	-0.09	-0.08	-0.14
Pro environ		1.06	1.09	1.08	1.09	1.09	1.10	1.11	0.83
		-0.07	-0.08	-0.08	-0.08	-0.08	-0.09	-0.08	-0.12
Pro EU		1.01	1.01	1.00	1.05	1.05	1.06	1.06	0.81
		-0.07	-0.07	-0.07	-0.08	-0.08	-0.08	-0.07	-0.12

	(1)	(2)	(3)	(4)	(5)	(6)	(7)	(8)	(9)
Pro B'ess	1.09	1.08	1.07	1.08	1.08	1.07	1.08	1.15**	1.32**
	-0.07	-0.07	-0.08	-0.08	-0.08	-0.08	-0.08	-0.08	-0.18
More/Less Equality	1.09	1.09	1.07	1.11	1.11	1.11	1.11	1.01	0.97
	-0.07	-0.08	-0.08	-0.09	-0.09	-0.09	-0.09	-0.07	-0.14
Left-right	0.99	0.98	0.97	1.00	1.00	1.00	1.00	0.97	0.97
	-0.04	-0.04	-0.04	-0.04	-0.04	-0.04	-0.04	-0.07	-0.08
Father FF		4.73***	3.25***	2.95***	2.95***	3.07***	3.27***		1.76*
		-0.76	-0.57	-0.52	-0.53	-0.56	-0.58		-0.54
Attachment			11.25***	10.19***	10.15***	9.59***	19.32***		5.93***
			-3.11	-2.86	-2.85	-2.71	-8.54		-2.11
Economy				0.77***	0.77***	0.79***	0.76***		1.21
				-0.07	-0.07	-0.07	-0.06		-0.2
Health				0.91	0.91	0.91	1.03		0.87
				-0.07	-0.07	-0.07	-0.07		-0.12
Housing				0.98	0.98	0.97	0.91		0.70***
				-0.07	-0.07	-0.07	-0.06		-0.09
Crime				0.97	0.97	0.97	0.97		1.2
				-0.07	-0.08	-0.08	-0.07		-0.18
Leader best					1.22	1.16	1.08		1.32
					-0.31	-0.30	-0.26		-0.44
Party contacted						2.14***	2.35***		0.78
						-0.36	-0.36		-0.23
Constant	0.50*	0.47	0.33**	0.21***	0.22**	0.17***	0.22**	0.65	0.86
	-0.21	-0.24	-0.18	-0.12	-0.13	-0.1	-0.13	-0.34	-0.97
Observation	1191	1191	1191	1191	1191	1191	1191	1191	283
R²	0.025	0.032	0.104	0.176	0.187	0.203	0.188	0.201	0.199

Note: cell entries are odds ratio with standard errors underneath; * significant at 05, ** significant at 01, *** significant at 001.

people to vote Fine Gael, the leader adds nothing. Given that leader popularity did bring supporters to most other parties, this means the Fine Gael leader was an electoral liability.

Contact was also important: the odds of a Fine Gael vote in houses canvassed by the party are more than twice as high as in those not visited. Even with an extensive set of controls, the importance of a home visit remains significant and strong, suggesting that there is little reason to see this simply as an indication that Fine Gael contacted its own supporters – a possibility raised in the Chapter 7. It seems more likely that the visit itself matters. It is, of course, possible that the visit activates candidate-centred rather than party-centred supporters, a point we take up later.

Looking at broader Fine Gael support, the main features of the previous analysis are reproduced. Other things being equal, the wider group of supporters comprise people more likely to be rural, better educated, pro-environment and also pro-private enterprise. They are also more likely to have been contacted by Fine Gael. The final column of coefficients reveal the difference between loyal Fine Gaelers and those who defect with their second preference. Values seem less important here although a pro-business ethos is clearly more pronounced among loyalists; contact matters less (suggesting this may be as much a candidate-centred factor as a party factor, as we have already seen in the Fianna Fáil analysis); and Michael Noonan had no more success in keeping FG voters than he had in attracting them in the first place.

Labour

Labour is now a broadly based party in demographic terms and in terms of values. None of the demographic variables and only two of the seven values measured have a significant impact: Labour voters are left wing and less nationalist. Together, these raise the R^2 from .01 to .05. Using the model in column 2, the difference in predicted support for the party between a voter located at the mid-point of the left-right and nationalism scales and one at the left, non-nationalist extreme is 26 points, from 9 to 34 percent, although there are few voters at these extreme points. The direction of the other value associations coincide with expectations that Labour would appeal more to a secular, less nationalist, more egalitarian, and pro-public enterprise voter, but none of the effects are significant. Party attachment is significant, but father's vote is not. While many Fianna Fáil and Fine Gael voters are born into their identity, Labour identifiers are self-made.

Adding in evaluations of the government's performance, we see that neither health nor the economy nor housing is significant. It should be remembered that the model used here is designed to predict Labour voters, and those voting for any opposition party may also have poor evaluations of the government. There is nothing that particularly singles out those who choose one opposition party over the others. Quinn is another leader who seems to have been unable to boost his party. He appears to have been a positive force, but the odds ratio is not a significant one, at least with respect to first preferences. Campaign contact did help: a home visit had a huge impact, pushing up the relative odds of voting Labour by a factor of almost 5: the predicted Labour vote is only 5 percent where there is no contact and 21 percent where contact takes place. Thus, while some visits are made to mobilise Labour voters, many are to persuade others to support Labour.

The main factors underlying broader Labour support, apart from fundamental loyalties, seem to be a less nationalist outlook and being more supportive of the EU – a somewhat unexpected outcome, but one which certainly separates Labour from smaller opposition parties as well as a disappointment with the government's record on the economy and on health. The difference in predicted support for the party between a voter who evaluates improvements in health and the economy as neutral and one who evaluates them both as very poor is 23 percentage points, from 16 to 39, all other things being equal.

We now turn our attention to the three smaller parties. The Progressive Democrats, Greens and Sinn Féin each won between 4 and 6 percent of the vote, so clearly our analysis here is based on very few cases. We continue to use the same statistical method for estimating the effects of the various factors. This is not ideal, not least because there are so few cases and the very skewed distribution of the support for these parties makes results potentially unreliable. However, we have also run the same models with an alternative procedure and the results are very similar to those discussed here and displayed in Appendix III.[6]

The Progressive Democrats

The Progressive Democrats are sometimes described as a 'niche' party, one that places a firm emphasis on clear policy positions, rather than appealing to a very broad spectrum of opinion and social position. They are certainly a party that appeals to the younger voters, with the relative odds of a voter under 40 supporting them almost twice those of a voter over 40 doing so. (The party was founded only in 1986.) It looks much more middle class and also more male, but given the small number of cases, not significantly so. Adding values, we see supporters tend to have, as might be expected, a clear pro-business ethos, but they

Table 9.3 Predicting the Labour vote

	LB	LB	LB	LB	LB	LB	LB	LB2
Under 40	0.91	0.79	0.80	0.86	0.86	0.88	0.83	0.79
	-0.21	-0.19	-0.20	-0.22	-0.22	-0.22	-0.22	-0.15
MC	1.56	1.39	1.37	1.49	1.42	1.42	1.35	1.39
	-0.47	-0.43	-0.42	-0.48	-0.46	-0.46	-0.46	-0.35
Self-emp'd	1.16	1.19	1.14	1.27	1.27	1.25	0.98	1.71
	-0.55	-0.57	-0.55	-0.64	-0.64	-0.63	-0.51	-0.60
Farmer	0.40	0.41	0.41	0.50	0.50	0.49	0.51	1.08
	-0.26	-0.26	-0.27	-0.33	-0.33	-0.32	-0.34	-0.41
Skilled	1.01	0.92	0.84	0.83	0.82	0.84	0.77	0.98
	-0.45	-0.42	-0.39	-0.41	-0.40	-0.41	-0.39	-0.35
Urban	1.21	1.07	1.02	1.03	1.01	0.99	0.97	1.06
	-0.27	-0.25	-0.24	-0.25	-0.25	-0.25	-0.25	-0.20
More educ	1.1	1.02	1.05	1.16	1.15	1.15	1.32	1.07
	-0.29	-0.28	-0.29	-0.33	-0.32	-0.33	-0.39	-0.23
Female	0.85	0.84	0.83	0.89	0.9	0.91	0.98	0.88
	-0.19	-0.19	-0.19	-0.21	-0.21	-0.22	-0.24	-0.16
Nationalist		0.80**	0.80**	0.84	0.85	0.85	0.87	0.76***
		(0.08)	(0.08)	(0.09)	(0.09)	(0.09)	(0.10)	(0.06)
Secular-rel		0.88	0.89	0.91	0.92	0.93	0.90	0.90
		-0.10	-0.10	-0.11	-0.11	-0.11	-0.11	-0.08
Pro environ		1.03	1.02	0.99	1.00	0.99	0.98	1.03
		-0.11	-0.11	-0.11	-0.11	-0.11	-0.11	-0.09
Pro EU		1.16	1.13	1.15	1.18	1.18	1.18	1.20**
		-0.12	-0.12	-0.13	-0.13	-0.13	-0.14	-0.10

	(1)	(2)	(3)	(4)	(5)	(6)	(7)	(8)
Pro B'ess		0.87	0.87	0.9	0.91	0.9	0.89	0.91
		-0.09	-0.09	-0.1	-0.1	-0.1	-0.1	-0.07
More/less equality		0.93	0.94	0.91	0.93	0.92	0.92	1.02
		-0.10	-0.10	-0.10	-0.11	-0.10	-0.11	-0.09
Left-right		0.82***	0.83***	0.85**	0.87**	0.87**	0.87**	0.86***
		-0.05	-0.05	-0.05	-0.06	-0.06	-0.06	-0.04
Father FF			2.19**	1.69	1.78	1.72	1.65	1.34
			-0.77	-0.65	-0.69	-0.67	-0.66	-0.45
Attachment				16.42***	16.87***	16.15***	15.51***	7.33***
				-9.14	-9.67	-9.26	-9.18	-4.28
Economy					0.82	0.83	0.81	0.83*
					-0.1	-0.11	-0.11	-0.08
Health					0.88	0.88	0.85	0.84**
					-0.1	-0.1	-0.1	-0.07
Housing					0.99	1	0.99	0.99
					-0.11	-0.11	-0.11	-0.08
Crime					1.05	1.06	1.06	0.99
					-0.13	-0.13	-0.13	-0.09
Leader best						1.51	1.78*	1.49
						-0.51	-0.6	-0.39
Party Contacted							5.15***	3.86***
							-1.35	-0.82
Constant	0.08***	0.4	0.36	0.18**	0.19*	0.18*	0.11**	0.44
	-0.05	-0.32	-0.29	-0.16	-0.17	-0.16	-0.1	-0.29
Observation	1069	1069	1069	1069	1069	1069	1069	1069
R²	0.019	0.056	0.061	0.102	0.110	0.112	0.167	0.124

Note: cell entries are odds ratio with standard errors underneath; * significant at 05, ** significant at 01, *** significant at 001.

do not think of themselves as being on the right. Allowing for values, farmers and middle-class voters are now more likely to be Progressive Democrats than are unskilled workers, and the urban appeal is also clearer. The R^2 is 0.11. Adding in party attachment hardly weakens any of these effects although they become less significant statistically: while the same tendency exists on average, there is more variation.

Evaluations of government performance are, surprisingly, unrelated to the Progressive Democrat vote. Although three of the four issue areas have an expected positive sign, meaning positive evaluations increase the likelihood of supporting the party, the effects are very slight. Mary Harney had a positive effect. The predicted Progressive Democrat vote is less than 3 percent among those for whom Harney is not considered the best leader and 11 percent where she is. Contact is a very strong factor: the predicted Progressive Democrat vote rising from 4 percent to 15 percent with contact.

Looking at broader Progressive Democrat support in the form of those who voted Progressive Democrat as their first or second party, the youth, urban and (middle) class bias is much more significant – though no stronger – but there is little sign of values being very important. Supporters are slightly less nationalist, but the pro-business concern is not a significant factor. Contact and Mary Harney remain as strong positive influences.

The Green party

The Greens, as Chapter 3 demonstrates, have the best-defined image of any party. The party is urban and its supporters better educated; and the odds of a person who is self-employed supporting the party are much greater than are those of an unskilled worker. With other demographic factors controlled, age is not a factor. Five of the seven value dimensions are significant, far more than for any other party. Support is more likely among the more secular, the more environmentally concerned, the more egalitarian, the less pro-EU and those on the left – and the introduction of values leaves the importance of the demographic factors largely unaltered. Party attachment matters a lot, but there are very few Green partisans.

Those critical of the government's housing record are much more likely to vote Green, but other evaluations are not significant. Trevor Sargent's popularity helped his party. Party contact mattered: the odds of a person from a contacted house voting Green being more than three times the odds of a non-contacted person doing so.

In terms of broader support, the pattern is much the same as for first preference votes. Contact, though, is twice as important; and there is, for the first time, a significant bias towards the party among those with pro-public enterprise views.

Sinn Féin

Sinn Féin is another small party that has a reasonably clear image in the public mind, at least in terms of its nationalism. The analysis suggests a party that is stronger among younger voters than older voters – the odds ratio is over 4 – but with no other clear demographic characteristics. The party is more likely to get the support of nationalist voters – although the odds ratio of 2 is hardly a huge effect – and is also relatively more attractive to those on the left and to voters more hostile to the EU. Despite that, and the party's often socialist rhetoric, there is no sign that its supporters are more egalitarian, or less in favour of private enterprise. These results remain the same even when party attachment is introduced.

There is nothing distinctive in the views of its supporters in terms of their evaluations of the government's record. Nor are assessments of Gerry Adams important, at least for first preferences. There is an extremely strong contact effect, as we saw in Chapter 7. This would seem to be more than a case of the party contacting its own supporters. Remarkably, when all variables are included, the impact of youth increases: all other things being equal, the odds of a person under 40 voting Sinn Féin are more than 4 times the odds of someone over 40 doing so.

The model of broader Sinn Féin support suggests a more significant role for Gerry Adams, and a broader age profile. Contact remains a highly significant factor: the expected Sinn Féin vote share (first and second party preferences) of those contacted, all other things held at their mean value, is 32 percent, as compared to 4 percent for those not contacted. As in the case of Fianna Fáil, when we look at first or second preference *party* voters there is a tendency for support to be linked with more nationalist and less egalitarian values.

Independents

Finally, we turn to those who did note vote for any party, but simply for an independent candidate. We know that independent candidates come in all guises: some focused on specific local issues, some broadly of the left, others disappointed at missing out on a party (and particularly a Fianna Fáil party) nomination. We, therefore, expect support for different candidates to vary hugely and for that reason it is very hard to predict within the electorate as a whole.

Looking at the demographic factors, Independents are relatively poorly supported by skilled workers and farmers: they do best among unskilled workers and the self-employed. There are no particular associations between any of the value scales and independent voting. Independent candidates are, as we would expect, more likely to win support among those with no party attachment. They also attract a disproportionate level of support from those unhappy with the government's record on the economy and housing. The effect of evaluations of the government's health record is almost significant, and becomes so when more controls are introduced. A candidate visit has a big impact, but those without any leader or party towards whom they feel warm are no more likely to vote independent than are other voters. In this respect, independent voting is not a general expression of anti-party sentiments. R^2 is only 0.13 with all items included, suggesting that those who support independents really are a varied bunch who defy easy categorisation.

This is equally true of those who give either a first or second vote to an independent. The R^2 is now only .12. The pattern of demographic effects is similar, but there is a slight antipathy to the EU and a slight left bias. Concerns about the government's management of the health service are also very significant, while concerns about its housing record are not. Independents in general therefore seemed to better reflect voter discontent with health than did the main opposition party.

Table 9.4 summarises these several models by showing the additional contribution made to the R^2 by each successive stage.[7] Looking first at the largest two parties, we see that much the strongest contribution is made by party attachment, indicated both by parental vote and, even more strongly, by the respondent's partisanship. In addition, competence increases the Fianna Fáil R^2 by 4 points and demographics are worth 3 points in the case of Fine Gael. When we look at the smaller parties we generally see that demographics (except for Labour) and

Table 9.4 Contribution of various factors to overall model success

	FF	FG	Labour	Greens	PDs	SF
Demographics	0.02	0.03	0.02	0.06	0.07	0.06
Values	0.02	0.01	0.04	0.12	0.03	0.09
Father's party	0.06	0.07	0.01			
Party attachment	0.08	0.07	0.04	0.03	0.03	0.17
Competence	0.04	0.01	0.01	0.02	0.02	0.01
Leader	0.00	0.00	0.00	0.00	0.02	0.00
Campaign contact	0.01	0.02	0.06	0.01	0.03	0.06
Overall	0.23	0.20	0.17	0.24	0.20	0.39

Note: cell entries are the increase in McFadden's R^2 at each stage.

values (except for the Progressive Democrats) are each much stronger. Attachment – as we have seen before – and contact are also remarkably high for Sinn Féin. Competence is important for the main government party, Fianna Fáil, but it does relatively little to explain voting for other parties.

No party was able to mobilise the discontented. Leaders make for little improvement except in the Progressive Democrats. They were often significant, but they did not add to the overall explanation. This really means that leadership popularity was largely the outcome of the forces seen earlier in each model that have an effect on vote through their impact on leader evaluations. Perhaps the most unexpected result is the very strong impact of the campaign factors for Labour, Progressive Democrats and Sinn Féin. The strength of partisanship is there in all parties, but in particular for Fianna Fáil, Fine Gael and Sinn Féin. This raises some questions about what partisanship means, since in the smaller and newer parties there has been relatively little time for such attachments to build up. We consider this in more detail in the Conclusion. In general, while all these various elements make significant contributions to explaining party support, the most obvious result is that few make strong ones.

Leaders

The analysis here took a conservative approach to leader popularity, using a measure that assumed that party evaluations had an effect on leader evaluations, but that the reverse could not occur. Would our conclusions have been different had we used a different approach, which allowed for both a direct and an indirect effect of leader popularity on the vote? As an alternative, we entered both the top leader and the top party variables into our models, instead of the adjusted top leader measure. By doing this we allow each to have an influence independent of the other, making no assumption about which is primary. These results, not shown here, encourage broadly the same conclusions. In particular, such an analysis still suggests that Noonan made no positive contribution to his party's vote. It also suggests that Ahern, and Harney were positive influences for their parties. The effects are of comparable magnitude. Adams has no significant impact in either analysis. Quinn now has a slight positive impact, but this is significant only at the one-star level. As in the previous analysis both Adams and Quinn contribute significantly when second preferences are added. The only difference is in the case of the Green party leader, whose impact is significant only on combined first and second preferences, while in

Table 10.5 the leader had a significant effect also on first preferences. The magnitudes of the effects are comparable. For instance, taking the example of Fianna Fáil, the impact on expected party support of moving the leader variable from minimum to maximum is 15 points in the case of the adjusted measure and 17 points with the unadjusted measure.

If we go a step further and include only the top leader factor in an otherwise full model, without any adjustment, and without including the top party variable, then the results suggest very strong positive effects for all parties, even for Fine Gael. For Fianna Fáil the minimum–maximum effect is now 40 points. However, this assumes that the models already contain sufficient controls for the advantage accruing to a leader of, say, Fianna Fáil *because* he is the leader of Fianna Fáil. This is an unreasonable assumption – a position we established in Chapter 6. But only if we take this position will we find that leaders have very substantial effects indeed on their party's vote, close to three times as great as those we find with more conservative approaches. This seems quite unreasonably high. To illustrate: let us suppose Ahern had been a little less popular, and that only 42 percent thought he was the best leader, rather than the 65 percent who actually did so. This would parallel that party's actual support level. In that case, and using a model including just the top leader (plus all other variables previously used), the expected Fianna Fáil vote would have been 10 percentage points lower. In contrast, the model with top leader and top party suggests a drop of only 4 percentage points.[8] Given that Fianna Fáil's support has varied only between 39 percent and 42 percent over the last three elections, under two different leaders, and substantial variations in popularity (see Chapter 6), this seems implausibly high.

Candidates and parties

For the most part, this more sophisticated statistical analysis has confirmed the conclusions of the previous chapters. While some effects decline once we allow for the importance of others, they do so in an expected manner that does not in any way undermine their relevance. Even when we control for general party attachments, the short-term importance of government evaluations, leader evaluations and campaign contact remains clear, if not always strong. Many associations between values and vote also survive all controls, which is testament to their robustness, even if, for most parties, most of these associations are weak. Demographic factors can always be expected to fall away once we control for the sort of factors that we think account for why middle-class people support party X, or young people support party Y, such as values or the lack of traditional loyalties. For the most part, they do fall away, although some patterns of demographic effects persist, casting doubt on either the adequacy of the explanation or the sufficiency of the control.

One major factor which has received relatively little direct attention here is the focus of the voter and the extent to which the voter really bases his or her judgement on parties or on candidates. As argued in Chapter 8, many voters seem almost indifferent to party, while other voters are indifferent to candidates. This manifests itself in patterns of voting on the ballot paper, but it should also manifest itself in the sort of factors that underlie 'party' choice. A vote for a Fianna Fáil candidate looks just like a vote for the Fianna Fáil party, but requires a rather different explanation.

Much of this book has been about parties and voting for parties. A focus on candidates would require that we ask a different set of questions, ones directed far more to candidate–voter relationships and less to candidate–party and party leader ones. If the argument is correct that people do vote for candidates, candidate-centred voters will be much more idiosyncratic in their 'party' choice than those who vote for parties in a more deliberate way. It could be that the relative weakness in previous statistical explanations of party choice in Ireland (as well as those here) stems from the absence of any strong theory and of measures of candidate appeal. Future research will have to come to terms with this. Here we underline the problem, by showing that we can account for the behaviour of party-centred voters much more easily than for those who focus on the candidate.

A simple way to do this is to examine the effectiveness of the statistical accounts offered earlier in this chapter (Tables 9.1–9.3, and III.1–III.4) for each of the different types of voters identified in Chapter 8, those who focus on party and those who focus on the candidate. If it is true that some voters are unconcerned about party as many of our respondents report, and as our analysis of ballot patterns with respect to lower preferences might indicate, then we can expect to find that the adequacy of the statistical models will be much greater for party-centred voters than for candidate-centred ones. Arguably, the sorts of variables we identify should perform very poorly when voters are candidate-centred, since values, party attachments and leader considerations will matter little. But they should perform very well when voters really care about the party, rather than the candidate. We examined the accuracy of the predictions made by each model according to our identification of candidate-centred or party-centred voters in Chapter 8. (This was based on the two questions asked of respondents: did you

Table 9.5 Accuracy of model predictions, by party and type of vote

	Model predictions for candidate-centred voters	Proportion of each party's voters in candidate-centred sample	Model predictions for party-centred voters	Proportion of each party's voters in candidate-centred sample
Greens	0.10 (.05)	0.01	0.31 (.10)	0.05
SF	0.37 (.09)	0.03	0.77 (.08)	0.07
FF	0.56 (.02)	0.39	0.70 (.02)	0.51
Labour	0.22 (.04)	0.11	0.28 (.05)	0.09
PDs	0.20 (.04)	0.05	0.58 (.10)	0.04
FG	0.31 (.02)	0.30	0.58 (.04)	0.22

Notes: validated voters only; cell entries in columns 1 and 3 are model predictions with standard errors in brackets; models used are final first preference estimations from Table 9.1–9.3 and III.1–III.4; voter type from Table 8.1.

vote for a party or a candidate, and would you have voted for the same candidate if they had represented a different party?)

Table 9.5 shows the predicted likelihoods of actual Fianna Fáil, Fine Gael, Labour, Green, Progressive Democrat and Sinn Féin voters supporting their respective parties plus the proportions of each party's voters in the candidate- and party-centred groups. If our models were perfect representations of behaviour, all likelihoods would be 1. As the models are less than perfect, all likelihoods will be considerably less than that. What is interesting is whether we can more accurately estimate which party a voter supports when they say they are choosing a party than we can when they say they are choosing a candidate. It should be recognised that the likelihoods will naturally vary across parties, with supporters of larger parties having higher probabilities than those of smaller ones. To make this clearer: if we knew nothing about someone we would give a higher probability to the chance that they would vote Fianna Fáil than we would to the chance that they would vote for the Labour Party.

The results for the smaller parties are based on very few cases so the most important results are those for Fianna Fáil and Fine Gael. Two points are important. First, in each case the models work better on party-centred voters. The probabilities rise – very sharply in most instances – when we contrast the prediction for candidate-centred and party-centred voters for each party. This demonstrates very clearly that we can explain the choice of some voters very much better than others, with the source of this difference being the heterogeneity of voters with respect to candidates. The models discussed earlier in this chapter were not very successful in identifying who voted, for instance for Fianna Fáil, and who did not. What this analysis indicates is that this failure is due in no small measure to the fact that many voters are not really choosing a party at all, but are choosing a candidate. It is the needs of the constituency that seems to be their principal focus, not the direction of the national government. When we focus attention on the party-centred voters the models perform very well, for both large and small parties. This can be seen by comparing columns 3 and 4. Column 4 shows the proportion of party-centred voters who support that party. This is also the proportion that would be expected if the model performed no better than randomly; comparing column 3 with column 4 tells us how well the model performs relative to a model based on guessing at random.

The second point is that, when we contrast column 1 with column 2, we see that the probabilities for candidate-centred voters are in almost all cases much higher than the share of the (candidate-centred) vote received by the respective parties. Even among candidate-centred voters the identification of choice is very much better than random! The exception is Fine Gael. For that party the model in Table 9.2 performs no better than a random guess in terms of identifying Fine Gael voters. This means that the models earlier in this chapter do a reasonable job in identifying most party's voters even when such voters say they care most about the candidate.

Perhaps such voters do care more about the candidate, but this is not to say that party does not matter, or that the candidates they prefer will not tend to be from a particular party. Only the contact variable in the models estimated could really be said to tap the candidate factor directly. The obvious implication is that while voters may see candidates as central, most voters still have a predisposition to favour candidates of some parties over others. There is an alternative interpretation, which is that, for many voters, their evaluation of a party is influenced by the evaluations of its candidates. A good candidate can improve the image of his party and a poor one can hurt it. In practice, it may well be that both processes operate. Fine Gael is the exception here. How far this is due to the circumstances of the campaign is uncertain, but it seems likely that this played a part. What is clear is that without, candidate-centred voters, Fine Gael would have suffered an even heavier defeat.

Assessing which of these two processes is most important is a task for future research. Each indicates a different causal path, one leading from parties to candidates and the other flowing from candidates to parties. One way to establish which of these is more plausible would be to trace the party support of such voters when that particular candidate was no longer available. If the first interpretation were true then most of these voters would stick with the same party. If the second were true, we would expect much higher rates of change in party support. It is hoped that the 2007 election study, when some of the same respondents will be re-interviewed, will help us sort out these rival interpretations. At this point, we can only admit the real possibility that the extent of candidate-centred voting identified in Chapter 8 is an overestimate and that, while candidates are undoubtedly important, party-based reasons for first preference votes are much more widespread that previous survey evidence might suggest.

We can, though, look at candidates a little more closely. If some voters are picking candidates, what determines the sort of candidates they will be inclined to favour? We explored this in Chapter 8, and showed that more successful candidates were ranked more highly on a number of criteria that summarise different potential roles for a TD. It appeared that working on behalf of the local area was the most important, but this conclusion was based merely on comparing the mean values on each scale according to how a candidate was ranked on the ballot paper. We also saw that party was important, with most voters linking best party with best candidate. Here we want to see whether these conclusions are born out by multivariate analysis. Predicting candidate support is obviously more complex than predicting party support. There are many more candidates and we have data from only a few individuals with respect to each of them. We proceed by treating the candidate evaluations, gathered using the 0–100 thermometer scales, as the variable to be explained. We choose this over ballot rating, which is obviously more directly important, because this provides us with information on all (non-independent) candidates. Most voters cast only a limited number of preference votes, as we saw in Chapter 2, so we have little information from these about how a voter evaluated most candidates.[9] Moreover, as we saw in Chapter 8, about 90 percent of voters do give a first preference to the candidate they like best.

Our objective here is largely to assess the importance of leaders, parties and the criteria about TD roles for candidate evaluations. However, to do that we need to control for the influence of as many other factors as we can. Drawing on previous research (Marsh 1981, 1987; Laver *et al.*, 1999) we have included several items of background information on each candidate relevant to their political experience, including whether or not the candidate is an incumbent TD and whether or not the candidate holds government office, in addition to the party and leader evaluations appropriate to each candidate and whether or not the respondent is close to the candidate's party. We also include whether or not the candidate called at the respondent's house, whether party workers allied to the candidate called and, of course, the party of the candidate. Finally, we add the relative position on the ballot paper of the candidate, since there is some evidence that being more highly placed confers an advantage (Robson and Walsh, 1974). The key question is, in general, what explains which candidates the voters like and, specifically, how important in their evaluations are the several roles we have identified in Chapter 8?

Table 9.6 illustrates the results. These are simple Ordinary Least Squares (OLS) regressions. A coefficient indicates the expected increase (or decrease) in candidate evaluation that comes from a 1-point increase in the variable in question. All the rating variables have been transformed to 0–10 scales to make it easier to compare their impact on candidate evaluations, which are also transformed onto a 0–10 scale. The number of observations used in each estimation is large because the data has again been stacked, meaning that the unit of observation is each candidate for each respondent. The first model looks at all candidates who were evaluated, up to 12 in each case. There is a big range here and most of the included variables have highly significant effects. The first point of interest is that the party of the candidate is important. All the

Table 9.6 A model of candidate evaluations

	Candidate evaluations		
	(1)	(2)	(3)
FG	0.80***	0.63***	0.54***
	−0.07	−0.10	−0.10
Green	0.38***	0.33*	0.42**
	−0.08	−0.15	−0.14
Labour	0.81***	0.61***	0.45***
	−0.07	−0.11	−0.1
PD	0.52***	0.49**	0.43**
	−0.1	−0.16	−0.15
SF	0.20*	0.62***	0.51***
	−0.08	−0.15	−0.15
Close to party of the candidate	0.47***	0.22*	0.13
	−0.07	−0.09	−0.08

Table 9.6   *(Cont'd)*

	Candidate evaluations		
	(1)	(2)	(3)
Rating of candidate's party	0.46***	0.32***	0.24***
	−0.02	−0.03	−0.03
Rating of candidate's leader	0.13***	0.10***	0.10***
	−0.02	−0.02	−0.02
Incumbent	0.46***	0.35***	0.24**
	−0.06	−0.09	−0.09
Incumbent minister	0.54***	0.50***	0.36***
	−0.09	−0.11	−0.10
Incumbent minister of state	0.21*	−0.12	−0.03
	−0.1	−0.14	−0.13
Incumbent local councillor	0.27***	−0.10	0.07
	−0.07	−0.12	−0.11
Incumbent senator	0.47***	0.28	0.16
	−0.14	−0.18	−0.18
Candidate in 1997 election	0.08	−0.04	−0.02
	−0.05	−0.09	−0.08
Candidate visited home	1.10***	0.70***	0.44***
	−0.06	−0.07	−0.07
Worker from candidate's party visited home	0.11*	0.01	−0.05
	−0.06	−0.08	−0.07
Ballot order	−0.02*	−0.02	−0.01
	−0.01	−0.01	−0.01
Good for respondent's area			0.19***
			−0.02
Good at contributing to national political debate			0.07***
			−0.02
Close to respondent's political views			0.04*
			−0.02
Constant	1.01***	3.38***	2.11***
	−0.10	−0.20	−0.20
Observations	9883	3182	3182
R-squared	0.45	0.25	0.34
MSE	1.91	1.70	1.59

Notes: *** $p < 0.001$, ** $p < 0.01$, * $p < 0.05$; validated voters only. Role criteria are weighted by salience, as in Table 8.8. All ratings transformed to 11 point scales; OLS estimations: robust clustered standard errors.

coefficients are positive, from Sinn Féin at +0.18 to Fine Gael at +0.80. Fianna Fáil is the reference category, so a Fine Gael candidate is evaluated 0.8 points higher than a Fianna Fáil candidate, all other things being equal. In fact, candidates from all other parties were evaluated more highly than Fianna Fáil candidates. This may seem unlikely, but it is because the Fianna Fáil *party* is generally evaluated more highly than other parties, as is its leader. This really means that candidates in parties other than Fianna Fáil did better than we might expect given other considerations. Effectively, Fianna Fáil is a stronger *party*.

Other party characteristics are also significant. Attachment – closeness to a party – and evaluations of the candidate's party each has an impact, with party evaluations having a very big impact indeed. A shift from 0–10 on the party scale is associated with a shift of +4.6 points on the candidate evaluation scale. Leaders have much less impact, less than a third of that of the candidate's party. Political experience matters, but merely having stood in 1997 is in itself of little value. Candidate visits are very important, worth in excess of 1 point on the evaluation scale; visits by party workers alone are barely helpful, having less than a tenth of the impact of candidate visits. Finally, there is a very slight ballot order effect: those at the top of the list get 0.24 more points than those at the bottom, at least 12 places below them (i.e. 2.4 on the original 0–100 thermometer scale). The R^2 here indicates that 45 percent of all variance has been explained, and the average error is less than 2 points so the model performs reasonably well.

In the second and third set of estimates we look at the smaller group of candidates, up to four for each respondent, on whom we sought further evaluation. A judgement that a candidate is good for the area is much more important than judgements on either of the other two roles, while the third role, sharing the respondent's views, is barely significant. The full range of scoring on the first of these is associated with almost a 2-point increase on the evaluation scale, comparable in impact to that of the candidate's party. Performing on national issues, though less important, is associated with a corresponding increase of 0.7 points. For the most part, the same factors are important in much the same ways, but most effects are smaller. Comparing columns 2 and 3, as well as 1 and 3, we can see how far this is due to the smaller sample and more restricted range of evaluations, and how far it is due to the inclusion of the additional three role variables. The party differences observed before still hold, as do the leader and party evaluation effects, but all are a little weaker. Incumbency matters less in itself, and incumbent ministers – who are reputed to be very good for their areas – do a little less well once the role evaluations are included, as we

might expect. Councillor, senators and ministers of state are not significant factors for this reduced sample. Visiting, at least by candidates,
remains important, but, like ministers, lose one-third of their independent impact once the role evaluations are included. In other words,
ministers, and those who make contact, are evaluated more positively
on these three roles. Overall, the R^2 is lower – there is less variance –
but the average error is well under 2.

In general, it is clear that the partisanship of a candidate is associated clearly with their evaluation and hence likely success.[10] Leaders
matter much less than parties, but the personal record and experience
of the candidate is important. Voters think constituency service is much
more important than being good in the Dáil, or sharing the voter's view-
points. This also underlines the message of Chapter 7 that contact by a
candidate remains important. It is more important than, for instance,
incumbency or even ministerial office. This is a preliminary exploration
of the basis of candidate popularity, but it is sufficient to confirm some
bits of political folk wisdom and to raise doubts about others.[11] It
confirms the widespread view that constituency service and being visible is very important, and underlines the importance of party for the
candidate. However, it also suggests that ministers of state have no
great advantage and that candidates whose names being with 'W' are
hardly disadvantaged compared with those who names start with 'A'.

Alternative scenarios

In the final section of this chapter we return to the question of party
choice and use the set of party choice models from Table 9.1–9.3 (and
Appendix III) once more in order to look again at the 2002 election
and ask what made the difference that pushed 2002 beyond the recent
norm, with a small increase in Fianna Fáil support and a sharp drop in
Fine Gael's vote and the re-election of a government for the first time
since 1969. We have argued that the odds seem to have been stacked
against the main opposition parties and in favour of those in government. Evaluations were broadly good, at least on the issues that seem
to have mattered most to voters (the economy) and while health appeared
to be a problem, its impact seems to have been smaller than many
thought it might be. The government leaders were well ahead in personal popularity. We might also add to this the organisational advantage of Fianna Fáil during the campaign, with more party workers to
knock on more doors, particularly with the Fine Gael organisations
somewhat disheartened by campaign setbacks and polling results that
did little to suggest that the electorate would reject the government or

boost Fine Gael. One way to explore what made the difference in 2002 is to ask how outcomes might have been different. For instance, if Fine Gael had had a more popular leader, or been able to expose government weaknesses on the economy or knocked on more doors, would the party have done much better? Such counterfactual questions go to the heart of our explanation of the 2002 election.

We look first Fianna Fáil. How would Fianna Fáil have fared had the economy been a little less rosy, its leader a little less popular and the organisation a little less effective? On a five-point scale from −2 to +2 the average evaluation on the economy was 0.8 and on health −0.3. What if things had been not quite so good? The standard deviation of economic evaluations is 0.97, and health 1.13. We drop each mean evaluation by half a standard deviation, by 0.48 in the case of the economy and 0.56 in the case of health, a relatively small movement. Sixty-five percent thought Ahern the best leader. Only 13 percent thought Noonan was best. We can narrow that gap, placing both on an equal footing at 39 – something that appeared to be the case in 1997. And the party contacted 33 percent of voters. We will drop this to 30 percent. Under this slightly different scenario the Fianna Fáil vote would have been about 5 percent lower, making it a very bad, rather than a very good election.[12] This illustrates the potential importance of short-term factors in voting behaviour, which may be greater now, as party attachment seems much less widespread.

For Fine Gael we assume exactly the same set of values as for Fianna Fáil. This would have added less than 2 percent to the Fine Gael vote. It would still have been a bad election. This simulation underlines how little Fine Gael gained from poor evaluations of the government's record, or from its own leader. Even potentially effective short-term forces, therefore, were of little value to the party. While it was true that the circumstances were helpful to the incumbent coalition, it is very apparent that the main opposition party was unable to take much support from those who were dissatisfied. Such support went instead to the smaller parties and independents. As one wag put it, it was an election that saw the Opposition voted out of office!

The models in this chapter tell us a number of things about the 2002 election. One clear one is that support for all parties is multi-faceted. There is no simple explanation for any party's support. While there are few marked demographic features, political values are factors for at least some voters, particularly in the case of the smaller parties. Competence and campaign contacts each play a significant role for most parties. The argument that parties also rely on traditional, family-based loyalties also gets a fair degree of support. Parental voting, particularly for Fianna Fáil and Fine Gael, does influence the next generation, and party attachment, perhaps stemming from childhood socialisation as well as from the accumulated experiences of adulthood, has a major impact on the vote. Leaders matter too, but are far from being the dominant factor.

We have no reason to think that at this level of interpretation – what factors matter most – the models will change very much for – the next election. However, they may each change in the weight of the effect the each has on the result. Parties will seek to use campaign to alter distribution and weight of the factors determining vote choice to their advantage. We would expect that the distribution of many of the underlying factors would be different in a future election (such as competence, leaders and organisation activity) while others should vary little. Change is unlikely in the case of the demographics, the values and the enduring party attachments. Political campaigns will seek rather to shift the distributions of short-term factors in their favour. New leaders may be more popular and the appeal of old ones tarnished; credit and blame for progress, or the lack of it on major issues will be debated; and party organisations may be in better or worse shape than in 2002. A further aspect of the campaign will be the determination of parties to explain why they should benefit from any of the government's inadequacies, or why they are the best parties to represent values such as nationalism, the promotion of pro-business policies or the defence of the environment.

Notes

1 For the various questions see Appendix IV: Nationalism A12_2, A12_4, A12_3, C6_1; Secular/Religious C25_1, A11_1, B44_7, B44_5, E26; Environment A11_2, A12_8, B44_8a, A11_7; EU B44_6, B44_2, B44_9a; Privatisation B44_4, B44_1, B44_3; Equality C27_1, A11_4, A11_6, A11_3. The factor analysis was run only on voters and was a principal components analysis with varimax rotation.

2 For instance, we used logistic regression to estimate the relationship between (Y) whether or not the FF leader was the top leader and (X) whether or not FF was the top party, calculated the predicted value (Y-hat) and substracted this from Y.

3 When a factor has a positive effect, the table will show the odds as greater than 1. When a factor is negative, it will be shown by a figure of less than 1. An odds ratio of 2 is the positive equivalent of 0.50: a figure of 2 indicates that a factor makes voting for the party more likely, while a figure of 0.50 makes it less likely, but in each case the effect is equivalent. We will translate some of the more interesting effects into percentage

point increases in the share of the vote for particular parties, showing how groups who differ on the variable of interest are predicted in the model to be more or less in favour of the party we are interested in.

4   Kennedy and Sinnott (2006), employing the same approach to constructing value scales and using a multivariate analysis, found significant effects. However, their dependent variable was a 10-point scale of likely Fianna Fáil support, which may be more nuanced than the more stark indicator of voting for the party or not. There are tendencies in these directions, but they are not significant at this point. It is also possible that the nationalist-unionist dimension is weak because Fianna Fáil are in the centre, with Fine Gael on one side and Sinn Féin on the other, but in a separate analysis we found little support for that explanation.

5   Except where it is stated otherwise, simulations were made using the sbpost routine for Stata 9 by Scott Long. All other variables here and in each subsequent simulation are held at their mean values.

6   The alternative procedure was Rare Effects Logit.

7   The Psuedo R^2 used here is McFadden's. This is the most conservative of possible R^2 terms. It represents the percentage improvement in the log likelihood from the intercept only model to the full model in each case. Hence it resembles the better known OLS R^2 in having a percentage reduction in error (PRE) interpretation.

8   We use this model as a contrast because it is not possible to consider an equivalent setting for the top leader variable in the actual model in Table 9.1, as that is constructed in quite a different way. For this simulation, which was done using CLARIFY, all other variables were set at their mean values.

9   The correlation between evaluations and actual first preference vote totals is 0.31. It should be remembered that there are less than 100 respondents per constituency and fewer still rating any one candidate.

10 The correlation is fairly strong at −.53.

11 This analysis was repeated using the ballot rankings. The results were much the same in respect of which factors were more or less important.

12 See note 8. We again use models including top leader and top party rather than those that use the adjusted party variable only. This makes it easier to manipulate the leader variable in a transparent way and yet makes little difference to the outcomes of the simulations.

10

And those who do not: the problem of low and declining turnout

Our account of Irish electoral behaviour is, so far, radically but un-avoidably incomplete. It is radically incomplete because it leaves out the largest single block of registered electors, namely those who did not vote (non-voters account for an estimated 37 percent of the registered electorate, while the next largest grouping – Fianna Fáil voters – makes up only 26 percent). The incompleteness is unavoidable because many of the variables and especially the techniques necessary to study turnout/ abstention are largely the same as those used in analysing vote choice. Accordingly, these variables and techniques were first introduced and explained in the context of analysing how people voted, with the delib-erate intention of then applying them to the problem of explaining turnout.

According to the official returns for each election, turnout in Irish general elections from 1969 to 1981 held more or less steady at 76 to 77 percent (see Figure 10.1). Since then, it has fallen in three phases: between 1981 and 1982, between 1987 and 1989 and between 1992 and 2002. Based on the electoral register, the cumulative decline has been 13 percentage points over two decades (see Appendix I, note 1, p. 234). The declining trend in general elections is, with just two excep-tions, mirrored in declining levels of turnout at other types of elections, namely presidential, local, and European (see Figure 10.1).[1] Presiden-tial turnout went from 62 percent back in 1973 to 45 percent in 1997. Local election turnout fell from 65 percent in 1979 to 51 percent in 1999 before recovering to 59 percent in 2004. In the case of the two European elections that were not held concurrently with other elections (1984 and 1994), turnout also declined, albeit by a slight margin.[2]

Ireland's turnout of 69 percent in the general election of 2002 puts it close to the bottom of the European league table of voter turnout. To be precise, in national elections between 2000 and 2004 in the 25 member states of the European Union, Ireland ranked ninth lowest.

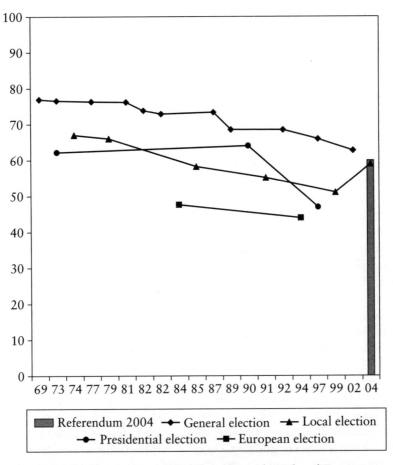

Figure 10.1   Turnout in general, local, presidential and European Parliament elections in Ireland, 1969–2004 and in 2004 referendum on Irish citizenship

It was well ahead of the UK on 59 percent, but well behind countries such as Denmark, Sweden, Austria, the Netherlands and France, all of which had turnout of 80 percent or more.

Measuring and explaining voter turnout

Before drawing any inferences from these comparisons and before going into the Irish case in detail, we need to consider the issue of how to measure turnout.

Examining turnout by means of sample surveys, like the one on which this book is based, has advantages and disadvantages. They are less accurate than aggregate data, but much richer in terms of the range of independent variables that can be considered.[3] They also avoid the 'ecological problem', that is, the problem of making inferences about relationships between variables when the variables are measured at different levels. However, the inaccuracies found in survey data on voter turnout are always in the same direction: towards an overestimation of turnout. The overestimate in the survey is 15 percentage points. Fortunately, the fact that the sampling frame for household selection is based on the electoral register makes it possible to compare actual and reported voting and to adjust the data so that they reflect actual behaviour (see Appendix I). The adjusted estimate of turnout in 2002 is 74.6 percent, giving an overestimate of 5.7 percentage points. While the adjustment does not eliminate the discrepancy between turnout as reported in the official returns and turnout as estimated from our sample data, the wide range of variables and the (relative) ease of inference involved when using individual-level data mean that it is well worth pursuing the issue of the sources of turnout via this route.

Research in this area has tended to respond to the problem of the wide range of influences on turnout by spawning mutually exclusive explanations. Thus, for example, Blais notes that, in addition to the rational choice approach (which is his main concern), 'there are four alternative explanations for why people vote. These are the resources and mobilisation models, and what could be called the psychological and sociological interpretations' (Blais, 2000: 12). While he notes that there is some overlap and some complementarity between these various approaches, his review of the theoretical explanations suggests that these are alternative or competing accounts. Similarly, Franklin argues that the many theories that have been proposed to explain variations in political participation 'essentially boil down to explanations involving three different features that distinguish people from one another: resources, mobilisation, and the desire to affect the course of public policy (what we shall call "*instrumental motivation*")' (Franklin, 1996: 219). Clarke *et al.* (2004) split the explanatory options into an individual rationality framework and a sociological framework, each with several subdivisions. Thus there is no current agreement on the proper explanatory categories. This lack of agreement about the independent variables that influence turnout is related to what is arguably an even more fundamental problem, namely the failure to recognise that abstention comprises, not one, but two dependent variables.

Two sorts of abstention

People fail to vote for two quite different sets of reasons, thus giving rise to two different kinds of abstention. The two kinds are revealed by an open-ended question that asks respondents who claimed not to have voted what was their main reason for not voting and following this up with a supplementary question probing for 'any other reasons'. Based on a coding of responses to these two questions, one can distinguish between 'circumstantial' and 'voluntary' abstention (Blondel *et al.*, 1998: 40–54).[4] In the case of circumstantial abstention, the individual is subject to circumstances on the day or at the time of the election that prevent him or her getting to the polls. Examples include being away from home, being ill, being tied up at work or being registered in a constituency that is distant from one's current place of residence. Voluntary abstention, on the other hand, has to do with the attitudes and perceptions of the individual, for example, attitudes of lack of interest or distrust in, or dissatisfaction with, politics, or specific perceptions of there being insufficient choice among the parties or candidates on offer, or a feeling that one's individual vote has no consequences. It should be emphasised that the distinction is not an absolute one. This is because circumstantial factors and voluntary factors interact with each other. Thus, the same difficult circumstances that inhibit one elector from voting will be readily overcome by another elector with a higher degree of motivation. On the other hand, some obstacles to voting simply cannot be overcome, no matter how high the motivation and some electors will never participate no matter how easy or propitious the circumstances, the reason being that they have no desire whatsoever to vote.

Circumstantial abstention

Circumstantial abstainers outnumber voluntary abstainers by 2 to 1 (10 percent of the sample cited a circumstantial reason while 5 percent gave a voluntary reason).[5] The circumstances involved vary substantially. Almost one-half of all circumstantial abstainers cited absence from home as their reason for not voting, with approximately one quarter of these referring specifically to being on holiday as the reason for the absence from home. A further one-in-four gave lack of time as their reason – lack of time arising from work ('busy, would have, but did not get home in time'; 'working double shift, no time') or from family commitments ('new baby arrived'; 'had no one to baby-sit my six children'; 'couldn't get to voting station due to caring for my aunt'). Thirteen percent of circumstantial abstainers said they did not vote because of illness or infirmity ('suffering from bad flu'; 'incapacitated due to old age'). The remaining categories of circumstantial abstention were quite small – registration and voting card problems (7 percent – 'couldn't find voting card and thought it was necessary'), bad weather (5 percent – 'lashing rain'; 'weather too bad for going out of doors'), and difficulty in getting to the polling station (3 percent – 'nobody came to bring me out to vote'; 'because it was wet and I had no way of getting to the polling station' and, from a respondent dependent on a wheelchair, 'couldn't get there, no one came to collect me'). Six percent of circumstantial abstainers reported that they did not have a vote.

Voluntary abstention

By far the most frequently cited reason for voluntary abstention is simple lack of interest, this being the reason given by over 50 percent of voluntary abstainers. 'I couldn't be bothered' is the classic statement of this attitude. Others elaborated slightly, as in 'I have no interest – I don't follow politics' or the respondent who linked his lack of interest to deficiencies in the system ('I have no interest in politics; it makes no difference who gets into the Dáil').[6] Lack of interest can also be specific to the election in question as with the respondent who said 'no interest this time'.

Dissatisfaction with or distrust in politics and politicians is the second most frequent source of voluntary abstention but, at 28 percent of all voluntary abstainers (and 9 percent of all abstainers), it is a long way behind lack of interest.[7] Some expressed their dissatisfaction with politics forcefully and, well, robustly ('It's a lot of bullshit. I don't believe in any of them. They all talk shite'). Other dissatisfied abstainers spoke more in sorrow than in anger ('What difference would it make? Have a look around here; it's awful'). There were, not surprisingly, instances of the standard complaint of broken promises that is levelled at all politicians ('They promise you the moon and the stars and when the time comes they do nothing for you'). However, lack of confidence or trust in politicians is not quite as sweeping as often assumed. It can also lead to quite complex decisions not to vote, as in the case of the respondent who explained: 'I did not want Fianna Fáil to get an overall majority and I have no faith in the other parties.'

Signalling a theme that we return to later in this chapter, almost one in five voluntary abstainers referred to their own state of knowledge of politics in general or of parties or candidates in particular as their reason for not voting ('didn't understand anything about the system' or – in the case of a relatively recently arrived immigrant who was conscious that it takes time to catch on to what politics in a society is all about: 'I've only been living in Ireland for four years so I don't know enough about the political parties and their policies).' The redrawing of constituency boundaries and creation of new constituencies can also affect people's level of knowledge as in the case of the respondent who explained his abstention on the basis that, 'This area was changed and I didn't know the candidates.' Finally, small, but significant, minorities of respondents lay the blame on what they see as structural flaws in the party system or in the electoral system/elections as such, referring either to the lack of choice on offer ('no differences between parties, no real choice'; 'no point in voting, they're all the same') or to their belief that their vote has no consequences. In the latter vein, one respondent came up with an interesting rational choice calculation of the inconsequentiality of voting: 'Nobody approached me for a vote, so, when nobody did, I figured it wasn't worth giving.'

Given these reports by abstainers themselves as to why they did not vote, what more is there to say? Do these reports not provide a sufficient explanation of abstention? Unfortunately, in the case of the great majority of abstainers, whether circumstantial or voluntary, the answer is 'no', because most of the accounts given by the respondents are radically incomplete. They are incomplete, first, because, given the nature of the question asked and the time and space allocated to the question within the interview, the responses represent only the first line or two of what could, and probably should, be a long narrative about how people's background, circumstances and relationship to politics affected their decision not to vote. Our open-ended question is useful in getting an inkling of what is in that narrative, but an inkling is all that it produces. The second reason why the accounts given by respondents only provide a very incomplete explanation is that they are subjective accounts and, as such, even if they were fully elaborated on, would be likely to miss some of the very many aspects of the individual's background and outlook that directly or indirectly affect whether or not they turn out to vote. Despite these limitations, the evidence from these responses plays an important role in our exploration of the sources of abstention in that the distinction between circumstantial and voluntary abstention to which they give rise is a key element in constructing a typology of the causes of turnout/abstention.

Four kinds of factors affecting turnout

The first step in devising this typology is to distinguish between voter facilitation and voter mobilisation (Blondel *et al.*, 1998: 246–57). Facilitation is anything that makes it easy to vote. Mobilisation is anything that makes an individual want to vote. This distinction has the merit of being related to the behavioural distinction between circumstantial and voluntary abstention that we have just been considering. Thus, effective facilitation lowers circumstantial abstention and inadequate facilitation increases it. Likewise effective mobilisation lowers voluntary abstention and inadequate mobilisation increases it. But there are also potential interaction effects – effective mobilisation may overcome inadequate facilitation or inadequate mobilisation may be offset by effective facilitation. Be that as it may, the main point is that, in devising a comprehensive typology of the variables affecting voter turnout/abstention, it is useful to start with the distinction between facilitating turnout and mobilising turnout, understanding both these terms in a broad sense.

The second step in the construction of a typology of the factors affecting turnout is based on taking account of the location of these two variables, that is taking account of the fact that the processes of facilitation and mobilisation operate both at the level of institutions or organisations and at the level of individuals. Cross-classifying the two distinctions (facilitation versus mobilisation and institutional level versus individual level) leads to the fourfold typology of influences on turnout presented in Figure 10.2. Thus *institutional facilitation* consists of the practical administrative arrangements that govern the way in which elections are conducted (e.g., the arrangements for voter registration, the month in which the election takes place, whether polling takes

| | *Location of the variable* | |
Nature of the effect	*Institutional level*	*Individual level*
Facilitation	*Institutional facilitation*	*Individual facilitation*
	Attributes of the administration and regulation of elections that make it easy to vote	Attributes of individuals' circumstances that make it easy to vote
Mobilisation	*Institutional mobilisation*	*Individual mobilisation*
	Attributes of the political system and of the political process that make people want to vote	Attributes of individual electors' political outlooks that make them want to vote

Figure 10.2   A typology of the variables affecting voter participation/abstention

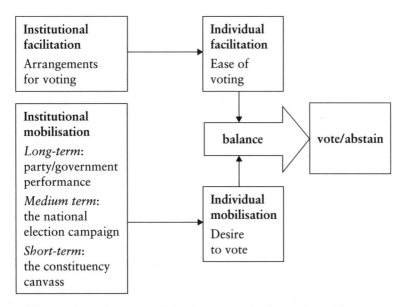

Figure 10.3   A model of the determinants of voter participation

place on a weekday or at the weekend, the hours of polling, the accessibility of polling stations, the availability of postal voting, etc.). *Institutional mobilisation* ranges from the long-term performance of parties, governments and representative institutions to the immediate efforts of parties and candidates to get out the vote. *Individual facilitation* refers to how easy or difficult it is for the individual to vote. Finally, *individual mobilisation* is the sum of the attitudes and perceptions that make people want to vote. A simplified model of how these four factors affect turnout is presented in Figure 10.3.

The advantages of this facilitation-mobilisation framework can be illustrated by considering the relationship between turnout and age – probably the most striking and puzzling of all the relationships thrown up by the analysis of individual-level turnout. Reported turnout among young people (those aged 18–24) in the 2002 election was 54 percent (see Table 10.1). It rose to 65 percent in the age group 25–34, to 73 percent in the age group 35–44, to 77 percent among 45 to 54-year-olds and reached a peak of 79 percent among those aged 55–64. Only in the final age group – those aged 75 and over – does one find a significant falling off in the level of turnout (to 67 percent).

Application of the facilitation-mobilisation framework to these striking age contrasts shows that the composition of abstention varies in different age cohorts (see Table 10.1). Thus, while circumstantial abstainers

Table 10.1 Electoral participation and types of abstention by age (%)

	Age group						
	18–24	25–34	35–44	45–54	55–64	65–74	75+
Voted	54	65	73	77	79	77	67
Circumstantial abstainer	20	13	10	7	5	10	14
Voluntary abstainer	15	9	3	3	3	2	4
Abstainer – other or no reason given	11	13	14	14	13	12	15
Total	100	100	100	100	100	100	100
N	296	402	459	532	442	242	171

outnumber voluntary abstainers by more than 3 to 1 among people aged 35 and over, the ratio is only 1.6 to 1 among 25 to 34-year-olds and 1.3 to 1 among the under 25s. In terms of the framework presented in Figures 10.2 and 10.3, this higher rate of voluntary abstention among young people in general suggests that failures of mobilisation are a major factor in the very low levels of turnout in the younger age cohorts. At the same time, it is clear that circumstantial abstention and, by implication, inadequate facilitation affect young people as well and, in particular, affect students. Facilitation is also a factor at the other end of the generational spectrum in that, having dipped as low as 5 percent among 55 to 64-year-olds, circumstantial abstention rises to 10 percent among those aged 65 to 74 and to 14 percent among those over 75.

The analytical message in all of this is that institutional factors, whether they be facilitating or mobilising, affect the probability of turning out to vote by interacting with individual characteristics to produce different effects for different categories of individuals. This can be further illustrated by looking at the processes of facilitation and mobilisation in the 2002 election.

Processes of voter facilitation

Administrative arrangements for voting are never perfect. Ideally, for example, every eligible voter would be registered to vote based on his or her current place of residence. In practice, some people end up being registered at an address other than that of their current residence. This

Table 10.2 Electoral participation and types of abstention
by place of registration (%)

	Registered to vote at this address	Registered to vote at another address
Voted	73	44
Circumstantial abstainer	9	32
Voluntary abstainer	5	9
Abstainer – other or no reason given	13	15
Total	100	100
N	2462	59

is most likely to occur in the case of young people who live away from their parental home and in the case of people who have recently moved residence. While the numbers of people with a discrepancy between residential address and registration address is small, the phenomenon illustrates again how personal characteristics (being young, being mobile) interact with administrative arrangements (the registration process) to, in this case, reduce the ease of voting. The consequences are evident in Table 10.2, which shows a 29 percentage point difference in turnout between those for whom residency and registration coincide and those for whom the direct link between where they live and where they vote is broken.

As well as affecting different age groups in different way, arrangements for voting interact with occupation in a way that makes certain occupational categories more prone to abstention and others less so. This tends not to become evident if we simply adopt the standard approach of treating occupation as an indicator of social status. In this approach, the contrast in turnout across occupational groups is usually found to be quite marginal. Instead, Table 10.3 takes account of both employment status and occupational category, arranging the employment and occupational categories in order of increasing levels of turnout from left to right. The lowest level of turnout and the highest level of *circumstantial* abstention are found among students, suggesting that institutional facilitation does not work well in this case. The next lowest level of turnout is found among the unemployed. Here, however, the ratio of circumstantial to voluntary abstention is 1 to 2 (it is 2 to 1 among students). Thus, whereas student abstention is due more to low facilitation and less to low mobilisation, abstention among the unemployed is less a result of lack of facilitation and more due to low mobilisation.

Table 10.3 Electoral participation and types of abstention by employment situation and self-employed/employee occupation (%)

	Student	Unemployed and seeking work	Manual	Non-manual	Retired/long term sick or disabled	Engaged in home duties	Farmer	Total
Voted	56	66	67	70	74	78	84	72
Circumstantial abstainer	24	7	9	11	11	9	4	10
Voluntary abstainer	12	13	9	5	3	2	4	5
Abstainer – other or no reason given	8	14	15	14	13	11	9	13
Total	100	100	100	100	100	100	100	100
N	107	91	450	914	443	402	104	2511

Table 10.3 also shows that, while the absolute level of turnout among those with manual occupations is the same as that among the unemployed, the mix of voluntary and circumstantial abstention is quite different. Thus, the ratio of circumstantial to voluntary abstention among those with manual occupations is 50:50 in comparison to 1:2 among the unemployed. When we move from manual to non-manual occupations, the absolute level of turnout does not change that much, but the ratio of circumstantial to voluntary abstention swings decisively in favour of circumstantial abstention. This suggests that low turnout in the middle-class electorate is more a function of low facilitation than of low mobilisation.

The ratio of circumstantial to voluntary abstention is particularly high in the next two categories in Table 10.3, namely among the 'retired and long-term sick and disabled' and those 'engaged in home duties'. The reasons for problems in voter facilitation among the first of these two categories are obvious. The reasons for the predominance of facilitation problems in the case of those in the 'home duties' category are less obvious, but the finding does suggest that something in the home-duties occupational role imposes constraints on voter participation. Finally, we should note that the ratio of circumstantial to voluntary abstention (and facilitation to mobilisation) returns to 50:50 among farmers, reflecting equally low levels of both forms of abstention in this occupational group, the members of which have the highest propensity to vote of any occupational category.

Processes of voter mobilisation

Elections are episodic. Between episodes, parties get on with the business of governing or of opposing the government. In doing so they lay down a record of performance that contributes to their long-term image. In similar fashion, representative institutions themselves generate an image that reflects their role and their performance. Individuals respond to all of this by learning from experience to like or dislike certain political parties and/or certain political institutions. Some go on from this to form a long-term attachment to or identification with a party (see Chapter 4). For some individuals, indeed, party attachment may precede the possibility of voting or any real experience of party performance. This occurs when party attachment is inherited from parents, a common occurence, as shown in Chapter 4.

The data in Table 10.4 are certainly compatible with the notion that voter turnout can be affected by voting history. Thus, turnout in the current generation varies from 76 percent among those coming

Table 10.4 Electoral participation and types of abstention by parental electoral involvement (%)

	Voting and intense support	Voting only (both parents)	Voting only (one parent)	Don't know how/whether either parent voted	Neither voted/One did not and other dk	Total
Voted	76	73	67	64	50	72
Circumstantial abstainer	9	9	10	13	18	10
Voluntary abstainer	3	5	8	8	23	5
Abstainer – other or no reason given	12	13	15	14	10	13
Total	100	100	100	100	100	100
N	1125	581	141	580	40	2467

from a strongly political family background (where parental voting was accompanied by intense support for a party) to 67 percent among those coming from families in which only one parent voted, but without any particular intensity, to 64 percent among those from an apolitical background (where the offspring do not know how or whether their parents voted). Though the number of cases is too small for the evidence to be any more than suggestive, it is worth noting that turnout falls to 50 percent among those whose parents did not vote at all.

While some people thus have a headstart in the political mobilisation process, the key long-term mobilising factor is the individual's own experience of politics and the political system. For a proportion of the electorate, such political experience results in the development of a sense of attachment to a political party and that sense of attachment is associated with higher turnout. Thus, 80 percent of those who feel very close to a party report having voted in 2002. The other end of the scale is defined by those who say that they are not close to any party, not even, on prompting, a little closer to one of the political parties than to the others. Sixty-seven percent of those without any attachment to party as measured in this way report that they voted.

It should be noted, however, that the notion of 'think[ing] of yourself as close to any political party?' is a rather demanding criterion and is likely to elicit a positive response only from those who have a really strong sense of party attachment.[8] The stringency of the initial measure of party attachment is somewhat compensated for by the supplement-ary question that was put to those who said they were not close to a party: 'Do you feel yourself a little closer to one of the parties than to the others?' As we have seen in Chapter 4 (Table 4.1), this supple-mentary question brings a further one-quarter of the electorate into the category of having some degree of attachment to a party. However, even this measure leaves almost 50 percent of the electorate without any apparent relationship to a political party. In order to deal with this limitation, we presented respondents with a virtual 'feeling ther-mometer' that required them to rate each of the parties in terms of the warm or cold feelings elicited by the party in question. We have used this question in several previous chapters. The responses indicate that far more people feel some degree of warmth towards the political parties than is indicated by the party attachment question. When attitude to the parties is measured in terms of thermometer ratings, only 4 percent of respondents make absolutely no differentiation between the parties and 67 percent show a range of warm/cold feelings towards the parties of 50 degrees or more. This estimate of two-thirds of respondents having some significant affective relationship with the parties must be

Table 10.5 Electoral participation and types of abstention
by range of feeling towards parties (%)

	Range of feeling towards parties						
	0	1 to 20	21 to 40	41 to 60	61 to 80	81 to 100	Total
Voted	54	63	68	75	77	76	72
Circumstantial abstainer	15	13	13	10	8	8	10
Voluntary abstainer	20	8	8	4	1	3	5
Abstainer – other or no reason given	11	16	12	12	14	13	13
Total	100	100	100	100	100	100	100
N	105	167	555	793	589	296	2505

born in mind in assessing the implications of low levels of party attachment that we have considered elsewhere in this book.

The relationship between this party-feeling thermometer and turnout is shown in Table 10.5. Turnout ranges from a low of 52 percent among the small minority who make no differentiation whatsoever between the parties to a high of 75 to 77 percent among those who show a range of feeling towards the parties of 40 percentage points or more. In between, turnout goes up as the range of feelings towards the parties increases. The differences in turnout at these various levels of differentiation between the parties are accounted for mainly by changes in the rate of voluntary abstention, which goes from 21 percent among those with no sense of party difference to 1 percent among those who register a range of feeling towards the parties of between 60 and 80 percentage points.

It is also worth noting that the relationship between a person's range of feeling towards the parties and his or her turnout is stronger among those with low levels of political knowledge than it is among those with medium to high levels of knowledge. As Table 10.6 shows, at low and medium levels of political knowledge there is a 25 percentage point difference in the rate of turnout between those with a wide range of feeling towards the parties and those whose feelings towards the parties are largely undifferentiated. Among those with a high level of knowledge, on the other hand, there is only a 13 percentage point difference and among those with the highest level of knowledge, the difference in the rate of turnout is only 10 points.

In interpreting the significance of these findings regarding the relationship between party attachment and range of feeling towards parties, on the one hand, and voter turnout on the other, one should bear in mind

Table 10.6 Electoral participation by range of feeling towards parties controlling for level of political knowledge

Level of political knowledge	Range of feeling towards parties						
	0	1 to 20	21 to 40	41 to 60	61 to 80	81 to 100	Total
Low	36.1	53.8	53.9	66.1	70.5	72.1	61.7
	(36)	(52)	(152)	(177)	(122)	(61)	(600)
Medium	51.7	61.5	68.2	70.7	72.9	79.3	70.4
	(29)	(39)	(148)	(205)	(133)	(87)	(641)
High	61.1	75.0	74.7	79.7	81.5	78.1	78.1
	(18)	(36)	(150)	(222)	(168)	(73)	(667)
Very high	77.3	65.0	76.2	80.4	80.1	73.3	77.6
	(22)	(40)	(105)	(189)	(166)	(75)	(597)

Notes: Main entry in each cell is the percentage in that category reporting having voted in 2002.
Entry in brackets is the N of cases on which the percentage is based.

the extent to which, as revealed in Chapter 8, the Irish electorate is motivated not just by party preferences, but also by candidate preferences. Do such preferences also affect voter turnout? Once again, the first step in answering this question is to find out whether there is a relationship between the range of feeling that an individual may display towards the candidates and that individual's propensity to vote. As we have seen, almost everyone (i.e. 96 percent) shows some degree of preference between the parties as this is measured on the feeling-thermometer. The rate of differentiation drops slightly when we turn to feelings towards candidates. In this case, the proportion showing at least a minimal degree of variation in feeling is 86 percent. Parties also elicit stronger feelings than do candidates. Whereas 49 percent of respondents show a range of 60 degrees or more between the parties, only 34 percent show such a range as between the candidates.[9] However, while differentiation between candidates may be less then differentiation between parties, it is still substantial – 50 percent of the electorate show a range of warmth of feeling towards candidates of at least 50 degrees. The question is: does this variation affect turnout? On the face of it and bearing in mind the necessary qualifications about multiple and overlapping causation, the answer is yes. In 2002 turnout among those who are entirely neutral towards the candidates was 58 percent; among those for whom the range of feeling towards the candidates was between 80 and 100 degrees, turnout was 83 percent (see Table 10.7).

Table 10.7 Electoral participation and types of abstention
by range of feeling towards candidates (%)

	_	_	Range of feeling towards candidates				
	0	1 to 20	21 to 40	41 to 60	61 to 80	81 to 100	Total
Voted	58	70	72	73	76	83	72
Circumstantial abstainer	15	12	11	10	8	4	10
Voluntary abstainer	15	4	5	4	1	3	5
Abstainer – other or no reason given	13	14	12	13	15	9	13
Total	100	100	100	100	100	100	100
N	359	256	643	671	422	216	2567

Voter mobilisation is about more than the long-term performance of parties and candidates. Most obviously, it is also, or even more, about campaigning, canvassing and communicating the message and the appeal of the parties and candidates. During the campaign itself, parties and candidates undertake all sorts of efforts to get their messages across to the electorate and the evidence indicates that a substantial part of the electorate sits up and takes notice. In the case of the most prevalent and visible manifestation of the election campaign, the electorate could not but at least notice the candidate posters that festoon every other lamppost and telegraph pole. Our survey indicates that candidate posters are 'looked at' by the vast majority (82 percent) of potential voters. The next most prevalent means of communication in the 2002 election approximates to the notion of a two-step flow of communication, that is, campaign communication through people discussing the election with family, friends and acquaintances. Such discussions are fuelled by the extensive coverage of the campaign in the media, particularly on television and radio. Experience of this interpersonal form of campaign communication was reported by 74 percent of respondents.

The substantive messages the parties wish to convey are contained primarily in campaign leaflets and in party or candidate advertising in newspapers.[10] Sixty-five percent of the electorate claim to have read campaign leaflets, but exposure drops to 50 percent in the case of party/candidate advertisements in newspapers. The other two channels of communication examined in the INES survey were the most traditional (public meetings) and the most modern (the internet). The evidence indicates that the traditional has all but disappeared and that the particular form of modernity involved in the latter has yet to arrive as both public meetings and the internet show very low levels of penetration (4 and 6 percent, respectively).

The effect on turnout of attending to the campaign in any of the ways just considered is modest, the difference in rates of turnout ranging from no difference at all as a result of accessing campaign information on the internet to a 12 percentage point difference in turnout between those who did, or did not, discuss the election with family, friends or acquaintances. There is, however, some evidence that campaign exposure has a cumulative effect – the rate of turnout goes from 55 percent among those who have no exposure at all to the campaign to 77 percent among those exposed to the campaign via five or six channels of communication. However, the big difference is between those with no exposure and those with at least one form of exposure (the rates of turnout for these groups were, respectively, 55 percent and 70 percent).

As we have seen in Chapter 7, Irish elections are characterised by an exceptional degree of contact between parties/candidates and individual electors and households. The bulk of this contact is based on what is referred to as 'the canvass' or 'the campaign on the doorstep'. This is particularly extensive in Ireland. Turnout ranges from 62 percent among those not contacted at home by any of these means (candidate called at home, party worker called at home, party worker phoned home) to 75 percent among those who were contacted in at least one of these ways and to 80 percent among the small group of electors who were contacted in all three ways (see Table 10.8). Perhaps surprisingly, turnout does not increase in proportion to the number of candidates or parties that call at the voter's home; what matters again is whether or not any contact at all was made.[11] It is also quite striking that the

Table 10.8 Electoral participation and types of abstention by extent of candidate/party worker/phone contact at home (%)

Range of feeling towards Parties	Extent of candidate/party worker/phone contact at home				
	No contact	One type contact	Two types contact	Three types contact	Total
Voted	62	73	74	80	72
Circumstantial abstainer	15	8	10	8	10
Voluntary abstainer	9	5	4	1	5
Abstainer – other or no reason given	14	13	12	11	13
Total	100	100	100	100	100
N	511	1127	843	86	2567

Table 10.9 Electoral participation by extent of candidate/party worker/ phone contact at home controlling for range of feeling towards parties

Range of feeling towards Parties	Extent of candidate/party worker/phone contact at home		
	No contact	Some contact	Total
Low	52.9	70.2	67.3
(range = 0 to 3)	(68)	(326)	(394)
Medium	73.9	75.2	75.0
(range = 4 to 7)	(176)	(1001)	(1177)
High	74.2	79.6	78.9
(range = 8 to 10)	(66)	(431)	(497)

Notes: Main entry in each cell is the percentage in that category reporting having voted in 2002.
Entry in brackets is the N of cases on which the percentage is based.

strength of the association between turnout and *which* party or parties made the contact does not vary as between the main political parties. It does, however, vary as between contact by parties and contact by independents, the latter being associated with a significantly higher rate of turnout.

The impact of contact on turnout also depends on the level of prior mobilisation of the individual in question having a bigger effect when an individual's sense of party differentiation is low. As Table 10.9 shows, among those with a low range of inter-party differentiation, turnout varies from 53 percent of those who have not been contacted to 71 percent among those who have been contacted by either party workers or a candidate on at least one occasion. However, contact seems to make no difference at all for those with medium levels of party differentiation and is associated with only a 5 percent increase in turnout among those with high levels of party differentiation. In short, contact makes a difference when it adds something to the experience of the individual and makes either no difference, or very little difference, when it is addressed to those with an already high degree of mobilisation.

Sources of circumstantial and voluntary abstention

The foregoing analysis of the determinants of voter turnout suffers from the major limitation that the sources of turnout/abstention are undoubtedly multivariate while the analysis so far has been bivariate.

As indicated in Chapter 9, the time has come to attempt to sort out the interlocking processes of causation that lead people to vote, or not to vote. The first step is to separate the underlying questions, the two distinct questions being what are the sources of circumstantial abstention and what are the sources of voluntary abstention. In line with the interpretation put forward so far in this chapter, we would expect that circumstantial and voluntary abstention would be subject to largely different patterns of causation. To be specific, we would expect that facilitation effects would be more evident in the case of the former and that mobilisation effects would play the most prominent role in relation to voluntary abstention. The qualification 'largely' should be underlined. As noted at the outset of this chapter and as is central to the approach presented in Figure 10.3, the likelihood of the occurrence of circumstantial abstention is relative to the strength of mobilisation and vice versa. Accordingly, we should expect to find some evidence of association between weak mobilisation and circumstantial abstention and between poor facilitation and voluntary abstention.

In order to establish a benchmark against which the sources of circumstantial and voluntary abstention can be assessed, Table 10.10 begins with an analysis of abstention as a whole. Reflecting the fact that a good deal of abstention is circumstantial, the model on the left-hand side of Table 10.10 shows that three of the four facilitation variables have statistically significant and fairly substantial effects. The exception is student status, which, on this evidence (that is, without distinguishing between the two kinds of abstention), we would conclude is unrelated to abstention. Even more contrary to expectation is the apparent finding that two key mobilising factors – parental party attachment and own party attachment – are also, apparently, unrelated to electoral participation. The medium-term indicators of political mobilisation – campaign exposure and candidate differential – also have only very modest effects on undifferentiated abstention. Indeed, the only mobilisation variable with a substantial effect is short-term contact through the door-to-door canvass.

The results set out in the models that address the two types of abstention are more informative and more in line with expectations. In the case of circumstantial abstention, the two most clearly circumstantial variables (being registered at another address and being over 75 years old) have substantial effects. Consistent with the theory, neither of our main indicators of long-term political learning (parental participation and own party identification) plays any role in relation to circumstantial abstention. However, there is some evidence of medium-term mobilisation having some effect on circumstantial abstention. It is

Table 10.10   Logistic regression of total abstention, circumstantial abstention and voluntary abstention

	All abstainers	Circumstantial abstainers	Voluntary abstainers
Facilitation effects			
Registered at another address	3.01***	5.11***	1.97
	0.88	1.77	1.18
Student	0.96	1.32	0.91
	0.22	0.39	0.36
Farmer	0.59	0.43	1.24
	0.17	0.22	0.68
Aged over 75	2.63***	4.32***	9.11***
	0.59	1.43	5.07
Mobilisation effects			
Parental party attachment	0.92	0.98	0.72*
	0.05	0.09	0.11
Own party attachment	0.98	0.95	0.70**
	0.04	0.06	0.09
Age	0.82***	0.76***	0.59***
	0.03	0.04	0.05
Campaign exposure	0.86***	0.89*	0.59***
	0.03	0.05	0.05
Candidate differential	0.84***	0.77***	0.71***
	0.03	0.04	0.05
Contacted at home	0.63***	0.61**	0.59*
	0.07	0.10	0.13
R^2	0.06	0.08	0.24

Notes: cell entries are odds ratios with standard errors underneath; * significant at .05, ** significant at .01,*** significant at .001.

particularly noteworthy that the strongest mobilisation effect derives from the short-term contact variable, with lack of such contact contributing significantly to circumstantial abstention. This may reflect the problem of those who need transport or other assistance to get to the polling station; if there is no contact with the household, such assistance is much less likely to be arranged.

For obvious reasons, most interest in the analysis of abstention centres on the voluntary variety. By and large, and as anticipated, facilitation variables play little or no role in this case. Given the extent of discussion at election time of the failure of young people to get out and vote, it is worth underlining the finding that, while student status has a negative effect on facilitation, it shows no evidence of being associated with voluntary abstention and appears, therefore, to be unrelated to political mobilisation.

Among the socio-demographic variables included in the model, being aged 75 or over is the only one that is strongly related to both circumstantial and voluntary abstention. This suggests that a combination of poor facilitation and failing mobilisation contributes to the decisive downward shift in voter turnout in this age group that was evident in Table 10.1.

Our primary interest in the voluntary abstention model (right-hand side of Table 10.10) is in the impact of the indicators of political mobilisation. The results confirm the expectation that having (had) parents with who are (were) strong supporters of a party and having a sense of party identification oneself substantially reduce the likelihood of abstention. However, in addition to these long-term factors, campaigning also matters: abstention is significantly affected by overall campaign exposure and by having been contacted at home. Taking all of these effects into account, candidate differential has only a relatively small effect. Note, however, that the age effect displayed in Table 10.1 persists even when all the facilitation and mobilization variables included in the model on the right-hand side of Table 10.10 are taken into account. Our interpretation of this residual age effect is that age is acting as a proxy variable for length of political experience and for what one might regard as a life-cycle process of political mobilisation.

Conclusion

Ireland experienced a 10 percentage point drop in general election turnout between 1981 and 2002 and is now ninth from the bottom of the turnout league table comprising the 25 member states of the European Union. This chapter began the analysis of the causes of low turnout by distinguishing between circumstantial and voluntary abstention, noting that the former outpaced the latter by a ratio of at least two to one. The distinction between the two types of abstention leads to a fourfold typology of the causes of abstention. The typology is arrived at by combining a distinction between facilitation (which addresses circumstantial abstention) and mobilisation (which addresses voluntary abstention), with a distinction based on whether these two kinds of causes of voter turnout operate at the institutional or individual level.

Bivariate analyses of the relationship between turnout/abstention and a wide array of facilitating and mobilising variables illustrate the

processes at work and identify several points at which individual characteristics and experiences interact with each other or with institutional
variables to tilt the facilitation-mobilisation balance in the direction
of turnout or in the direction of abstention. Multivariate analysis confirmed the utility of the facilitation-mobilisation distinction and demonstrated that the two kinds of abstention are products of quite different
patterns of causation. Thus, for example, circumstantial abstention is
made more likely by the individual being registered at a different address
and being aged over 75, but is reduced by being a farmer. Consistent
with the underlying distinction, circumstantial abstention is only
minimally affected by mobilisation variables; the only really substantial
mobilisation effect on circumstantial abstention is that of having been
contacted at home in the course of the house-to-house canvass that is
such a striking feature of Irish election campaigns.[12]

Voluntary abstention, on the other hand, is mainly affected by mobilisation variables, such as coming from a strongly political family,
feeling close to a party, having a high level of campaign exposure and,
again, being contacted at home. Having strong preferences between
candidates makes a small additional contribution to reducing voluntary
abstention. Even when all this has been taken into account, there remains
a strong and somewhat complex age effect – voluntary abstention reduces
with each passing decade of increasing age, but only up to age 75; thereafter, the age effect is negative as electors encounter more and more
obstacles to turning out to vote.

Can anything be done to reverse the declining turnout trend? The
argument in this chapter is first that, yes, something can be done and,
second, that the levers are to be found in a combination of voter
facilitation and voter mobilisation, with the former being essentially in
the hands of policy makers and administrators, and the latter in the hands
of politicians and party activists. In terms of numbers of abstainers, it
might seem that the emphasis should be on facilitation and on circumstantial abstainers, as these outnumber voluntary abstainers by 2 to 1.
However, as suggested above, this is where the interaction between
facilitation and mobilisation comes into play and gives primacy to
voter mobilization – if voters do not want to vote, then all the facilitation in the world will not induce them to do so.

Notes

1   Figure 10.1 omits subnational and supranational elections that were
    combined with other more important contests. Thus, it omits turnout in
    European Parliament elections in 1979 (when EP elections were combined

with local elections), in 1989 (when they were combined with national elections) and in 1999 and 2004 when they were again combined with local elections). In the case of the local elections of 2004, the graph includes both turnout in the local elections and turnout in the referendum on citizenship held on the same day as the evidence suggests that the referendum rather than the local elections may have been the factor behind the increase in turnout (see note 3 below).

2 The two exceptions to these downward trends were turnout in the presidential election of 1990, which at 64 percent was up two points on 1973 and turnout in the local elections of 2004, which was 8 percentage points higher than turnout in the previous local elections (1999). The increase in the 1990 presidential election, while small, was significant because it was against the trend. The reasons for the increase are related to the stature of the candidates and the dramatic political developments that unfolded during the campaign (see Marsh, 1992). However, the more substantial increase in turnout in the local government elections of 2004 is open to contrary interpretations. One is that it represents a decisive revival in local democracy. Another is that it was due to the voters rising up in rebellion against the incumbent Fianna Fáil-Progressive Democrat government and turning out in their droves to register their protest. The third interpretation is that the increase was because there was a referendum on the right to citizenship on the same day and that it was this issue that drew the voters out in unusually large numbers. While it is difficult to be certain about the matter, the evidence points in the direction of the third or referendum explanation. If this is so, then we can conclude that the overall trend in turnout remains downwards and that the apparent recovery in 2004 was due to special circumstances.

3 Accuracy of aggregate data of course, as estimates of turnout, depends on the quality of the electoral register. Relying on reported turnout by constituency as our source of data also gives rise to limitations on the number and type of variables or causes of turnout that we can examine, the causal variables being confined to the basic socio-demographic characteristics collected in the census. Finally, constituency-level or aggregate data provide particular challenges when it comes to making inferences about behaviour. This is because the data refer to the behaviour of aggregates, but our main interest is in the behaviour of individuals. In short, aggregate data may not be wholly accurate and are subject to considerable limitations when it comes to making inferences about the sources of electoral participation.

4 Analogously but using precoded responses Marsh (1991) proposed a distinction between non-voters by accident and non-voters by design.

5 The full array of responses was: voters 72 percent, circumstantial abstainers 10 percent, voluntary abstainers 5 percent and other/no reason given 13 percent. The source of the relatively large proportion of 'no reasons given' lies in the adjustment of the data by reference to the marked electoral

registers. Cases reassigned from voted to not voted were, for obvious reasons, not asked the 'Why did you not vote?' question.

6 However, when prompted by the interviewer for other reasons for his abstention, this same respondent added that he was away for the weekend. Despite giving this circumstantial reason, this respondent was categorised as a voluntary abstainer. This is because, as explained earlier, a voluntary reason trumps a circumstantial one.

7 This suggests that, contrary to much speculation and to what might have been expected on the basis of the long-running tribunals of inquiry into particular cases of political corruption, apathy rather than alienation is the main source of voluntary abstention.

8 For a discussion of the measurement problems involved, see Sinnott, 1998.

9 Far more respondents evaluate all parties than evaluate all candidates.

10 Political advertising on television/radio is banned but there is provision for free air-time in the form of 'party political broadcasts' on radio and television.

11 Thus, turnout increases by 11 percentage points as between those who were not contacted by any party or candidate and those who were contacted by one party or candidate; however, it only increases another 3 percentage points with contact from additional parties or candidates.

12 As pointed out in the text, for those without transport or with a disability of some sort, being contacted at home may be seen as a facilitation, rather than a mobilisation, variable.

11

Conclusions

In the opening chapter of this book we argued that Irish electoral behaviour was of particular interest in the comparative study of electoral choice. The Irish case combines an electoral system that provides candidates with a strong incentive to campaign for and develop a 'personal vote' with a party system that is increasingly independent of stable social and psychological underpinnings. There is, therefore, considerable potential for candidates, as well as short-term forces like leaders and government performance, to have a big impact on the voter's choice. How important are parties in such a context? Here we review our findings before going on to consider the broader implications of our results for an assessment of the electoral process. We start by considering the basis of support for parties and then deal with the balance between parties and candidates.

Whyte's (1974) observation that Irish parties were 'without social bases' has prompted much research and there have been many qualifications to that statement. Our own findings, based on arguably better measures of class and a more comprehensive set of other socio-demographic and attitudinal measures, qualify the remark still further, but in essence it remains true. In fact, it may be truer now that it has ever been. Mair (1979) pointed out that while there was little to discriminate Fianna Fáil from 'the rest', it was still the case that Labour and Fine Gael were quite different (in terms of the urban versus rural, working class versus middle, and non-farmers versus farmers distinctions). Despite this social division, government was either Fianna Fáil or a Fine Gael and Labour coalition, so the political representation of those divisions was essentially absent. However, in contemporary Ireland, Labour looks more like Fine Gael (and indeed Fianna Fáil) than it used to. Hence, there are three similar parties and not just two similar blocs. There are differences between the three parties, notably in terms of the educational levels of their voters, and there are some urban–rural contrasts but, in purely social class terms, they are all very similar. The qualification must be made that the newer members of the party system are less broadly based. The Progressive Democrats, Greens and Sinn Féin all appeal rather more to some social groups than others, although even these parties are not quite so sectional as may sometimes be believed. The Progressive Democrats are far from being solely middle class, and Sinn Féin is far from being solely working class. These parties are also more urban, and attract younger voters: a group that is increasingly detached from the old party system (Laver, 2005). Even so, in terms of potential future coalitions these differences are likely to be more visible within a government than between government and opposition.

Value divisions are typically thought to stem from social divisions, cleavages being both sociological and attitudinal. This is an area that has been explored far less than the class basis of parties has, because data availability has to date been limited. The analysis here brought together both a battery of questions relating to many areas of potential value conflict and information on how the voters perceived each party's stance on these matters, and indeed on how they perceived the parties in general. The analysis reported is thus more comprehensive than any previous exploration of value divisions between Irish parties. It showed that the basis for party competition about values is limited. Most voters and most parties are located (by voters) in much the same place on most of the dimensions we considered. There is potential for partisan conflict on the secular–religious dimension, best manifested by views on abortion, which are quite polarised. Certainly, voters vary a lot on such issues, but the parties do not, arguably because the institution of the referendum has allowed this issue to be dealt with, even if ineffectively, outside the party system (Sinnott, 2002).

The one issue on which parties and voters do seem to be separated is the environment, but the voters, who are far more environmentalist than the parties, see little difference between most parties – the Greens are an exception – on that issue. When parties do differ it is the smaller parties that stand out. Value orientations tell us much more about support for the smaller parties, including Labour, than they do about support for the big two. It is clear that perceptions of left and right are more important for voters' choice than are other value sets. Those who see themselves as being on the left tend to vote for parties that see themselves as left, and those who see themselves as being on the right support the centre right parties. However, it is also striking that left and right lack clear definition and so do not imply any obvious polit- ical direction. A Fine Gael+Labour government would be seen as more left wing than a Fianna Fáil+PD government, but it is far from evident what implications that might be expected to have for the policies and priorities of either government. Nor do voters apparently see parties in broad ideological terms, and only the Green party was identified with a particular policy focus. This is obviously an area that demands further research to find out what left and right mean to voters.

Party systems underpinned by social or cultural cleavages can be expected to be fairly stable and to be able to provide an electoral channel for the expression of different interests. In the absence of such cleavages, stability can still be maintained through attachments to parties. The USA is a prime example in this respect. Ireland could be another, as party attachment could fulfil the function that it does in the US (Shively, 1979). Party attachment, or identification, is at least a familiar idea in Ireland, where it is common to hear of people and their families 'being' Fianna Fáil or Fine Gael. While there have been studies exploring party identification in Ireland prior to this one (e.g. Carty, 1983; Marsh, 1985a; Sinnott, 1995) we were able to link attachment with a much richer set of data on voting behaviour and attitudes to (and evaluations of) parties. We discovered some important features of such attachment in Ireland. On the one hand, attachment is linked to voting stability, with identifiers more likely to remain loyal both across elections, by voting over time for the same party, and within parties across candidates. It helps explain party voting. It also has clear, if diminishing, roots in the family. Attachment to the party by the voter provides much the strongest correlate of vote choice for both Fianna Fáil and Fine Gael, and in the case of Labour it is also quite strong. There are two caveats.

The first is that we cannot be sure that attachment itself is stable, that is does not, to a significant degree, 'travel' with the vote rather than determine it. The plausibility of the view that party attachment does precede vote is supported by the fact that the meaning of people 'being' Fianna Fáil or Fine Gael is easily understood in public discourse, and by the fact that such attachment is more important in the older parties that have had time to build such attachment. Sinn Féin is an outlier here. Its support is also strongly driven by attachment despite the fact that it is a new electoral organisation. The second caveat is that attachment is so low in Ireland. As we have seen, it has been declining for at least the last 20 years, and probably for longer (Mair and Marsh, 2004). When only a quarter of voters indicate relatively strong attachments, the plausibility of an explanation of stable electoral choice based on party identification is obviously limited. There are two possibilities, which are not mutually exclusive. The first is that identification can no longer explain stability, and that recent election results indicate that the party system is now unstable and may change considerably over the next few elections, particularly in its non-Fianna Fáil components. The second is that Irish voters remain much more attached to their parties than it appears. In other words, the measurement itself may be flawed. The clear weakness of attachment in a cross-national perspective, and the steadiness of the decline in a cross-time perspective, may cast doubt on the 'flawed measurement' argument, but it could still be true that, while Irish voters do not think of themselves as being 'close' to a paricular party, they have a strong predisposition to support one. Both this, and the real stability of attachment, will be the subject of future research.

The chapters on political cleavages and party attachment focus on the enduring characteristics of voters and their links with parties. If we ask why Fianna Fáil does so well, the strength of party attachment – subject to the caveats above – provides an answer. But if we want to know why Fianna Fáil did so well in 2002, and why the main opposition parties did so poorly, we need a more limited short-term focus and the chapters on issues, leaders and, to a lesser extent, campaigning all provide that. In the absence of any basis for voting on packages of policies, we concentrated in our cleavages chapter on issues of 'policy competence', the perceived ability of each party to run the economy and various public services efficiently. Once again, we were able to look much more comprehensively at the importance of particular policy issues than any previous analysis, but we concentrated on looking for evidence that the governing parties were rewarded for having done a generally good job and explored the extent to which the government would get credit for things which had gone well and the blame for things that had gone badly. While this was a significant factor in the 2002 result, it was nowhere near as strong an influence as party attachment. We took a conservative view on the importance of policy competence in our multivariate analysis by controlling for party attachment. If competence assessments have a significant short-term influence on attachments then we will have underestimated the importance of things like the economy and the health service in 2002.

Even so, our more detailed analysis of these issues did suggest clearly that the competence issue worked to the advantage of the government. Most voters thought it had done a good job. Where evaluations were negative, as they were on crime, voters did not necessarily blame the government for the worsening situation. Even when they did, as in the case of health, there was little confidence in the ability of any alternative government to do a better job. Moreover, the areas in which the government was weak, such as transport, were simply not important enough to voters to make any difference. In assessments of performance voters rate the economy as most important; it was in good shape and the government, and particularly Fianna Fáil, reaped the reward. This is no surprise, given the widespread international support for the existence of an 'economic vote'. What is surprising is that the opposition parties were generally unable to capitalise on government weaknesses. The government itself admitted in its election slogan that it had 'more to do'. Neither Fine Gael nor Labour was able to channel the expression of discontent. It is striking that even among those who said the government had done a 'bad' job, Fianna Fáil won more votes than Fine Gael. All opposition parties picked up the votes of some of the disaffected and disappointed, but no single party served as a focus for such feelings. Fine Gael and Labour have since concluded that their failure to provide a coherent alternative government during the 2002 campaign was a very significant factor in this, and accordingly agreed to present a common programme for the 2007 election. It may be that in such a situation, where the choice is more clearly between alternative governments, there will be a stronger link between performance evaluations and vote choice.

If the performance of the economy provides us with one explanation why 2002 was a particularly good year for Fianna Fáil, the popularity of the respective party leaders provides us with another. Of the two potential candidates for Taoiseach, the incumbent, Bertie Ahern, enjoyed a huge lead over his rival, Michael Noonan. The gap between them was greater than at any previous election in the last 25 years. It is apparent in our analysis that leaders had a limited impact on their party's fortunes. Most had a positive impact, but there is little to suggest that Irish elections are a presidential-style battle between likely leaders of government, however much the parties' national election campaigns and the media cast elections in such a light. And this version of events leaves little room for the leaders of minor parties. Our data allow a much more nuanced exploration of the impact of leaders on the vote than has been possible previously, as they contain separate and relevant evaluations of each of the leaders and of their parties. Again, we have been conservative here, assessing the impact of leaders only after controlling for other party evaluations, but it was clear in Chapter 6 that where the popularity of leaders and parties diverge, and they often do, voters follow parties rather than leaders. This is not to say that a popular leader is not an asset, but that the asset is one that makes a only marginal difference to vote totals. A marginal change can make a difference between whether a government wins a majority or not. In that respect, the return of the Fianna Fáil-PD government was secured by the popularity at the time of the leaders of those two parties relative to alternatives. However, there is nothing to suggest that the victory was essentially that of the Ahern-Harney parties rather than of Fianna Fáil and the Progressive Democrats. Fianna Fáil certainly placed a huge emphasis on its leader, Bertie Ahern, in 2002, but we have shown here that perceptions of the advantage this conferred have been exaggerated.

The local campaigns, centred rather more on candidates, supplemented the leader focused national campaigns. The data available here allowed us to detail contact by specific parties and specific candidates, to assess the extent of the door-to-door canvass and to establish how closely such contacts are related to vote choice. Local campaigns seem to contribute to votes for all parties, with a visit to a voter's home associated significantly with support for the party in question. This is particularly so for the smaller parties, who are forced by the lack of resources to campaign only in some areas and naturally can be expected to pick those areas in which they are likely to do well. Campaign contact is also important for the larger parties, whose canvassing is much less targeted. It is quite possible that the occurrence of contact indicates a number of other factors that are more important than the contact itself. This is particularly so given that candidate contact is so much more important than contact by party workers. There is ample evidence to show how candidates tend to win more support close to their home areas, areas where they will generally be better known and where they may well have done more constituency work (Sacks, 1976; Parker, 1982). It seems likely that candidate contact will be more frequent in areas closer to the candidate's home base and, if so, reports of contact will pick up the importance of locality in general as well as of the contact that specifically relates to a single visit. This is also a question for further research. In any case, such an interpretation does little to change the main conclusion drawn from our results, which is that party support depends in part on the local, personal linkages established by its candidates and party workers. This also helps to explain why the bigger parties remain bigger: they have a much more extensive presence in most areas.

This naturally brings us back to the second major question to be addressed here: What is the relative importance of candidates and parties as determinants of vote choice? This has been a long-standing puzzle in the analysis of Irish electoral behaviour. In contrast to most previous research, which could look only at a single measure, we were able to draw on a very wide variety of evidence. This does not all point to the same conclusions. The various analyses carried out in Chapters, 2, 8 and 9 point in somewhat different directions and the question of how many voters are attracted primarily to candidates and how many to parties cannot be answered precisely. What is very clear, though, is that elections are not simply about parties. When we ask them, the voters tell us that directly and it is also evident in the way ballots are marked, in the differences between voters' evaluations of candidates and their parties and in the strong tendency of voters to follow the candidate rather than the party when the two diverge. Candidate-centred electoral systems enable voters to put their trust in a candidate. Many Irish voters do that: the average voter rated their first choice at 79 on a 0–100 scale. At a time when politicians in general rate lower than just about any other occupational group in terms of public standing, this is significant. Conventional wisdom sees a personal rating of this kind as being a function of a candidate's ability, or perceived ability, to provide strong constituency (or sub-constituency) service, and our analysis in Chapter 9 certainly supports that interpretation.

On the question of how many voters are candidate-centred, much of our analysis seemed to indicate that a large minority of voters saw themselves as attracted primarily by candidates and a smaller minority saw themselves as essentially party-centred. Yet in Chapter 8 we saw that, for most voters, the best party has the best candidate(s). In contrast to the picture for leaders and their parties, there is little divergence between candidates and their parties. We also saw in Chapter 9 that even those who seem to be most candidate-centred are likely to make party choices that are predictable in terms of party-centred factors. Two explanations for this combination of results are offered. The first is that even candidate-centred voters have a predisposition to support a candidate from a particular party. This does not imply that they will go on to support the other candidates of that party, or that they would not follow that candidate should he or she leave their party, but it does mean that candidate-centred voters are not necessarily neutral when it comes to party. The second explanation is that the parties are able to build their own local reputations on the evaluations of their candidates. This may be particularly important for newer parties. The right candidate can bring in voters who will see themselves as supporting the party, even though the first step in the process is for those voters to support the candidate. The durability of such support is another matter. Can parties keep this support with a different candidate? Again, this requires more research, looking at the way party support changes as its candidates change.

What this analysis of party versus candidate also indicates is that while candidate-centred voters may be predisposed to support their

candidate's party, such voters are also more idiosyncratic in their voting behaviour than those who are party-centred. One of the difficulties
faced in any analyses of Irish voting behaviour is in making room for
the candidate factor in models of electoral behaviour. Candidate-centred
voting introduces an important degree of heterogeneity, meaning that
some people decide to vote on some factors and others decide to vote
on the basis of others. This is a problem for all electoral analysis in all
countries, but in Ireland it is greatly compounded by candidate effects.
We showed in Chapter 9 how great an impact this heterogeneity has
on our ability to explain party choice. In the case of the Fine Gael vote, for
instance, we found that our model identified party-centred Fine Gael
voters almost twice as effectively as candidate-centred ones. This is much
more pronounced for most of the smaller parties and even in Fianna Fáil,
there is a 25 percent improvement in our ability to identify a Fianna
Fáil voter as we move from candidate- to party-centred respondents.

Our analysis suggested that the balance between candidate and party
varies across parties. There is a marked contrast between Fianna Fáil
and Fine Gael. In Fianna Fáil, party is much the stronger element: more
of its first preference voters go on to vote for further candidates of the
party, more of them rate party above candidate and fewer report, when
asked directly, that the candidate is most important to them. Furthermore, our Fianna Fáil model was relatively successful at predicting a
Fianna Fáil choice among candidate-centred voters. In contrast, Fine
Gael voters stand out in rating candidate above party, and our Fine
Gael party model failed to improve on a random guess in identifying
candidate-centred voters whose first preference choice was a candidate
from that party. This is consistent with the evidence of aggregate transfer votes that has generally suggested that Fianna Fáil voters show
more solidarity. Moreover, Fianna Fáil has long been seen as the stronger
and more cohesive force in Irish politics. Nevertheless, the difference
we have discovered should be seen against the background of the 2002
election. This election was a low point in Fine Gael fortunes, so its
weakness relative to its candidates might be expected. The gap could
well be much narrower on another occasion. More generally, among
the other parties it is the Greens and Sinn Féin who have a stronger
party-based appeal to their voters and the Labour Party and the PDs
whose appeal is less party centred. Of course, the Greens and Sinn Féin
also have much more distinctive party images, as we have seen in
Chapter 3.

We must be careful in drawing conclusions on the evidence of just
this single election study. Most recent Irish elections have shown a

trend towards or away from a particular party. We have shown how the findings here fit with the analyses of previous elections, based on opinion polls as well as on studies such as Eurobarometer. There were obviously some unusual features about 2002, such as the unusually high level of satisfaction with the government, the gap between the party leaders in terms of approval, and the exaggerated lead for Fianna Fáil over its rivals in the polls. The tide certainly ran against Fine Gael in 2002, and this may mean that as a party Fine Gael looks weaker than it might have had this study been done in 1997, or in 2007. There were other features of 2002 that are not common to all Irish elections, such as the free-for-all competition between potential coalition partners. We expect later election studies to discover that some of our findings are unique to 2002, but we would argue that, in broad terms, what we have found in 2002 would also have been found in 1997 and will be found in 2007.

Essentially, these results indicate that electoral competition in Ireland is largely between parties who have little ideological or sociological identity, and where support still owes more to long established loyalties than to any other factor. At the same time, these parties rely significantly on their candidates. Many voters put more emphasis on, and have more faith in, the candidate who represents them rather than the party. While newer parties resist elements of this characterisation, at least to the extent that they have a clearer identity and focus, all parties must be alert to the importance of their candidates. What does this mean for our assessment of the capacity of Irish elections to involve the electorate, and to aggregate and reflect the wishes and preferences of the voters and to hold politicians accountable?

Irish elections have been performing badly with regard to involving the electorate, with declining turnout since 1982 and, currently, a low rank in the international turnout stakes (in 2002 Irish general election turnout was ninth from the bottom among the 25 members states of the EU). Our analysis locates the sources of low turnout in the twin processes of facilitation and mobilisation. It also locates the responsibility for these two processes – among election policy makers and administrators in the case of the former and, for the latter, among party leaders and political activists.

Schattschneider started his classic work on party government (1942: 1) by asserting that 'modern democracy is unthinkable save in terms of the parties'. He was writing about the USA, but the assertion has been equally true of Ireland. Parties organise the government's majority in parliament through the whip system, ensuring that it is a party government that is formed and a party government's legislation that makes up the bulk of legislation passed by the Dáil. However, at the level of what Key (1966) called 'the parties in the electorate', the unthinkable is now a little closer to the forefront of our consciousness. Parties are becoming weaker, in terms both of how people vote and the reasons they vote as they do. They may still determine how things work after the election, but there are serious questions to be asked about how effectively parties can express the will of the electorate. In this respect there are further democratic purposes we might look for in elections. Powell (2000) identifies two: the mandate function and the function of accountability. The mandate function provides a link between the broad policy preferences of the electorate and the future direction of government. Parties can bring this about by offering competing platforms and whichever party wins will then implement its programme. This does, of course, also require that voters choose parties on the basis of these programmes (Katz, 1986b) and, while there is evidence that parties do make great efforts to implement those platforms in office (Mansergh, 2004; Mansergh and Thomson, 2007), in recent years there has been considerable unpredictability when it comes to the question of which parties will govern together after the election.

The Fianna Fáil+PD government in 1989 and the Fianna Fáil+Labour coalition in 1992 were post-election deals that surprised many observers and even the 1997 Fianna Fáil+PD government required the support of independents. The post-election coalition in 2002 was different, at least in as much as the two parties expressed a willingness to govern together again even though they ran separate campaigns, with the Progressive Democrats being particularly critical of their erstwhile partners. We have also found little in the evidence considered here to suggest that voters choose their parties on broad policy grounds. This is really possible only when policies can be linked together and made into a coherent package, labelled in terms of values or, more commonly, ideologies, as otherwise the information requirements placed on the average voter will be unrealistic, a point made by one of the most influential proponents of the mandate theory, Anthony Downs (1957). The fact that voters do not choose on policy grounds is not necessarily because they are unwilling; it may be that they are not offered much of a choice. There is a realisation that some parties are centre right and some centre left, so that could be a significant basis for choice, but most voters see themselves as centrist and many reject the concepts of left and right altogether, or are unfamiliar with them. Nor is it at all clear what 'left' and 'right' mean in terms of policy. This is understandable given that the two largest parties, the twin poles of alternative governments, are both perceived to be on the right. It is in this respect that the Irish party system remains unusual, and it is hardly surprising to find that vote choice is relatively particularistic (van der Eijk *et al.*, 1992).

The mandate function is forward looking. Accountability is backward looking. Elections give the electorate the opportunity to hold politicians accountable. The election is judgement day, when the electorate considers whether or not to trust their politicians again on the basis of what they have done since the previous election. This does not require any great knowledge on the part of the voter. Certainly, it makes fewer demands on voter knowledge than does the mandate model. The holding of governments to account seems to have operated in Irish elections quite effectively – or a least quite frequently – given the turnover in governments since 1973. Even so, all elections since 1987 have returned a Fianna Fáil-led government. Without a coherent and cohesive opposition, it is probably the case now that elections do not give the electorate as much opportunity to replace a government as they once did. This process also demands that voters choose on the basis of governmental performance, and while we certainly find firm evidence that voters take this into account, it is also obvious from the findings in this book that this is far from being the most powerful determinant of the vote.

These two functions, the forward-looking one of policy choice and the backward-looking one of accountability, can be thought about at two quite different levels; the national and the local. At national level, voters may choose a government on the basis of what it might do, or return a government for a second term because it has done a good job. At local level the voter selects a candidate. This can be done to promote a local policy package, or it can be done because a candidate has performed well in the previous term. The concern in either case is with the well-being of the voter's own area. This is perfectly rational from the voter's perspective, if somewhat old fashioned as a theory of representation (Thomassen, 1994). Indeed, given an expectation that whoever governs will make little difference at national level, it might be the only rational basis for voting.[1] However, it does create a difficulty if we want to trace a clear connection between local choices and national *policy* priorities.[2] Many theorists argue that democracy requires strong coherent parties that offer clear policy alternatives and implement them: the so-called Responsible Party Model of government (Ranney, 1962). But this concept of the electoral process will still be invalid if the electorate makes its choices on the basis of the candidate that can best deliver concrete benefits for their home area.

Our evidence indicates that parties can serve to link the local with the national, so that local judgments are translated into national ones. The fact is that, for most voters, the best party and the best candidate coincide. In any event, whichever of these motivations is primary for the individual voter, the TDs elected in this process do address the national issues of choosing a Taoiseach and approving the membership of the government when they get to Dáil Eireann, and they do so along party lines. And so the part-fact, part-fiction of responsible and accountable party government is maintained. It is vital, however, that those who seek to interpret and understand Irish elections should keep the underlying complexities of Irish electoral behaviour firmly in mind. There is a potential conflict between the local and the national, and political leaders and party strategists know only too well that while party-oriented voters can generate a swing that may put them and their party into power, any gains made in this realm will be secure only as long as their winning candidates continue to meet the needs of their constituencies.

Notes

1 Although a majority feel that who is in government does make a difference: see Q.10, Appendix IV.
2 Of course there are other forms or styles of representation: Thomassen (1994: 21–2) cites service responsiveness – the ombudsman role – and allocation responsiveness, getting things for the area, both of which are important in Ireland, although only ministers are likely to be able to achieve the latter directly.

Appendix I: details of the survey

The Irish National Election Study (INES) 2002 is based on a survey of a representative sample of Irish people. The survey was conducted by the Economic and Social Research Institute (ESRI) after the election and was based on face-to-face interviews. Persons 18 years or older were interviewed and no regions of the country were excluded from the sample frame.

Persons residing in institutions were excluded. Military personnel were included provided they lived at a private address and were excluded if their primary address was an institution. Note that almost all military personnel in Ireland live in private households. In total, approximately 2.7 percent of the Irish population live in institutions. No other persons were excluded from the sampling frame.

A three-stage clustered sampling approach was used for sample selection. In the first instance a random sample of PSUs (Primary Sampling Units) was selected. In the second, a random sample of households was selected. In the third, a random person within the household was selected. The sampling frame used was the most up-to-date national electoral register. Electors are recorded in the electoral list in 'polling books'. For sample selection purposes these polling books are reconstituted into area units known as District Electoral Divisions. There is a total of 3,400 DEDs in Ireland. These DEDs are the most spatially disaggregated area units for which census data are available and form the standard PSU building block for random sample selection. Once the Electoral Register had been restructured into the District Electoral Division structure a random sample of 220 PSUs was selected. Each PSU was made up of the DED or aggregate thereof using a minimum population threshold criteria. A sample of 25 addresses was selected from within each of the 220 PSUs. This was the second stage of sampling. Households were randomly selected from within the PSU. Individuals were then selected from within households using the 'next-birthday' rule. This was the third stage of sample selection.

A sample line was designated non-sample if any of the following applied: it was a non-residential sample point; all members of the household were ineligible; the housing unit was vacant; or there was no answer at the housing unit after five call-backs. No non-sample replacement methods were used. No letter was sent to the respondent prior to the study and there were no payments or gifts used. However, as an incentive, respondents were entered into a lottery, which had eight prizes.

Response rate

Total number of sample lines issued	4674
Number of refusals	909
Number never contacted (no contact)	216 (could not locate/demolished)
Other non-response	834 (not available during fieldwork; ill; bereavement in household etc.)
Number of lines of non-sample	166 selected but not issued
Total number of completed interview	2715 (52 of which not used in analysis due to incomplete data)
Total number of questionnaires analysed	2663
Response rate	60% (2663/(909+834+2715))

Sample weights

The weights were constructed using a minimum information loss routine with marginal constraints based on age, gender, principal economic status, region, marital status, level of educational attainment, household size (number of persons aged 18 years and over). Because the PSUs were selected from the electoral register, larger households had a disproportionately higher probability of selection than smaller households. This was addressed in the reweighting scheme by including a dimension on household size. This weighting scheme adjusts for both design and non-response effects. A further adjustment was made to bring the vote shares of the parties in line with recorded vote shares in the election. This weighting was used in all analyses in the book, except for the analyses in Chapter 9 where no weights were used.

Just over 150 interviewers worked on the survey. Approximately 40 percent are male. In terms of age distribution, approximately 20 percent are aged less than 30 years. A further 40 percent are aged between 31 and 40 years and the remainder are aged 51 or over. In terms of interviewer training, the following points are relevant. A pilot stage was held for the project. This involved interviewer briefing for half a day. Debriefing took place after the pilot. Interviewers were given half a day briefing for the main study. The first three completed questionnaires from each interviewer were checked immediately by data coding staff with detailed written comments sent back to the interviewer. Rebriefing of selected interviewers was carried out where necessary.

When were the interviews completed?

Figure I.1 shows when the INES interviews were carried out. Because these were face to face with individuals in designated households they could not be completed within a few weeks. However, interviews started a few days after the election and 20 percent were completed within the first month, two-thirds within two months, 90 percent were completed within two and a half months, and almost every interview was carried out within four months. The fact that interviewing was done over so many weeks obviously gives rise to concerns that there may be biases in the responses associated with the time of the interviews. Accordingly,

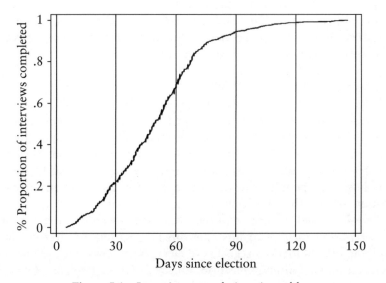

Figure I.1 Interview completion timetable

some simple checks were carried out. Public support for Fianna Fáil and satisfaction with the government had declined very sharply by the time that the first post election poll was published in late September (*Irish Times*, 28 September 2002). It was seen to be due to severe cutbacks in government spending after the election. This might well mean that fewer Fianna Fáil voters would have admitted their support for the party as it became clear there was no money left in the government's coffers. However, there is no significant relationship in our data between the timing of the interview and support for Fianna Fáil. Nor do we find any link between voting and the timing of interviews, using either the report of voting or the validated voting measure.

How long did each survey take to complete?

On average, each survey took an hour to complete. Half of the surveys were completed between 54 and 106 minutes. One quarter took less than 54 minutes and one quarter took more than 106 minutes, with five percent taking less than 25 minutes another 5 percent taking more than 1 hour 35 minutes.

Reported turnout

In the 2002 Irish National Election Study, 81 percent of respondents report that they voted. However, the level of electoral participation is 69 percent.[1] Ireland is not unique, as over-reporting of participation is common in many countries. On average, reported turnout exceeds official turnout by 26 percentage points in the British general elections, 40 percentage points in the American presidential elections, 42 percent in New Zealand general elections (Karp and Brockington, 2005; see also Swaddle and Heath, 1989).

The most common explanation for over-reporting is that some people give a socially desirable answer in order to cast themselves in a positive light. That is, people regard voting as a right and a responsibility of citizens and are reluctant to admit to an interviewer that they failed to carry out this duty. That said, over-reporting may also be due to a sampling bias: people who do vote are more willing to participate in election studies than those who do not vote.

We established the degree of over-reporting by comparing a respondent's reported turnout against the official registers of electors. In Ireland, the official marked registers of electors are available for inspection up to six months after an election. Of the 2663 respondents, 69 percent correctly reported that they voted and 16 percent correctly reported that they did not vote. A very small percentage of respondents – 3 percent – voted even though they reported that they did not. Comparing reported turnout with the official records allows us to identify the 12 percent of respondents who did not vote yet reported to the INES that they did vote.

It should be noted that the sampling procedure (by household) meant that when two members of a household share the same name it was not possible to identify the respondent. For example, the voting register may indicate that two individuals named Patricia Murphy live in the same household. One of these may have participated in the INES and one may have voted. Since it is not possible to distinguish between these two individuals, we code the respondent as having voted.

We found that over-reporting was close to random in terms of demographic and political features (see Table I.1) There is a lot of

Table I.1   Over-reporting of turnout by various demographic and political characteristics

	Validated voters	Reported voters	Difference
Old	53.2	53.4	−0.3
Young	46.9	46.6	0.3
Middle class	49.7	49.9	−0.3
PB	6.9	6.8	0.0
Farmer	10.1	9.6	0.5
Skilled workers	10.3	10.5	−0.2
Unskilled workers	23.2	23.2	0.0
Rural	53.2	52.7	0.5
Urban	46.8	47.4	−0.6
Less educated	41.1	41.7	−0.6
More educated	58.9	58.3	0.6
Male	47.6	47.5	0.1
Female	52.4	52.5	−0.1
FF	44.7	45.0	−0.3
FG	22.1	22.1	0.1
Green	4.4	4.3	0.1
Lab	9.4	9.3	0.2
PD	3.2	3.1	0.1
SF	4.9	5.0	0.0
Ind	9.9	10.0	0.0
Others	1.4	1.3	0.1
Total	100	100	

Note: Age, urban-rural and educated split at median: see Chapter 9.

research that tries to assess the impact of this over-reporting our ability to model vote choice and turnout, much of it finding that the over-reporting does not introduce any serious bias into the results. Our own preliminary analyses suggested that is also true of the Irish case but all analyses reported here of voters are limited to validated voters only.

Note

1 It should be emphasised that the basis used in calculating these turnout estimates is the electoral register. Of course, any errors in the register would distort the estimate of turnout, the most likely distortion being an underestimation of turnout because of a surplus of names on the register (O'Malley, 2001). There is in fact evidence of the occurrence of such a surplus since the early 1980s, indicating that our electoral-register-based estimates of turnout may be too low – probably by, on average, about 5 percentage points. Fortunately, the problems posed by inaccuracies in the electoral register can be overcome by using the voting-age population (VAP) as the basis for calculating turnout. Crucially the corrected figures confirm that there was a downward trend in turnout between 1981 and 1997, the cumulative drop over that period being 10 percentage points. However, the corrected figures also indicate that, rather than there suffering a further drop of 3 to 4 percentage points in 2002, as the official figures suggest, turnout actually increased marginally in 2002 (by one percentage point) bringing turnout in the election that is the main focus of this book to 69 percent. In Chapter 10 we used the voting-age population figures when dealing specifically with general election turnout but we have continued to use the figures based on the electoral register when comparing turnout across different electoral contests in Ireland (because we do not have voting-age population estimates for all the years involved). For a full discussion of these issues see Kavanagh and Sinnott, 2007.

Appendix II: the Irish electoral system

Electoral systems govern how people cast their votes and how votes translate into seats in parliament. The important features of the Irish electoral system are the electoral formula (proportional representation by means of the single transferable vote (PR-STV)) and multi-member constituencies (or district magnitude) In Ireland, PR-STV, was first applied in January 1919 for the election of Sligo Corporation. Proportional representation has written into the 1922 Constitution and the 1923 Electoral Act confirmed PR-STV as the Free State's electoral system. The 1937 Constitution outlines the electoral system in Article 16.2. In 1959, and again in 1968, Fianna Fáil governments sought to replace PR-STV with the plurality system, but the Irish people rejected both proposals.

From the voter's point of view, the PR-STV system is quite straightforward. The ballot paper lists the constituency candidates in alphabetical order and voters are required to indicate their order of preference among the candidates. Voters may indicate as many or as few preferences as they wish. However, each voter has only one vote ('single transferable vote'). The preference ordering on the ballot is a set of instructions to the returning officer as to what to do with that vote if a more preferred candidate does not require it. Before considering why a candidate may not require a vote, it is necessary to outline how the system works.

While the PR-STV is straightforward from the voter's perspective, the counting of votes and the allocation of seats is more complicated. Since the purpose of this Appendix is to provide a brief outline of the Irish electoral system, readers interested in a comprehensive discussion should consult Sinnott (2005). A candidate must win a quota to be sure of election. The calculation of the quota takes account of the number of valid votes and the number of seats available in the constituency:

Quota = [(Total Number of Valid Votes)/(Number of Seats + 1)] + 1

In a three-seat constituency, the quota is equal to a quarter of the valid votes plus one. Hence, only three candidates can reach the quota. For example, in a three-seat constituency, with four contesting candidates and 100 valid votes, three candidates can each achieve the quota of 26 votes leaving the fourth candidate with 22 votes. The quota reduces as the number of seats available to be won increases. In a four-seat constituency, the quota is equal to a fifth of the valid vote plus one, and in a five-seat constituency, the quota is a sixth of the valid vote plus one. The Constitution sets 3 as the minimum number of seats in a constituency and current practice has settled on 5 as the maximum.

The transfer of votes occurs when a candidate has a surplus of votes or when a candidate is eliminated. The returning officer deems a candidate elected when his or her number of votes is greater than (or equal to) the quota. The surplus is equal to the number of votes in excess of the quota won by the elected candidate. These surplus votes are not required to elect the candidate. The returning officer therefore transfers the surplus votes according to the preference ordering indicated on the ballots.

If no candidate exceeds the quota, the returning officer eliminates the candidate with the fewest votes. Since such a candidate cannot be elected, his or her votes are transferred to the remaining candidates in line with the next preference indicated on each ballot. It is important to emphasise that votes transfer only to candidates who are available to receive them. Elected or eliminated candidates do not receive transfers. For instance, when a voter's most preferred candidate is eliminated, and if their second and third most preferred candidates have been elected at earlier counts, their fourth most preferred candidate receives their transfered vote.

Despite the low district magnitudes (Katz, 1980), PR-STV in Ireland delivers a high degree of proportionality 'virtually as high as that produced by electoral systems that have the achievement of proportionality as their sole aim' (Gallagher, 1996: 519). That said, the larger parties do slightly better than the smaller ones. On average, the shares of seats won by both Fianna Fáil and Fine Gael are slightly greater than their shares of the vote, while the reverse is the case for the other parties.

Appendix III: multivariate analysis of support for small parties and independents

Table III.1 Predicting the Green party vote

Coefficient	Green	Green	Green	Green	Green	Green	Green 1 or 2
Under 40	1.06	0.78	0.90	0.92	1.02	0.96	1.26
	−0.35	−0.29	−0.34	−0.35	−0.39	−0.38	−0.38
Middle cass	1.44	1.33	1.21	1.23	1.28	1.22	1.35
	−0.69	−0.66	−0.60	−0.62	−0.65	−0.62	−0.52
Self-employed	3.44**	3.15*	2.63	2.97*	3.31*	3.21*	3.08**
	−2.11	−2.01	−1.73	−1.95	−2.2	−2.14	−1.6
Farmer	0.74	0.92	0.94	1.00	1.00	1.01	0.87
	−0.83	−1.04	−1.07	−1.15	−1.15	−1.16	−0.72
Skilled	1.17	0.96	1.05	1.07	1.13	1.07	0.59
	−0.85	−0.73	−0.8	−0.82	−0.87	−0.82	−0.38
Urban	2.07**	1.97*	2.02*	1.78	1.74	1.67	1.69*
	−0.73	−0.74	−0.78	−0.71	−0.69	−0.66	−0.51
More educ	2.80**	2.63**	2.56*	2.54*	2.40*	2.51*	2.04*
	−1.3	−1.27	−1.25	−1.24	−1.18	−1.24	−0.76
Female	1.43	1.25	1.36	1.46	1.49	1.49	0.98
	−0.46	−0.43	−0.48	−0.53	−0.54	−0.54	−0.27
Nationalist		1.04	1.10	1.02	1.03	1.03	1.12
		−0.16	−0.17	−0.17	−0.17	−0.17	−0.14
Secular-religious		0.80	0.87	0.92	0.95	0.94	0.88
		−0.13	−0.15	−0.16	−0.17	−0.17	−0.12
Pro environ	1.98***	1.79***	1.79***	1.77***	1.80***	1.75***	1.51***
	−0.33	−0.31	−0.31	−0.31	−0.32	−0.31	−0.20
Pro EU	0.70**	0.70**	0.71**	0.70**	0.70**	0.69**	0.67***
	−0.11	−0.11	−0.11	−0.12	−0.12	−0.12	−0.09

	(1)	(2)	(3)	(4)	(5)	(6)	(7)
Pro business		0.82	0.86	0.89	0.89	0.88	0.77*
		-0.14	-0.15	-0.16	-0.16	-0.16	-0.11
More/less equality		0.69**	0.71**	0.75*	0.76	0.74*	0.75**
		-0.11	-0.12	-0.13	-0.13	-0.13	-0.1
Left–right		0.84*	0.85	0.86	0.86	0.86	0.91
		-0.08	-0.08	-0.09	-0.09	-0.09	-0.07
Party attachment			7.37***	9.47***	7.93***	7.32***	4.23**
			-4.57	-6.18	-5.37	-5	-2.65
Economy				0.83	0.84	0.86	0.86
				-0.15	-0.15	-0.16	-0.12
Health				1.07	1.1	1.1	0.93
				-0.19	-0.2	-0.2	-0.13
Housing				0.66***	0.67**	0.67**	0.81*
				-0.1	-0.11	-0.11	-0.1
Crime				1.18	1.21	1.19	1.15
				-0.22	-0.23	-0.23	-0.17
Leader best					1.94	2	1.93*
					-0.91	-0.95	-0.73
Party contacted home						3.03*	4.49***
						-1.87	-2.26
Constant	0.00***	0.00***	0.00***	0.00***	0.00***	0.00***	0.01***
	0	-0.01	0	0	0	0	-0.01
Observation	915	915	915	915	915	915	915
R²	0.064	0.180	0.207	0.231	0.236	0.244	0.216

Table III.2 Predicting the Progressive Democrat vote (cell entries odds ratios and standard errors)

Coefficient	PD	PD	PD	PD	PD	PD	PD 1 or 2
Under 40	1.78	1.69	1.72	1.61	1.92	2.20*	1.86**
	−0.64	−0.66	−0.69	−0.65	−0.8	−0.92	−0.58
Middle class	2.66*	2.36	2.45	2.41	1.99	2.19	3.07**
	−1.52	−1.38	−1.44	−1.44	−1.19	−1.36	−1.36
Self-employed	2.01	1.84	2.16	2.54	2.33	2.13	1.29
	−1.62	−1.5	−1.78	−2.11	−1.92	−1.82	−0.89
Farmer	3.5	3.66	3.36	4.06*	3.31	2.86	1.45
	−2.72	−2.92	−2.76	−3.39	−2.77	−2.47	−0.98
Skilled	0.98	0.99	1.13	1.08	0.86	0.93	0.95
	−0.88	−0.89	−1.03	−1	−0.8	−0.87	−0.64
Urban	2.15*	2.08*	1.99	2	2.03	1.84	1.83*
	−0.88	−0.88	−0.85	−0.86	−0.88	−0.81	−0.6
More educ	1.56	1.49	1.43	1.41	1.27	1.19	0.93
	−0.72	−0.72	−0.72	−0.71	−0.64	−0.62	−0.34
Female	0.62	0.73	0.76	0.78	0.71	0.61	0.69
	−0.2	−0.25	−0.27	−0.28	−0.26	−0.23	−0.19
Nationalist		0.91	0.89	0.89	0.89	0.87	0.83
		0.14	0.14	0.14	0.14	0.15	0.14
Secular–religious		0.9	0.91	0.91	0.88	0.87	0.96
		−0.15	−0.15	−0.15	−0.15	−0.16	−0.13
Pro environ		0.94	0.96	0.96	0.97	1	0.97
		−0.16	−0.16	−0.17	−0.17	−0.18	−0.13
Pro EU		1.34	1.39*	1.36	1.36	1.37	1.11
		−0.25	−0.26	−0.26	−0.27	−0.28	−0.16

	(1)	(2)	(3)	(4)	(5)	(6)	(7)
Pro business		1.52**	1.50**	1.53**	1.49**	1.45*	1.19
		−0.28	−0.28	−0.29	−0.28	−0.28	−0.17
More/less equality		1.09	1.05	1.01	0.95	0.9	0.91
		−0.17	−0.17	−0.17	−0.17	−0.16	−0.12
Left–right		1.05	1.04	1.04	1.02	1.04	1.07
		−0.1	−0.1	−0.1	−0.1	−0.1	−0.08
Party attachment			7.56***	6.80***	6.95***	5.76**	2.9
			−5.13	−4.82	−5.05	−4.36	−2.07
Economy				1.22	1.22	1.3	1
				−0.23	−0.24	−0.26	−0.15
Health				1.13	1.12	1.16	1.21
				−0.21	−0.21	−0.22	−0.17
Housing				0.85	0.87	0.86	0.87
				−0.14	−0.15	−0.15	−0.11
Crime				1.31	1.28	1.24	1
				−0.27	−0.27	−0.27	−0.16
Leader best					2.59**	3.00**	2.69***
					−1.14	−1.37	−0.94
Party contacted home						4.58***	5.68***
						−2.04	−2.03
Constant	0.00***	0.00***	0.00***	0.00***	0.00***	0.00***	0.01***
	−0.01	0	0	0	−0.01	−0.01	−0.01
Observation	534	534	534	534	534	534	534
R²	0.073	0.107	0.133	0.148	0.163	0.196	0.160

Table III.3 Predicting the Sinn Féin vote (cell entries odds ratios and standard errors)

Coefficient	SF	SF	SF	SF	SF	SF 1 or 2
Under 40	4.56***	4.16***	4.01***	3.93***	4.02***	4.16***
	-1.79	-1.77	-1.94	-1.92	-1.98	-2.2
Middle class	0.6	0.81	1.04	0.99	0.99	1.05
	-0.24	-0.35	-0.54	-0.52	-0.52	-0.59
Self-employed	1	0.97	1.51	1.59	1.61	1.3
	-0.6	-0.61	-1.09	-1.16	-1.18	-0.97
Farmer	1.16	1.11	1.66	1.68	1.61	1.41
	-0.66	-0.66	-1.16	-1.2	-1.16	-1.09
Skilled	0.66	0.68	1.31	1.28	1.28	1.44
	-0.39	-0.42	-0.88	-0.86	-0.86	-1.03
Urban	1.44	1.3	1.44	1.39	1.39	1.3
	-0.48	-0.46	-0.59	-0.59	-0.59	-0.58
More educ	0.68	0.7	0.64	0.66	0.67	0.74
	-0.25	-0.27	-0.28	-0.29	-0.3	-0.34
Female	1.29	1.3	1.76	1.74	1.7	1.6
	-0.42	-0.44	-0.7	-0.68	-0.67	-0.67
Nationalist		1.99***	1.75***	1.83***	1.80***	1.79***
		0.37	0.35	0.37	0.37	0.39
Secular–religious		1.02	1.19	1.25	1.25	1.22
		-0.18	-0.24	-0.25	-0.25	-0.26
Pro environ		1.02	0.97	0.97	0.96	0.9
		-0.16	-0.17	-0.17	-0.17	-0.17
Pro EU		0.73**	0.73*	0.78	0.79	0.85
		-0.11	-0.13	-0.14	-0.14	-0.15

	(1)	(2)	(3)	(4)	(5)	(6)
Pro business		1.06	1.15	1.15	1.16	1.14
		-0.17	-0.21	-0.22	-0.22	-0.22
More/less equality		1.1	1.26	1.3	1.28	1.3
		-0.17	-0.23	-0.25	-0.25	-0.27
Left–right		0.74***	0.74***	0.74***	0.75***	0.76**
		-0.07	-0.08	-0.08	-0.08	-0.08
Party attachment			149.97***	164.87***	142.98***	72.58***
			-113.92	-128.34	-111.23	-57.87
Economy				0.76	0.78	0.76
				-0.16	-0.17	-0.18
Health				0.86	0.86	0.89
				-0.16	-0.16	-0.17
Housing				0.93	0.93	0.94
				-0.17	-0.16	-0.17
Crime				1.03	1.04	1.04
				-0.21	-0.21	-0.23
Leader best					1.85	2.01
					-0.95	-1.09
Party contacted home						9.10***
						-4.03
Constant	0.00***	0.02***	0.01***	0.01***	0.01***	0.00***
	0	-0.02	-0.01	-0.01	-0.01	-0.01
Observation	947	947	947	947	947	947
R^2	0.062	0.147	0.318	0.329	0.333	0.393

Table III.4 Predicting the Independent vote (cell entries odds ratios and standard errors)

Coefficient	IND	IND	IND	IND	IND	IND	IND 1 or 2
Under 40	0.91	0.9	0.88	0.89	0.87	0.83	0.79
	-0.18	-0.19	-0.19	-0.2	-0.19	-0.19	-0.15
Middle class	0.77	0.78	0.8	0.74	0.73	0.69	0.65**
	-0.18	-0.19	-0.19	-0.18	-0.18	-0.18	-0.14
Self-employed	0.78	0.84	0.86	0.89	0.78	0.71	0.72
	-0.3	-0.32	-0.34	-0.35	-0.32	-0.3	-0.25
Farmer	0.45*	0.44**	0.44**	0.44**	0.41**	0.44*	0.45***
	-0.18	-0.18	-0.18	-0.18	-0.17	-0.19	-0.15
Skilled	0.40**	0.40**	0.37**	0.35**	0.28***	0.27***	0.42***
	-0.17	-0.17	-0.16	-0.15	-0.13	-0.13	-0.14
Urban	1.09	1.1	1.08	1.04	1.03	1.01	0.9
	-0.21	-0.22	-0.22	-0.22	-0.22	-0.22	-0.16
More educ	1.2	1.26	1.25	1.24	1.24	1.32	1.38*
	-0.27	-0.29	-0.29	-0.29	-0.29	-0.32	-0.27
Female	0.94	0.9	0.85	0.86	0.85	0.84	0.94
	-0.18	-0.18	-0.17	-0.17	-0.17	-0.18	-0.16
Nationalist		0.98	0.99	1.02	1.02	0.98	0.97
		0.09	0.09	0.10	0.10	0.10	0.08
Secular–religious		1.01	1.01	1.04	1.05	1.01	0.98
		-0.1	-0.1	-0.11	-0.11	-0.11	-0.09
Pro environ		0.86	0.89	0.88	0.89	0.9	0.92
		-0.08	-0.08	-0.08	-0.08	-0.09	-0.07
Pro EU		0.89	0.91	0.97	0.98	0.98	0.89
		-0.08	-0.08	-0.09	-0.09	-0.1	-0.07

	(1)	(2)	(3)	(4)	(5)	(6)	(7)
Pro business		0.94	0.94	0.93	0.93	0.93	0.97
		-0.08	-0.08	-0.08	-0.09	-0.09	-0.07
More/less equality		1.01	1.01	1.07	1.09	1.1	1.07
		-0.09	-0.09	-0.1	-0.1	-0.11	-0.09
Left–right		0.93	0.94	0.97	0.96	0.96	0.91*
		-0.05	-0.05	-0.05	-0.05	-0.06	-0.04
Party attachment			1.90***	1.81***	1.81***	1.85***	1.85***
			-0.37	-0.35	-0.36	-0.39	-0.31
Economy				0.76***	0.77**	0.77**	0.81**
				-0.08	-0.08	-0.09	-0.07
Health				0.86	0.87	0.85	0.81***
				-0.08	-0.09	-0.09	-0.07
Housing				0.87	0.85*	0.82**	0.92
				-0.08	-0.08	-0.08	-0.07
Crime				0.95	0.98	0.96	1.05
				-0.1	-0.1	-0.1	-0.09
Like no party					1.65	1.73	1.18
					-0.55	-0.6	-0.36
Like no leader					0.91	0.91	0.9
					-0.3	-0.32	-0.27
Called to home						5.91***	6.30***
						-1.41	-1.33
Constant	0.14***	0.20**	0.16***	0.16**	0.18**	0.13***	0.37
	-0.07	-0.13	-0.11	-0.12	-0.13	-0.1	-0.23
Observations	1191	1191	1191	1191	1180	1180	1180
R²	0.011	0.019	0.033	0.058	0.115	0.126	0.117

Appendix IV: questionnaire with frequency distributions (%)

Section A

A1 First, I'd like to ask you a general question. What do you think has been the single most important issue facing Ireland over the last five years?

A2 How good or bad a job do you think the Fianna Fáil/Progressive Democrat government did over the past five years in terms of [the Main issue mentioned at A1 above]. Did they do a:

Very good job	Good job	Bad job	Very bad job	Don't know
12	49	24	10	5

A3.1a Looking back on the recent general election campaign in May of this year, could you tell me if a candidate called at your home?

Yes	No	Don't know
56	35	9

A3.1b **Which candidates?**

FF	FG	GRN	LAB	PD	SF	IND	OTH
57	40	3	21	7	12	13	3

A3.2a **Did a party worker (or representative of an independent candidate) call to your home?**

Yes	No	Don't know
52	34	14

A3.2b **From which party(ies)?**

FF	FG	GRN	LAB	PD	SF	IND	OTH
62	49	8	28	9	21	22	4

A3.3a **Did a party worker (or representative of an independent candidate) phone your home?**

Yes	No	Don't know	No phone
6	82	9	3

A3.3b **From which party(ies)?**

FF	FG	GRN	LAB	PD	SF	IND	OTH
36	28	3	11	12	8	11	1

A4 **Did you read election leaflets put in your letterbox or given to you on the street/shopping centres etc?**

Yes	No	Don't know
64	36	+

A5 **Did you look at advertisements in newspapers on behalf of the candidates or parties?**

Yes	No	Don't know
49	51	+

A6 **Did you attend public meetings related to the election?**

Yes	No	Don't know
4	96	+

A7 **Did you look at candidates' election posters?**

Yes	No	Don't know
81	19	+

A8 **Did you see information about political parties and candidates on the Internet?**

Yes	No	Don't know
5	95	+

A9 **Did you discuss the election with family, friends or acquaintances?**

Yes	No	Don't know
72	28	+

A10   In general, do you think that being contacted by candidates or party workers is helpful or unhelpful for people making up their minds how to vote?

Helpful   Unhelpful
60   40

A11   I will now read out a series of statements. These cover a range of different areas and topics and I would like you to tell me how strongly you Disagree or Agree with each. For each statement I read please tell me whether or not you Strongly disagree; Disagree; Slightly disagree; Neither agree nor disagree; Slightly agree; Agree; or Strongly agree. [Int. show card A1]

Strongly disagree	Disagree	Slightly disagree	Neither agree nor disagree	Slightly agree	Agree	Strongly agree

1 It would be better if more people with strong religious beliefs held public office.

| 15 | 37 | 6 | 17 | 7 | 15 | 4 |

2 I would be willing to accept a cut in my standard of living in order to protect the environment.

| 8 | 29 | 9 | 11 | 16 | 25 | 3 |

3 Ordinary working people get their fair share of the nation's wealth.

| 19 | 44 | 8 | 5 | 7 | 15 | 2 |

4 Income tax should be increased for people on higher than average incomes.

| 3 | 19 | 6 | 9 | 10 | 41 | 12 |

5 There is one law for the rich and one for the poor.

| 3 | 11 | 2 | 7 | 11 | 44 | 23 |

6 There is nothing wrong with some people being a lot richer than others.

| 5 | 14 | 4 | 11 | 12 | 49 | 6 |

7 Many of the claims about environmental threats are exaggerated.

| 8 | 36 | 9 | 15 | 10 | 20 | 3 |

A12 I will now read out some more statements. Please tell me to what extent you Disagree or Agree with each statement [Int. show card A2]

Strongly disagree	Disagree	Slightly disagree	Neither agree nor disagree	Slightly agree	Agree	Strongly agree

1 There should be very strict limits on the number of immigrants coming to live in Ireland.

| 2 | 11 | 5 | 5 | 12 | 42 | 23 |

2 The British government should continue to have a lot of say in the way Northern Ireland is run.

| 10 | 32 | 8 | 15 | 8 | 24 | 2 |

3 The long term policy for Northern Ireland should be to reunify with the rest of Ireland.

| 1 | 7 | 3 | 18 | 10 | 48 | 13 |

4 The British government should declare its intention to withdraw from Northern Ireland at a fixed date in the future.

| 2 | 12 | 4 | 21 | 10 | 41 | 11 |

5 People should not have to put up with travellers' halting sites in their neighbourhood.

| 2 | 15 | 8 | 13 | 10 | 37 | 14 |

6 Asylum seekers should have the same rights to social services as Irish people.

| 10 | 24 | 9 | 9 | 12 | 33 | 3 |

7 My first priority is to provide for myself and my family, even if this means doing things that harm the environment.

| 5 | 34 | 10 | 14 | 10 | 23 | 5 |

8 I would be willing to pay much higher taxes in order to protect the environment.

| 11 | 35 | 10 | 11 | 16 | 15 | 2 |

Section B

B1   As you may know, many people did not vote in the recent
        general election. How about you? Did you vote in the general
        election in May?

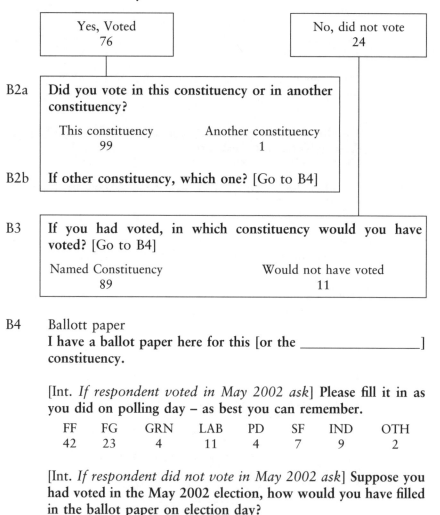

Yes, Voted 76	No, did not vote 24

B2a   **Did you vote in this constituency or in another
        constituency?**

        This constituency   Another constituency
               99   1

B2b   **If other constituency, which one? [Go to B4]**

B3   **If you had voted, in which constituency would you have
        voted? [Go to B4]**

        Named Constituency   Would not have voted
               89   11

B4   Ballott paper
        **I have a ballot paper here for this [or the _____]
        constituency.**

        [Int. *If respondent voted in May 2002 ask*] **Please fill it in as
        you did on polling day – as best you can remember.**

FF	FG	GRN	LAB	PD	SF	IND	OTH
42	23	4	11	4	7	9	2

        [Int. *If respondent did not vote in May 2002 ask*] **Suppose you
        had voted in the May 2002 election, how would you have filled
        in the ballot paper on election day?**

FF	FG	GRN	LAB	PD	SF	IND	OTH
23	20	9	20	11	3	6	9

        [Int: B5 and B6 to be filled out by interviewer]

B5   Interviewer: **Was ballot paper filled out?**

Yes [go to B9]	No
86	14

B6   **Was ballot paper not filled out on grounds of confidentiality or no interest in politics/doesn't vote?**

Refused on grounds of confidentiality	Doesn't vote/no interest in politics [go to B9]
47	53

B7   **If I gave you the ballot paper and asked you to fill it out and not show it to me but instead put it into a sealed envelope and give it back to me at the end of the interview would you be willing to fill it out?**

Yes [give ballot and go B9]	No [go to B8]
4	96

B8   **Could I ask which party you gave your first preference vote to? [go to B9]**

FF	FG	LAB	PD	GRN	SF	OTH	IND	Refused
18	6	4		4			1	67

[Int. ask B9 to B21 only if respondent voted in general election in may this year (yes at B1) – if respondent did not vote (no at B1) go to B22]

B9   **If you were voting today, would you give your first preference to the same party as you did in the election in May?**

Yes [go to B11]	No	Voted for Independent [go to B16]
94	4	2

B10   **Which party would you give your first preference to today? [go to B11]**

FF	FG	LAB	PD	GRN	SF	OTH	IND
33	17	17	7	10		1	14

B11 Did the political party to which you gave your first preference vote in the election ask people in this area to vote for their candidates in a particular order?

Yes	No	Don't know
24	67	9

B12 And did you vote for the candidates in that order?

Yes	No
36	64

B13 Which would you say was more important in deciding how you cast your first preference vote in the general election in May of this year – the party or the candidate him/herself?

Party	Candidate
38	62

B14 When did you decide which PARTY to give your first preference vote to in the general election in May this year?

Before the election campaign	In the first two weeks of the campaign	In the last week of the campaign	On the day of the election	Don't know
70	12	11	5	1

B15 Was there any time during the general election campaign when you seriously thought you might give your first preference vote to a different PARTY?

Yes	No	Don't know
15	82	3

B16 When did you decide which CANDIDATE to give your first preference vote to in the general election in May this year?

Before the election campaign	In the first two weeks of the campaign	In the last week of the campaign	On the day of the election	Don't know
65	13	14	7	1

B17 Was there any time during the general election campaign when you seriously thought you might give your first preference vote to a different CANDIDATE?

Yes	No	Don't know
16	82	2

B18   Thinking about the CANDIDATE you gave your first preference vote to, what was the *main* reason you voted for that particular CANDIDATE rather than any other CANDIDATE?
[Int. Please record *main* reason only. Do not leave blank]

B19   And what other reasons did you have for giving your first preference vote to that CANDIDATE?
[Int. If none write NONE. Do not leave blank]

B20   If this candidate had been running for any of the other parties would you still have given a first preference vote to him/her?

Yes	No	Depends on the other party
47	36	17

B21   On the day of the election how likely did you think it was that the candidate you gave your first preference vote to would be elected? Was it: [Int. show card B1]

Definitely/very likely	Quite likely	Not very likely	Definitely wouldn't
45	42	12	1

[Now go to Q24]

Int. ask B22 and B23 only if respondent did *not* vote in general election in May (No at B1)

B22   What was the *main* reason why you did not vote? Please describe as fully as possible.
[Int. Please record *main* reason only. Do not leave blank]

B23   Any other reasons why you did not vote? [Int. If none, write NONE. Do not leave blank]
[Int. make sure *all* respondents from B24 on]

B24   Did you vote in the previous general election in 1997?

Yes	No	Don't know/can't remember
70	26	5

B25   Which party did you give your first preference vote to in the 1997 general election?

FF	FG	GRN	LAB	PD	SF	IND	Don't know/can't remember
47	20	1	9	2	2	4	15

B26   **Did you vote in the referendum on the Treaty of Nice held in June of last year (2001)?**

Yes	No [go to B28]	DK/can't remember [go to B28]
54	41	5

B27   **Did you vote Yes, in favour or No, against the treaty?**

Yes, in favour of the treaty	No, against the treaty
41	59

B28   **There will be another referendum on the Nice Treaty before the end of this year. Imagine that you are voting in that referendum. Would you definitely vote in favour of the Nice Treaty, probably vote in favour, not sure either way, probably vote against or definitely vote against the Nice Treaty? [Int. show card B2]**

Definitely in favour of the Nice Treaty	Probably in favour of the Nice Treaty	Not sure either way	Probably against the Nice Treaty	Definitely against the Nice Treaty	Don't know
19	11	28	9	10	24

B29   **Did you vote in the recent Abortion referendum in March this year?**

Yes	No [go to B31]
64	36

B30   **Did you vote Yes, in favour or No, against the amendment?**

Yes, in favour of the amendment	No, against the amendment	Don't know/refused
35	57	9

[Int. If ballot paper *has* been filled out ask B31, B32 and B33. If ballot paper *has not* been filled out skip to B34]

B31   Candidates have different strengths and weaknesses. I would like you to think about the candidates to whom you gave your 1st, 2nd, 3rd and 4th preference votes on the ballot paper you have filled out for me a few moments ago. For each of these candidates I would like you to indicate on the scale on this card how good you think each candidate would be in terms of *working for this area*, where '0' means you think that candidate would not be very good at working for this area and '10' means you think that candidate would be very good at working for this area. [Show Card B3 and write in candidates names] For each candidate you may indicate any number between 0 and 10.

	0	1	2	3	4	5	6	7	8	9	10	DK	Missing
	not very						*very good*						
	good at						at working						
	working for						for this						
	this area						area						
Cand 1	+	1	+	1	1	5	4	9	17	12	32	4	15
Cand 2	1	1	1	2	2	8	8	11	15	9	16	7	20
Cand 3	1	1	1	3	4	9	8	9	10	5	9	8	34
Cand 4	1	1	1	2	3	6	4	5	4	3	3	6	63

B32   **And how good do you think each candidate would be in terms of contributing to national political debate? [Card B4]**

	0	1	2	3	4	5	6	7	8	9	10	DK	Missing
	not very						*very good* at						
	good at						contributing						
	contributing						to national						
	to national						political						
	political						debate						
	debate												
Cand 1	+	+	1	2	2	6	6	9	15	12	23	9	16
Cand 2	1	+	1	2	3	8	7	11	14	8	14	11	21
Cand 3	+	1	1	2	3	8	7	9	9	5	8	11	35
Cand 4	1	+	1	1	2	6	4	4	4	3	3	8	63

B33   **And how close do you think that each of these 4 candidates' political views are to your own? [Int. show card B5 write in candidate's names]**

	0	1	2	3	4	5	6	7	8	9	10	DK	Missing

	Political views are *not* very *close* to my own						Political views are *very* *close* to my own						
Cand 1	1	+	1	1	1	6	6	10	15	11	22	9	16
Cand 2	1	1	1	2	3	9	9	11	13	8	12	11	21
Cand 3	1	1	2	2	4	9	9	9	8	5	5	11	34
Cand 4	+	1	2	2	2	7	4	4	4	2	2	8	63

B34 **Thinking about the candidate whom you gave your first preference vote to, how often, if ever, have you spoken to the candidate?** [Int. Tick (✓) one box only]

Often	Occasionally	Once or twice	Never
19	24	26	31

B35 **Have you contacted any TDs, Councillors or Senators from this constituency, in the last 5 years?**

Yes	No	Don't know
28	71	1

B36 **Was this contact with TDs, Councillors or Senators?** [Int. Tick (✓) all that apply]

TDs	Councillors	Senators
62	31	7

B37 **Was the contact made by letter; phone; a visit to a clinic; or through another person?** [Int. Tick (✓) all that apply]

Letter	Phone	Visit to a clinic	Through another person
18	33	42	7

B38 **Was this contact on your own behalf; on behalf of a friend or family member; or on behalf of a committee or organisation to which you belong?** [Int. Tick (✓) all that apply]

Self	Family/friend	Committee/organisation
59	23	17

B39 **What was the main reason for the contact? Please describe as fully as possible.**

B40 **Thinking in general of the contact you had with these representatives, if similar circumstances arose in the future, do you think you would approach them or not?**

Yes	No	Don't know
87	10	3

B41   How interested would you say you are in politics – are you:
[Int. please tick (✓) one box only]

Very interested	Somewhat interested	Not very interested	Not at all interested
13	43	31	13

B42   **I will now read out some more statements. Please tell me to what extent you Disagree or Agree with each statement** [Int. show card B6]

Strongly disagree	Disagree	Slightly disagree	Neither agree nor disagree	Slightly agree	Agree	Strongly agree

1 So many people vote, my vote does not make much difference *to who is in government.*

22	46	7	5	6	13	3

2 Whatever I think about the parties and candidates, I really do think it is my duty to go out and vote in a general election.

3	5	1	6	7	43	35

3 So many people vote, my vote does not make much difference *to which candidates are elected.*

22	48	7	5	5	10	2

B43   **If you did not vote would you feel very guilty, fairly guilty, not very guilty or not guilty at all?**

Very guilty	Fairly guilty	Not very guilty	Not guilty at all
27	38	19	17

B44   **On this card I have a number of opposing statements. People who agree fully with the statement on the left would give a score of '0'. People who agree fully with the statement on the right would give a score of '10'. Other people would place themselves somewhere in between these two views. Where would you place yourself on these scales? The first scale is as follows:** [Int. show card B7, and tick (✓) one box on each line]

0	1	2	3	4	5	6	7	8	9	10	DK

1 Business and industry should be *strictly regulated* by the state. / Business and industry should be *entirely free from regulation* by the state.

0	1	2	3	4	5	6	7	8	9	10	DK
6	4	6	6	5	28	9	8	8	4	9	8

2 Ireland's membership of the European Union is a *bad* thing. / Ireland's membership of the European Union is a *good* thing.

0	1	2	3	4	5	6	7	8	9	10	DK
2	1	1	1	2	12	6	9	19	14	29	5

3 *Public or semi-state companies* are the best way to provide the services people need. / *Private enterprises* are the best way of providing the services people need.

0	1	2	3	4	5	6	7	8	9	10	DK
6	6	9	7	5	24	7	7	8	6	8	7

4 Most of business and industry should be *owned by the state*. / Most of business and industry should be *privately owned*.

0	1	2	3	4	5	6	7	8	9	10	DK
2	3	2	4	2	23	8	11	15	9	15	6

5 Homosexuality is *never* justified. / Homosexuality is *always* justified.

0	1	2	3	4	5	6	7	8	9	10	DK
9	5	4	3	3	30	5	5	6	4	13	13

6 European unification has already *gone too far*. / European unification should be *pushed further*.

0	1	2	3	4	5	6	7	8	9	10	DK
3	3	4	4	5	22	10	10	13	7	10	9

7 God definitely *does not* exist. / God definitely *does exist*.

0	1	2	3	4	5	6	7	8	9	10	DK
3	1	1	1	1	12	3	5	8	9	52	4

8a We should protect the environment even if this damages economic growth. / We should encourage economic growth even if this damages the environment.

0	1	2	3	4	5	6	7	8	9	10	DK
12	10	12	13	8	25	5	3	3	2	3	5

8b **How important is this issue of the balance between the environment and economic growth for you personally?**

Very important	Fairly important	Not very important	Not at all important
35	50	11	4

9a Ireland should do all it can to *unite fully* with the European Union.								Ireland should do all it can to *protect its independence* from the European Union.			
8	7	8	8	7	22	7	7	8	4	8	6

9b How important is this issue of the European Union for you personally?

Very important	Fairly important	Not very important	Not at all important
20	53	21	6

B45   Thinking about the leaders of the two main parties at the general election in May of this year – Bertie Ahern and Michael Noonan. At the time, which of these two did you think would make the best Taoiseach? [Int. tick (✓) one only]

Bertie Ahern	Michael Noonan
88	12

B46   I would like you to think about changes in the economy in the area around here since the general election 5 years ago in 1997. Do you think this area has been doing better than the rest of the country; the same as the rest of the country or worse than the rest of the country?

Better than the rest of the country	Same as the rest of the country	Worse than the rest of the country
18	60	22

B47   Who is most responsible for any improvements in the economic situation around here over the last five years?

Government policies in general	The efforts of local TDs	Neither	There have been no improvements around here
34	24	24	19

B48 | Which TD in particular? |

B49   Still thinking about the area around here, what is the most important local problem for you personally? [Int: If none write NONE and go to B53 below]

B50   Is there any one party better able to deal with this problem than
       the others?

Yes	No
26	75

B51   Which party?

FF	FG	GRN	LAB	PD	SF	IND	OTH
43	15	14	10	3	10	2	2

B52   Thinking about all the CANDIDATES who ran in this constituency
       in the recent election in May of this year, which of them, if any,
       do you think is best able to deal with this problem?

             Named candidate   None of the candidates

B53   Some things about a TD may be more important than others.
       On a scale of 0–10 where 0 means 'not very important' and 10
       means 'very important' how important do you think it is that a
       TD should: [Int. show card B8]

0	1	2	3	4	5	6	7	8	9	10	DK

Not very important   Very important

1 Be good at working for *this* area

1	+	+	1	1	3	2	5	12	14	58	3

2 Be good at contributing to national political debate

1	1	1	1	2	6	7	12	17	13	37	4

3 Be close to your political views

3	1	2	4	3	14	8	11	13	11	26	5

B54 **I will now read out some more statements. Please tell me to what extent you Disagree or Agree with each statement [Int. show card B9]**

Strongly disagree	Disagree	Slightly disagree	Neither agree nor disagree	Slightly agree	Agree	Strongly agree

.1 Sometimes politics and government seem so complicated that a person like me cannot really understand what is going on.

| 6 | 21 | 7 | 8 | 16 | 34 | 8 |

2 The ordinary person has no influence on politics.

| 7 | 30 | 11 | 6 | 13 | 27 | 6 |

3 I think I am better informed about politics and government than most people.

| 7 | 34 | 11 | 24 | 11 | 13 | 2 |

4 In today's world, an Irish government can't really influence what happens in this country.

| 9 | 43 | 11 | 12 | 10 | 13 | 2 |

5 It doesn't really matter which political party is in power, in the end things go on much the same.

| 5 | 26 | 10 | 7 | 14 | 32 | 6 |

B55 **We have a number of political parties in Ireland each of which would like to get your vote. How probable is it that you will ever give your first preference vote to the following parties? Please use the numbers on this scale to indicate your views, where '1' means 'not at all probable' and '10' means 'very probable'.**
[Int. show card B10 and tick (✓) one box on each line]
How probable is it that you will ever give your first preference vote to . . .

	1	2	3	4	5	6	7	8	9	10	Missing
Fianna Fáil	13	4	4	4	11	4	9	10	11	28	1
Fine Gael	18	8	8	8	16	8	8	6	5	12	2
Green Party	19	10	9	8	17	9	8	8	5	6	3
Labour	17	8	9	10	16	9	8	7	5	7	3
Progressive Democrats	20	9	8	9	16	9	9	7	5	5	3
Sinn Féin	38	11	8	6	12	5	5	4	4	6	3
An Independent candidate	15	6	5	6	17	8	9	10	8	13	3

SPLIT A (B56)

B56   Thinking in general about the main political parties in Ireland, can you tell me what you think each of the parties stand for. [Int. show card B11]. Take Fianna Fáil first. What do you think Fianna Fáil stands for. Anything else? And what do you think Fine Gael stands for?

SPLIT B (B57)

B57   Some people think that we should protect the environment even if this damages economic growth. Other people think that we should encourage economic growth even if this damages the environment. On the 0–10 scale below where would you place the views of each of the following PARTIES? [Put a tick (✔) in one box on each line. Show card B12]

	0	1	2	3	4	5	6	7	8	9	10	DK
	We should protect the environment even if this damages economic growth.								We should encourage economic growth even if this damages the environment.			
FF	3	2	4	4	7	25	8	10	9	4	5	20
FG	2	1	4	5	7	25	9	10	6	3	2	27
GRN	23	15	12	6	3	9	2	2	4	2	4	19
LAB	2	2	3	6	10	26	8	5	5	1	2	30
PD	3	2	3	4	7	23	10	8	7	3	3	28
SF	4	3	4	5	5	19	5	4	5	1	2	42

B58   Some people think that Ireland should do all it can to unite fully with the European Union. Other people think that Ireland should do all it can to protect our independence from the European Union. On the 0–10 scale below where would you place the views of the following PARTIES?

	0	1	2	3	4	5	6	7	8	9	10	DK
	Ireland should do all it can to unite fully with the European Union.						Ireland should do all it can to protect our independence from the European Union.					
FF	11	9	12	7	6	12	4	5	6	4	6	19
FG	8	5	9	9	9	16	4	7	5	3	3	24
GRN	3	2	4	6	7	18	6	8	6	3	4	33
LAB	4	3	6	7	8	19	6	7	4	1	2	31
PD	7	6	9	9	6	13	5	5	6	3	3	29
SF	4	3	3	5	4	13	5	5	7	5	8	40

Section C

C1a   I'd now like to ask you how you feel about some Irish politicians, using what we call the 'feeling thermometer'. The feeling thermometer works like this: [Int. show card C1]

If you have a *favourable feeling* (a warm feeling) towards a politician you should place him/her somewhere between 50 and 100 degrees;

If you have an *unfavourable feeling* (a cold feeling) towards a POLITICIAN, you should place him/her somewhere between 0 and 50 degrees; and

If you *don't feel particularly warm or cold* (have no feeling towards the politician at all) then you should place him/her at 50 degrees.

Where would you place these Irish politicians?

	0–10	11–20	21–30	31–40	41–50	51–60	61–70	71–80	81–90	91–100	Missing
1AHERN, Bertie											
	6	2	3	5	16	11	13	21	10	10	2
2BRUTON, John											
	13	7	11	12	23	11	8	5	4	2	4
3HARNEY, Mary											
	12	6	7	9	23	15	11	9	3	2	3
4QUINN, Ruairi											
	14	7	12	14	25	12	7	4	1	1	5
5MCCREEVY, Charlie											
	12	7	8	12	22	14	10	8	2	1	4
6SARGENT, Trevor											
	17	7	9	11	28	10	6	4	1	+	10
7MARTIN, Micheál											
	9	5	7	10	25	13	10	9	4	2	8
8NOONAN, Michael											
	21	13	12	14	20	8	5	3	1	1	4
9ADAMS, Gerry											
	23	9	10	9	19	10	7	6	3	3	4
10MACDOWELL, Michael											
	15	7	9	13	28	9	5	3	1	1	11
11HOWLIN, Brendan											
	16	8	10	13	27	10	5	3	+	+	9
12'DANA' Rosemary Scalon											
	35	11	11	9	19	6	3	2	1	+	6

C1b **And where would you place each of the following political PARTIES?** [Show Card C2]

	0–10	11–20	21–30	31–40	41–50	51–60	61–70	71–80	81–90	91–100	Missing
Fianna Fáil											
	7	4	4	5	17	12	13	17	9	12	3
Green Party											
	10	6	9	12	24	14	11	7	2	1	5
Fine Gael											
	11	7	10	13	23	13	7	7	3	3	4
Labour											
	9	7	10	16	24	13	8	6	2	1	4
Progressive Democrats											
	12	7	8	12	24	14	10	7	2	1	5
Sinn FéinSinn Féin											
	28	11	11	10	16	7	5	4	2	2	5

C2   And where would you place these CANDIDATES who ran in your constituency in the general election in May? [show card C3] Interviewer. You MUST write name of constituency from prompt card here.

Int. If respondent voted in general election in May (Yes at B1, pg3) show card for appropriate constituency.

If respondent did NOT vote in general election in May (No at B1, pg3) but gave a constituency at B3 show appropriate constituency card. [Yellow reference card or from list of all candidates]

If respondent did NOT vote in general election in May (No at B1, pg3) and did NOT give a constituency at B3 show card for constituency in which interview is taking place. Show yellow reference card]
[Int. Please write in surname from card and record degree]

C3   **Which do you think would generally be better for Ireland nowadays?** [Int: read out and tick (✓) one box only]

To have a government formed by one political party on its own, or	To have a government formed by two or more political parties together in a coalition
20	80

C4   **Looking at the parties listed on this card could you tell me, if there had to be a coalition government, which combination of two or more parties would you most prefer?** [Int. Write in each party of the parties mentioned on a separate line below and also number of parties mentioned]. [Show Card C4]

C5   **Please look at the following possible coalition governments. Of these coalitions which one would you most prefer?** [Int. Show card C5 and tick (✓) one box only to indicate which coalition the respondent would prefer]

FF-GRNS	FF-LAB	FF-PD	FF-SF	FF-IND	FG-FF	FG-LAB-GRN
7	10	42	9	5	7	20

C6 With regard to the Northern Ireland problem some people think we should insist on a United Ireland now while other people think we should abandon the aim of a United Ireland altogether. Of course, other people have opinions somewhere between these extremes. Suppose the people who believe that we should insist on a United Ireland now are at one end of the scale, at '0', and the people who think we should abandon the aim of a United Ireland altogether are at the other end, at '10'. Where would you place yourself on this scale?

And what about the political parties? Where would you place the parties on the card in terms of their views on Northern Ireland? [Int. show card C6]

	0	1	2	3	4	5	6	7	8	9	10	DK
	Insist on a United Ireland now							Abandon the aim the aim of a United Ireland altogether				
Self	14	7	8	9	8	29	5	4	3	2	6	7
FF	8	7	10	10	11	23	5	4	3	1	2	17
FG	4	3	5	7	9	27	9	5	3	2	2	23
GRN	3	2	3	5	8	24	6	5	3	1	2	39
LAB	3	2	4	6	10	27	8	4	3	1	1	31
PD	4	4	6	7	11	24	6	5	3	1	2	27
SF	46	17	7	2	1	6	1	+	1	1	3	16

C7 How important is the issue of Northern Ireland for you personally? Is it:

Very important	Fairly important	Not very important	Not important at all
21	46	25	9

C8 Thinking back over the last five years – the lifetime of the 1997 to 2002 Fianna Fáil/Progressive Democrat government – would you say that the ECONOMY in Ireland over that period of time got a lot better; a little better; stayed the same; got a little worse; or got a lot worse?

Got a lot better	Got a little better	Stayed the same	Got a little worse	Got a lot worse	Don't know
41	40	9	7	3	2

C9   Do you think this was MAINLY due to the policies of that government or NOT MAINLY DUE to the policies of that government?

Mainly due to the policies of that government	Not mainly due to the policies of that government
64	36

C10   Was this due equally to both parties in government – Fianna Fáil and the Progressive Democrats, mainly due to the Progressive Democrats, or mainly due to Fianna Fáil?

Due equally to both parties	Due mainly to the Progressive Democrats	Due mainly to Fianna Fáil
85	2	13

C11   Which of the following parties, if any, would have handled the ECONOMY better?

No other party	Fine Gael	Labour	Greens	Sinn Féin
77	12	8	1	2

C12   Again, thinking back over the last five years of the Fianna Fáil–Progressive Democrat government, would you say that the HEALTH SERVICES in Ireland over that period of time got a lot better; a little better; stayed the same; got a little worse; or got a lot worse over that period?

Got a lot better	Got a little better	Stayed the same	Got a little worse	Got a lot worse	Don't know
4	22	23	23	27	2

C13   Do you think this was MAINLY due to the policies of that government or NOT MAINLY DUE to the policies of that government?

Mainly due to the policies of that government	Not mainly due to the policies of that government
79	21

C14   Was this due equally to both parties in government – Fianna Fáil and the Progressive Democrats, mainly due to the Progressive Democrats, or mainly due to Fianna Fáil?

Due equally to both parties	Due mainly to the Progressive Democrats	Due mainly to Fianna Fáil
88	2	10

C15   Which of the following parties, if any, would have handled the
      HEALTH SERVICES better?

No other party	Fine Gael	Labour	Greens	Sinn Féin
66	13	15	2	4

C16   Again, thinking back over the last five years of the Fianna Fáil–
      Progressive Democrat government, would you say that the
      HOUSING SITUATION in Ireland over that period of time got a lot
      better; a little better; stayed the same; got a little worse; or got
      a lot worse over that period?

Got a lot better	Got a little better	Stayed the same	Got a little worse	Got a lot worse	Don't know
12	31	13	18	22	4

C17   Do you think this was MAINLY due to the policies of that govern-
      ment or NOT MAINLY DUE to the policies of that government?

Mainly due to the policies of that government	Not mainly due to the policies of that government
73	27

C18   Was this due equally to both parties in government – Fianna
      Fáil and the Progressive Democrats, mainly due to the Progress-
      ive Democrats, or mainly due to Fianna Fáil?

Due equally to both parties	Due mainly to the Progressive Democrats	Due mainly to Fianna Fáil
90	2	8

C19   Which of the following parties, if any, would have handled
      HOUSING better?

No other party	Fine Gael	Labour	Greens	Sinn Féin
71	10	13	3	3

C20   Again, thinking back over the last five years of the Fianna Fáil–
      Progressive Democrat government, would you say that CRIME in
      Ireland over that period of time increased a lot; increased a
      little; stayed the same; decreased a little; or decreased a lot over
      that period?

Increased a lot	Increased a little	Stayed the same	Decreased a little	Decreased a lot	Don't know
56	28	9	4	1	2

C21   Do you think this was MAINLY due to the policies of that government or NOT MAINLY DUE to the policies of that government?

Mainly due to the policies of that government 46	Not mainly due to the policies of that government 54

C22   Was this due equally to both parties in government – Fianna Fáil and the Progressive Democrats, mainly due to the Progressive Democrats, or mainly due to Fianna Fáil?

Due equally to both parties 91	Due mainly to the Progressive Democrats 1	Due mainly to Fianna Fáil 7

C23   Which of the following parties, if any, would have handled CRIME better?

No other party 74	Fine Gael 12	Labour 6	Greens 2	Sinn Féin 7

C24   Could you tell me how honest you think each of the political parties is using the 0–10 scale on this card where 0 means you think that party is not very honest and 10 means you think that party is very honest? [Int. Show Card C7 and tick (✓) one box on each line]

	0	1	2	3	4	5	6	7	8	9	10	DK
	Not very honest								Very honest			
FF	11	6	8	8	8	19	8	10	7	4	6	6
FG	6	3	5	8	9	21	11	12	8	4	4	9
GRN	5	2	3	4	6	19	11	13	12	5	4	17
LAB	6	2	3	5	6	23	13	13	9	4	3	12
PD	8	3	4	5	6	19	10	14	9	5	4	12
SF	12	7	6	6	8	18	7	7	4	2	4	19

C25 | And now I'd like to ask you a question about abortion. People who fully agree that there should be a total ban on abortion in Ireland would give a score of '0'. People who fully agree that abortion should be freely available in Ireland to any woman who wants to have one would give a score of '10'. Other people would place themselves in between these two views. Where would you place yourself on this scale? [Int. show card C8].
And what about the political parties? Where would you place the parties on the card in terms of their views on abortion?

	0	1	2	3	4	5	6	7	8	9	10	DK
	There should be a total ban on abortion in Ireland.						Abortion should be freely available in Ireland to any woman who wants to have one.					
Self	20	5	6	4	4	18	5	7	6	3	16	6
FF	7	3	5	7	8	23	7	5	4	1	2	27
FG	5	2	4	7	9	23	7	5	3	1	12	32
GRN	4	2	3	4	7	18	5	5	3	1	2	46
LAB	3	1	2	4	7	20	7	7	5	3	3	38
PD	5	1	3	5	7	22	7	7	4	1	2	37
SF	5	1	3	4	5	17	4	3	3	2	4	51

C26 | How important would you say is this issue of abortion for you personally?

Very important	Fairly important	Not very important	Not important at all
31	41	21	7

C27	I would like you to look at the scale from 0 to 10 on this card. [Int. show card C9] A '0' means government should cut taxes a lot and spend much less on health and social services, and '10' means government should increase taxes a lot and spend much more on health and social services.

(a) where would you place yourself in terms of this scale?
(b) and where would you place the political parties on this scale?

	0	1	2	3	4	5	6	7	8	9	10	DK
	Government should cut taxes a lot and spend much less on health and social services.							Government should increase taxes a lot and spend much more on health and social services.				
Self	3	2	2	1	4	29	11	11	11	6	17	6
FF	1	1	2	3	6	25	11	10	8	3	6	23
FG	1	1	1	2	6	24	11	12	6	3	4	28
GRN	1	1	1	2	4	21	9	10	8	3	4	38
LAB	1	+	1	2	4	19	9	12	11	5	5	30
PD	2	1	3	4	7	24	10	8	6	3	4	29
SF	2	1	1	2	3	20	6	6	7	5	4	45

C28	How important is this issue of taxation and spending on health and social services FOR YOU PERSONALLY?

Very important	Fairly important	Not very important	Not important at all
40	49	9	3

C29   How good do you think each of the political parties would be at RUNNING THE COUNTRY if they were in government. Please rate each party on a scale from 0 to 10 where 0 means you think that party WOULD NOT BE very good at running the country and 10 means that you think that party WOULD BE very good at running the country. [Put a tick (✓) in one box on each line]

	0	1	2	3	4	5	6	7	8	9	10	DK
	Would not be very good at running the country.							*Would be* very good at running the country.				
FF	4	1	2	3	4	12	10	14	18	10	17	5
FG	5	2	5	7	10	20	15	11	8	4	4	8
GRN	8	4	7	11	11	17	10	7	4	1	1	18
LAB	4	3	5	8	13	21	12	11	7	2	2	12
PD	5	2	4	6	7	18	13	14	12	3	3	11
SF	19	8	8	9	8	13	6	4	3	2	2	17

Section E Socio-demographics

E1 **Since when have you lived in this constituency?**
Month: Year:

E2 **Since when have you lived at this address?**
Month: Year:

E3a **Are you registered to vote at this address?**

Yes	No	Don't know
95	4	1

E3b **Are you registered to vote at another address?**

Yes	No	Don't know
75	22	3

E4 **Sex of respondent**

Male	Female
49	51

E5 **Could I ask for your date of birth?**
Day: Month: Year:

E6a **Could I ask about your current marital status? Are you:**

Married	Separated	Divorced	Widowed	Never married
48	4	1	6	41

E6b **Are you currently living with your husband/wife?**

Yes	No
97	3

E6c **Are you currently living with another partner?**

Yes	No
12	88

E6d **Are you currently living with a partner?**

Yes	No
6	94

E7   **Which of the following best describes the highest level of education you have completed to date. [Int. Please tick (✓) one box only]**

None	Completed Primary	Junior/Inter/ Group or equivalent	Leaving Cert. or equivalent	Diploma or Certificate	University Degree or equivalent
1	23	23	25	16	12

E8   **During the last five years have you been unemployed and seeking work? By unemployed I mean available for and actively seeking work in contrast, for example, to someone who is engaged in home duties.**

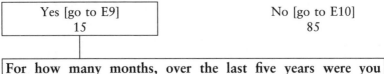

Yes [go to E9]	No [go to E10]
15	85

E9   **For how many months, over the last five years were you unemployed?**

E10   **Which of the following best describes your present situation with regard to employment: [Int. Please tick (✓) one box only]**

At work full-time (30hrs or more) [go to E13]	At work part-time (less than 30hrs weekly) [go to E13]	At work as relative assisting/unpaid family worker [go to E13]	Unemployed and seeking work [go to E11]	Student [go to E11]
47	10	1	4	7

Retired [go to E11]	Engaged in home duties [go to E11]	Long-term sick or disabled [go to E11]	Other, specify [go to E11]
9	19	3	1

E11   [Int: For people who are unemployed or coded 4–9 in question F7]
Did you ever work at any time in the past, even if not currently working now?

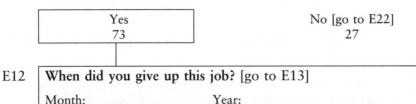

Yes	No [go to E22]
73	27

E12   **When did you give up this job? [go to E13]**

Month: Year:

E13   **What is/was your occupation? Please describe fully. If farmer, please record the number of acres farmed. If appropriate, please** record the rank or grade, e.g. Civil Service, Gardai, Defence Forces etc.

E14   Please describe as fully as possible the nature of the business activity of your employer.

E15   Do/did you work in the public or private sector? [Please tick one box only]

Civil Service	Local Authority, Health Board or VEC	Non-commercial semi-state body	Commercial semi-state body	Private sector
7	10	3	5	76

E16   Are/were you self-employed (including farmer) or are you an employee?

Self-employed	Employee
15	85

E17   How many people do/did you employ, including yourself?

E18   Are/were you a member of any trade union at this time?

Yes	No
33	67

E19   Do/did you normally supervise any other workers in your job?

Yes	No [go to E21]
30	70

E20   Approximately how many do you supervise? [go to E21]

E21   How worried are you that you might become unemployed in the next year?

Very worried	Somewhat worried	A little worried	Not at all worried
5	7	12	76

E22   When you were 16 what kind of work did your father do – what was his occupation? Please describe fully. If farmer please record number of acres farmed. If appropriate, please record the rank or grade, e.g. Civil Service, Gardai, Defence Forces etc.

E23   **What were some of your father's main duties at work? Please write in a description of his duties.**

E24   **With regard to your accommodation, could you tell me if it is . . .**
[Int. Please tick (✓) one box only]

Owner without a mortgage or loan (incl. LA tenant purchase)	Owner with a mortgage or loan (incl. LA tenant purchase)	Local Authority tenant	Private tenant	Other, please specify
47	32	9	7	6

E25   **Do you belong to any religious denomination?**

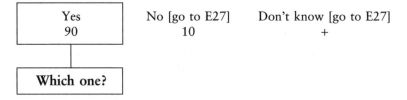

Yes	No [go to E27]	Don't know [go to E27]
90	10	+

Which one?

E26   **How often nowadays do you attend religious services?**
[Int: Show Card E1 and tick (✓) one box only]

Several times a week	Once a week	2 or 3 times a month	Once a month	Several times a year
8	46	9	6	14

Once a year	Less Frequently	Never	Refused	DK	NA
7	6	4	+	+	+

E27   **a) Have you ever lived outside the Republic of Ireland continuously for two years or more?** [Int. Please tick (✓) one box on each line]

No	Yes
82	18

What year did you return?

E27   **b) Are you a member of the GAA?**

Yes	No
16	84

E28   **Do you usually think of yourself as close to any political party?**

Yes [go to E29]	No [go to E31]	Don't Know [go to E31]
26	72	2

E29 **Which party is that?** Record all parties

First PARTY mentioned: If only one party mentioned [go to E33]

FF	FG	GRN	LAB	PD	SF	IND	OTH
54	24	3	8	2	9	1	+

Second PARTY (if volunteered): If more than one party mentioned [go to E30]
Note to reader: Two percent of respondents mentioned a second party

FF	FG	GRN	LAB	PD	SF	IND	OTH
21	7	16	12	15	22	6	2

Third PARTY (if volunteered): If more than two parties mentioned [go to E30]
Note to reader: Less than one percent mentioned a third party

FF	FG	GRN	LAB	PD	SF	OTH
		87	13			

E30 **Which party do you feel closest to**

FF	FG	GRN	LAB	PD	SF	OTH	No party identified [go to E34]
26	21	5	9	9	25		5

E31 **Do you feel yourself a little closer to one of the political parties than the others?**

Yes [go to E32]	No [go to E34]	Don't Know [go to E34]
36	56	7

E32 **Which party is that** [go to E34]

FF	FG	GRN	LAB	PD	SF	IND	OTH
55	17	7	10	5	3	+	2

E33 **Do you feel very close to this party, somewhat close, or not very close?**

Very close	Somewhat close	Not very close
34	58	8

E34   And now a couple of questions about how your parents voted when you were growing up; some people know about this while others do not. First your father, which party did he usually vote for or did he vote for various different parties? [Int. show card E2 and tick (✓) one box only]

Don't Know	FF	FG	LAB	PD	SF	WP/DL
31	38	17	6	+	2	+

CnaP	CnaT	Voted for different parties	Other	Did not vote
+	+	3	1	2

E35   [Int ask if 2–9 ticked in E34] **Would you say that he was a very strong supporter of this party?**

Yes	No
64	36

E36   And now your mother, which party did she usually vote for or did she vote for various different parties? [Int. show card E2 and tick (✓) one box only]

Don't Know	FF	FG	LAB	PD	SF	WP/DL
32	38	18	5	+	1	+

CnaP	CnaT	Voted for different parties	Other	Did not vote
+	+	3	1	2

E37   [Int ask if 2–9 ticked in E36] **Would you say that she was a very strong supporter of this party?**

Yes	No
57	43

E38   **1. Are you a citizen of Ireland?**

Yes, citizen of Ireland	No
99	1

E38   **2. Which country are you a citizen of?**

E39   **1. Can you tell me who was the leader of Fianna Fáil during the recent general election campaign?**

Charlie McCreevy	Brian Cowen	Charlie Haughey	Bertie Ahern	Missing
1	+	+	96	3

2. **The Green Party recently elected a leader for the first time. Could you tell me who that is?**

Patricia McKenna	John Gormley	Trevor Sargent	Roger Garland	Missing
3	8	64	3	22

3. **Who was the leader of Fine Gael during the recent general election campaign?**

Jim Mitchell	John Bruton	Michael Noonan	Alan Dukes	Missing
1	4	89	+	7

4. **Who was the Ceann Comhairle in the Dáil (Speaker of the Dáil) during the last Dáil 1997–2002?**

Sean Tracey	Des O'Malley	Sean Doherty	Seamus Pattison	Missing
24	5	7	32	33

5. **Who is Ireland's European Commissioner?**

David Byrne	Maire Geoghan Quinn	Barry Desmond	Padraig Flynn	Missing
45	6	4	18	28

E40 Are you the head of your household?

Yes [go to E46a]	No
53	46

E41 What is/was occupation of the head of the household? Please describe as fully as possible. If farmer please record the number of acres farmed. If appropriate, please record the rank or grade, e.g. Civil Service, Gardai, Defence Forces etc.

E42 Is he/she self-employed (including farmer) or are you an employee?

Self-employed	Employee
36	64

E43 How many people does he/she employ, including yourself?

E44 Does he/she normally supervise any other workers in his/her job?

Yes	No [go to E46a]
30	70

E45 Approximately how many do he/she supervise? [go to E46a]

E46 a) I would like to ask about the approximate level of net household income? This means the total income, after tax, PRSI and other statutory deductions, of *all* members of the household. It includes all types of income: income from employment, social welfare payments, child benefit, rents, interest, pensions etc. We would just like to know into which of four broad groups the total income of your household falls. I'd like to assure you once again that all information you give me is entirely confidential. [Int: Show Card E3 and tick (✓) one box below]

b) Card A: **Would that be:**
[Int: Show Card A, B, C or D from the yellow cards as appropriate. Tick ONE box only below]

Per week	Per month	Per year
Under €240	**Under €1050**	**Under €12,500**
Under £190	*Under £825*	*Under £10,000*
[Go to Q.A below, Show Card A]		
18		

Per week	Under €100	€100–150	€151–200	€201–240
	Under £85	*£86–110*	*£111–150*	*£151–190*
Per month	Under €430	€431–650	€651–850	€851–1050
	Under £370	*£371–475*	*£476–650*	*£651–825*
Per Year	Under €5150	€5151–7800	€7801–10500	€10201–12500
	Under £4500	*£4501–5700*	*£5701–8000*	*£8001–10000*
	5	29	31	35

Per week	Per month	Per year
€241–€450	**€1051–€2000**	**€12,501–€24,000**
£191–£360	*£826–£1570*	*£10,001–£19,000*
[Go to Q.B below, Show Card B]		
32		

CARD B: **Would that be:**				
Per week	€241–280	€281–350	€351–400	€401–450
	£191–220	*£221–270*	*£271–320*	*£321–360*
Per month	€1051–1200	€1201–1500	€1501–1700	€1701–2000
	£826–950	*£951–1150*	*£1151–1400*	*£1401–1570*
Per Year	€12501–14400	€14401–18000	€18001–20400	€20401–24000
	£10001–11500	*£11501–14000*	*£14001–16500*	*£16501–19000*
	24	29	23	24

Per week	Per month	Per year
€451–€700	€2001–€3000	€24,001–€36,000
£361–£570	*£1571–£2475*	*£19,001–£30,000*
[Go to Q.C below, Show Card C]		
25		

CARD C: Would that be:

Per week	€451–500	€501–570	€571–630	€631–700
	£361–400	*£401–450*	*£451–500*	*£501–570*
Per month	€2001–2150	€2151–2475	€2476–2700	€2701–3000
	£1571–1750	*£1751–2000*	*£2001–2200*	*£2201–2475*
Per Year	€24001–25800	€28501–29700	€29701–32400	€32401–36000
	£19001–21000	*£21001–24000*	*£24001–26000*	*£26001–30000*
	25	22	23	31

Per week	Per month	Per year
€701 or more	€3000 or more	€36,000 or more
£571 or more	*£2476 or more*	*£30,001 or more*
[Go to Q.D below, Show Card D]		
25		

CARD D: Would that be:

Per week	€701–825	€826–950	€951–1200	€1201 or more
	£571–650	*£651–750*	*£751–950*	*£951 or more*
Per month	€3001–3575	€3576–4100	€4401–5200	€5201 or more
	£2476–2800	*£2801–3200*	*£3201–4100*	*£4101 or more*
Per Year	€36001–42900	€42901–49000	€49001–62500	€62501 or more
	£30001–33500	*£33501–38500*	*£38501–49000*	*£49001 or more*
	25	23	24	27

E47   Could you tell me (a) how many persons living in the household are aged less than 14 years; (b) 14 to less than 18 years; (c) 18 years or more?

Less than 14 years	14 to less than 18 years	18 years or more
31	21	99

E48   Size of location in which household is situated:

Open country	Village (200–1499)	Town (1500–2999)	Town (3000–4999)	Town (5000–9999)	Town (10000+)
36	8	3	2	5	13

Waterford City	Galway City	Limerick City	Cork City	Dublin City	Dublin County
+	1	3	2	21	7

Drop-off questionnaire

Q1   To what extent do you think the following political parties are IN TOUCH WITH ORDINARY PEOPLE? Please rate each party on a scale from 0 to 10 where 0 means you think that party is NOT IN TOUCH with ordinary people and 10 means you think that party IS IT TOUCH with ordinary people. [Put a tick (✓) in one box on each line]

	0	1	2	3	4	5	6	7	8	9	10	DK
	Not in touch								*Not in touch*			
	with ordinary								*with ordinary*			
	people								*people*			
FF	5	1	3	6	6	14	10	15	15	8	11	6
FG	7	2	7	9	11	19	14	9	7	2	5	8
GRN	7	2	5	8	9	21	13	9	6	1	2	16
LAB	4	2	4	7	11	20	13	10	8	3	3	12
PD	7	2	6	7	8	19	13	13	8	2	3	13
SF	9	6	7	8	8	14	9	9	7	2	5	17

Q2   Please tell me to what extent you Disagree or Agree with each of the following statements. [Put a tick (✓) in one box on each line]

Strongly disagree	Disagree	Slightly disagree	Neither agree nor disagree	Slightly agree	Agree	Strongly agree

Compared to 10 years ago, Ireland is just as friendly a place now as it was then.

12	33	16	6	8	21	4

There is a lot more stress in people's lives today than there was 10 years ago.

1	3	1	3	10	50	32

People don't have enough time to spend with their families these days.

1	4	2	6	15	49	22

Q3   During the general election campaign in May of this year did you talk to other people to persuade them to vote for a particular party or candidate?

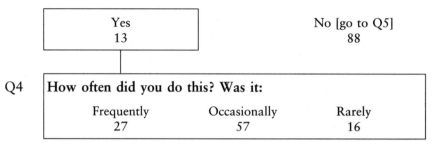

Yes	No [go to Q5]
13	88

Q4 | **How often did you do this? Was it:**

Frequently	Occasionally	Rarely
27	57	16

Q5   During the election campaign in May of this year did you show your support for a particular party or candidate by, for example, attending a meeting, putting up a poster, or in some other way?

Yes	No [go to Q7]
8	92

Q6 | **How often did you do this? Was it:**

Frequently	Occasionally	Rarely
30	48	22

Q7   During the election campaign in May did a candidate or anyone from a political party contact you to persuade you to vote for them?

Yes	No
53	47

Q8   Now thinking in general about the performance of the Fianna Fáil/Progressive Democrat government which was in office over the past five years – 1997 to 2002. *In general,* how good or bad a job do you think it has done over the past five years? Has it done a

Very good job	Good job	Bad job	Very bad job	Don't know
12	66	14	6	3

Q9   On the whole are you very satisfied, fairly satisfied, not very satisfied, or not at all satisfied with the way democracy works in Ireland?

Very satisfied	Fairly satisfied	Not very satisfied	Not at all satisfied
11	69	17	4

Q10   Some people say it makes a big difference who is in power. Others say that it doesn't make any difference who is in power. Using the scale below – where 1 means that it MARKS A BIG DIFFERENCE who is in power and 5 means that it DOESN'T MAKE ANY DIFFERENCE who is in power – where would you place yourself? [Put a tick (✓) in one box]

1	2	3	4	5	DK
It makes a big difference who is in power.			It doesn't make any difference who is in power.		
30	22	21	10	12	5

Q11   Some people say that no matter who people vote for it won't make any difference to what happens. Others say that who people vote for can make a big difference to what happens. Using the scale below – where ONE means that voting can make a big difference and FIVE means that voting won't make any difference to what happens, where would you place yourself? Put a tick (✓) in one box.

1	2	3	4	5	DK
Who people vote for can make a big difference.			Who people vote for won't make any difference.		
39	25	18	6	8	4

Q12   Could you tell me how strongly you agree or disagree with the following statement: Democracy may have problems but it's better than any other form of government.

Strongly agree	Agree	Disagree	Strongly disagree	DK
30	54	5	1	11

Q13   Thinking back to the party you voted for in the 1997 General Election, do you feel that that party did a good or a bad job over the last five years?

Very good job	Good job	Bad job	Very bad job	Voted for Independent in 1997	Didn't vote in 1997	DK
14	49	9	1	2	15	11

Q14   Thinking about how elections in Ireland work in practice, how
       well do you think they ensure that the views of voters are
       represented by TDs – very well, quite well, not very well, or not
       well at all?

Very well	Quite well	Not very well	Not well at all	DK
7	50	28	6	9

Q15   Would you say that any of the parties in Ireland represents your
       views reasonably well?

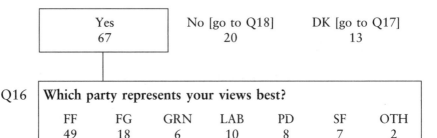

Yes	No [go to Q18]	DK [go to Q17]
67	20	13

Q16

Which party represents your views best?						
FF	FG	GRN	LAB	PD	SF	OTH
49	18	6	10	8	7	2

Q17   Regardless of how you feel about the parties, would you say
       that any of the individual party leaders at the election in May of
       this year represents your views reasonably well?

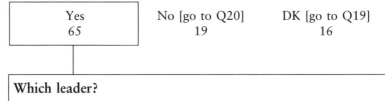

Yes	No [go to Q20]	DK [go to Q19]
65	19	16

Q18

Which leader?						
Bertie Ahern	Michael Noonan	Trevor Sargent	Ruairi Quinn	Mary Harney	Gerry Adams	Other
56	11	6	9	11	6	1

Q19   I'd like to know what you think about each of our political
       parties. Please rate each party on a scale from 0 to 10, where 0
       means you STRONGLY DISLIKE that party and 10 means that you
       STRONGLY LIKE that party. If you come to a party you haven't
       heard of or you feel you do not know enough about, just put a
       tick (✓) in the 'Don't know' box on the right. [Put a tick (✓) in
       one box on each line]

	0	1	2	3	4	5	6	7	8	9	10	DK
	Strongly dislike								Strongly like			
FF	6	3	3	3	5	17	8	12	14	8	16	3
FG	7	3	6	9	12	22	12	8	6	3	6	6
GRN	5	2	6	7	8	24	13	10	6	2	2	14
LAB	4	2	6	8	13	24	12	10	6	2	2	11
PD	6	4	6	6	11	20	15	11	6	2	2	10
SF	18	8	8	7	7	13	8	6	5	2	5	13

Q20 **In politics people sometimes talk of left and right. Where would you place Fianna Fáil on a scale from 0 to 10 where 0 means the left and 10 means the right?** [Please tick (✓) one box]

	0	1	2	3	4	5	6	7	8	9	10	DK
	Left								Right			
FF	1	+	1	2	3	20	9	13	10	6	7	27
FG	2	1	1	3	5	17	13	11	9	3	3	30
GRN	2	1	6	9	10	21	6	5	2	+	1	37
LAB	5	5	9	16	14	14	3	2	1	+	1	31
PD	1	1	1	3	4	16	9	13	11	4	3	31
SF	9	9	11	8	6	9	3	2	1	1	2	38

Q21 **Over the past 5 years or so, have you done any of the things below to express your views about something the government should or should not be doing?**

	Yes	No
1 Contacted a politician or government official either in person, or in writing or in some other way	22	78
2 Taken part in a protest, march or demonstration	7	93
3 Worked together with people who shared the same concern	18	82

Q22 **How much respect is there for individual freedom and human rights nowadays in Ireland? Do you feel there is . . .**

A lot of respect	Some respect	Not much respect	No respect at all	DK
15	53	24	4	5

Q23 How widespread do you think corruption such as bribe taking is amongst politicians in Ireland?

Very widespread	Quite widespread	Not very widespread	Hardly happens at all	DK
27	42	20	2	8

Q24 Where would you place yourself on a scale from 0 to 10 where 0 means the left and 10 means the right? Please tick (✓) one box.

0	1	2	3	4	5	6	7	8	9	10	DK
Left									Right		
1	1	3	4	6	29	8	8	8	3	5	25

Q25 Now turning to the problem of UNEMPLOYMENT. Thinking back over the last five years, the lifetime of the 1997 to 2002 Fianna Fáil – Progressive Democrat government, would you say that UNEMPLOYMENT in Ireland increased a lot; increased a little; stayed the same; fell a little or fell a lot over that period? [Please tick (✓) one box]

Increased a lot	Increased a little	Stayed the same	Fell a little	Fell a lot	DK
6	15	11	30	36	3

Q26 Do you think this was MAINLY due to the policies of that government or NOT MAINLY DUE to the policies of that government?

Mainly due to the policies of that government 64	Not mainly due to the policies of that government [go to Q28] 36

Q27 Was this due equally to both parties in government – Fianna Fáil and the Progressive Democrats – mainly due to the Progressive Democrats, or mainly due to Fianna Fáil?

Due equally to both parties	Due mainly to the PDs	Due mainly to FF
88	4	8

Q28   **Which of the following parties, if any, would have handled UNEMPLOYMENT better?**

No other party	FG	LAB	GRN	SF
73	10	13	2	3

Q29   **Again, thinking back over the last five years, during the 1997 to 2002 Fianna Fáil – Progressive Democrat government – would you say that the COST OF LIVING in the country as a whole increased a lot; increased a little; stayed the same; fell a little or fell a lot over that period? [Please tick (✓) one box]**

Increased a lot	Increased a little	Stayed the same	Fell a little	Fell a lot	DK
72	23	3	1	+	1

Q30   **Do you think this was MAINLY due to the policies of that government or NOT MAINLY DUE to the policies of that government?**

Mainly due to the policies of that government	Not mainly due to the policies of that government [go to Q32]
65	35

Q31   **Was this due equally to both parties in government – Fianna Fáil and the Progressive Democrats – mainly due to the Progressive Democrats, or mainly due to Fianna Fáil?**

Due equally to both parties	Due mainly to the PDs	Due mainly to FF
93	1	6

Q32   **Which of the following parties, if any, would have been better at dealing with THE COST OF LIVING?**

No other party	FG	LAB	GRN	SF
69	11	13	2	5

Q33   Thinking back over the last five years, would you say that
      the LEVEL OF TAXATION in the country as a whole has increased a
      lot; increased a little; stayed the same; fell a little or fell a lot
      over that period? [Please tick (✓) one box]

Increased a lot	Increased a little	Stayed the same	Fell a little	Fell a lot	DK
13	22	12	38	8	7

Q33   Do you think this was MAINLY due to the policies of that govern-
      ment or NOT MAINLY DUE to the policies of that government?

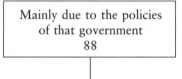

Mainly due to the policies of that government	Not mainly due to the policies of that government [go to Q35]
88	12

Q34   Was this due equally to both parties in government – Fianna
      Fáil and the Progressive Democrats – mainly due to the Pro-
      gressive Democrats, or mainly due to Fianna Fáil?

Due equally to both parties	Due mainly to the PDs	Due mainly to FF
82	10	8

Q35   Which of the following parties, if any, would have been better
      at dealing with THE LEVEL OF TAXATION?

No other party	FG	LAB	GRN	SF
76	10	10	2	3

Q36   Again, thinking back over the last five years, during the 1997 to
      2002 Fianna Fáil–Progressive Democrat government, would you
      say that TRAFFIC CONGESTION AND PUBLIC TRANSPORT in Ireland got
      a lot worse; got a little worse; stayed the same; got a little better
      or got a lot better over that period? [Please tick (✓) one box]

Got a lot worse	Got a little worse	Stayed the same	Got a little better	Got a lot better	DK
69	20	4	3	+	3

Q37 Do you think this was MAINLY due to the policies of that government or NOT MAINLY DUE to the policies of that government?

Mainly due to the policies of that government 51	Not mainly due to the policies of that government [go to Q38] 50

Q31 Was this due equally to both parties in government – Fianna
Fáil and the Progressive Democrats – mainly due to the Progressive Democrats, or mainly due to Fianna Fáil?

Due equally to both parties 93	Due mainly to the PDs 1	Due mainly to FF 6

Q38 Which of the following parties, if any, would have been better
at dealing with TRAFFIC CONGESTION AND PUBLIC TRANSPORT?

No other party	FG	LAB	GRN	SF
69	9	7	13	2

Q39 Thinking about the economy in Ireland in the past twelve
months, would you say that it has been. . . .

Very good	Good	Neither good nor bad	Bad	Very bad	DK
12	52	25	8	1	3

Q40 And how do you think the economy in Ireland will develop
over the next 12 months? Will it . . .

Get a lot better	Get a little better	Stay the same	Get a little worse	Get a lot worse	DK
2	16	31	35	8	9

Q41 How does the financial situation of your household compare
now with what it was 12 months ago? Has it . . .

Got a lot better	Got a little better	Stayed the same	Got a little worse	Got a lot worse	DK
3	27	43	20	6	2

Q42 How do you think the financial situation of your household will change over the next 12 months? Will it . . .

Get a lot better	Get a little better	Stay the same	Get a little worse	Get a lot worse	DK
2	14	48	21	5	10

Q43 How HONEST do you think each of the following politicians are, using the 0–10 scale below where 0 means you think that politician IS NOT VERY HONEST and 10 means you think that politician IS VERY HONEST? [Put a tick (✓) in one box on each line]

	0	1	2	3	4	5	6	7	8	9	10	DK
	Not very honest								Very honest			
Ahern	4	1	3	5	4	11	8	12	19	12	15	5
Noonan	5	2	5	7	6	14	8	14	15	8	10	7
Quinn	5	2	5	7	8	18	11	11	11	5	5	13

Q44 To what extent do you think the following politicians are IN TOUCH WITH ORDINARY PEOPLE? Please rate each politician on a scale from 0 to 10 where 0 means you think that politician is NOT IN TOUCH with ordinary people and 10 means you think that politician IS IN TOUCH with ordinary people. [Put a tick (✓) in one box on each line]

	0	1	2	3	4	5	6	7	8	9	10	DK
	Not in touch with ordinary people								*In touch* with ordinary people			
Ahern	8	4	8	11	11	17	11	8	7	2	2	10
Noonan	5	2	5	8	10	21	14	9	8	2	2	14
Quinn	2	1	3	3	3	9	8	13	22	11	20	3

Q45 How good do you think each of these politicians would be at RUNNING THE COUNTRY if they were in government. Please rate each politician on a scale from 0 to 10 where 0 means you think that the politician WOULD NOT BE VERY GOOD at running the country and 10 means that you think the politician WOULD BE VERY GOOD at running the country. [Put a tick (✓) in one box on each line]

	0	1	2	3	4	5	6	7	8	9	10	DK
	Would not be very good at running the country							*Would be* very good at running the country				
Ahern	2	1	3	3	3	9	8	13	22	11	20	3
Noonan	9	5	9	9	11	17	11	8	6	2	2	10
Quinn	5	2	6	8	11	22	13	9	7	1	1	15

Q46 How much you personally trust religious leaders? People who *do not trust them at all* would give a score of '0'. People who *trust them a lot* would give a score of '10'. Other people would place themselves somewhere in between these two views. Where would you place yourself on this scale? [Put a tick (✓) in one box on each line]

	0	1	2	3	4	5	6	7	8	9	10
	Do not trust at all								Trust a lot		
Religious leaders	13	6	7	8	9	20	9	9	8	4	6
Political parties	8	5	8	11	12	30	13	8	5	1	2
Gardai	5	3	4	5	9	14	12	16	16	9	8
Business leaders	8	6	9	9	14	24	14	9	4	1	1

Q41a Please record your date of birth:

Q42b Please tick to indicate male or female:

Male	Female
48	52

References

Adshead, Maura (2004) 'Still the Counterfactual? Lipset and Rokkan Cleavages in Ireland.' Paper presented to the Political Studies Association (PSA) Annual Conference, University of Lincoln, 6–8 April.

Anderson, Christopher J. (2000) 'Economic Voting and Political Context: A Comparative Perspective', *Electoral Studies* 19: 151–70.

Barry, Frank (ed.) (1999) *Understanding Ireland's Economic Growth.* New York: St. Martin's Press.

Bartels, Larry M. (2002) 'Beyond the Running Tally: Partisan Bias in Political Perceptions', *Political Behavior* 24: 117–50.

Bartolini, Stefano and Peter Mair (1990) *Identity, Competition, and Electoral Availability: The Stabilisation of European Electorates 1885–1985.* Cambridge: Cambridge University Press.

Bean, Clive (1993) 'The Electoral Influence of Party Leader Images in Australia and New Zealand', *Comparative Political Studies*, 26: 111–32.

Bean, Clive and Anthony Mughan (1989) 'Leadership Effects in Parliamentary Elections: Australia and Britain', *American Political Science Review* 83, 1165–79.

Beck, Paul A., Lawrence Baum, Aage R. Clausen and Charles E. Smith (1992) 'Patterns and Sources of Ticket Splitting in Subpresidential Voting', *American Political Science Review* 86: 916–28.

Beck, Paul A., Russell J. Dalton, Steven Greene and Robert Huckfeldt (2002) 'The Social Calculus of Voting: Interpersonal, Media, and Organizational Influences on Presidential Choices', *American Political Science Review* 96: 57–73.

Benoit, Kenneth and Michael Marsh (2003) 'For a Few Euros More: Campaign Spending Effects in the Irish Local Elections of 1999', *Party Politics* 9: 561–82.

Benoit, Kenneth and Michael Marsh (2004) 'Campaign Spending in the Irish Local Government Elections of 1999', *Irish Political Studies* 18: 1–22.

Benoit, Kenneth and Michael Laver (2005) 'Mapping the Irish Policy Space: Voter and Party Spaces in Preferential Elections', *Economic and Social Review* 36(2): 83–108.

Benoit, Kenneth and Michael Marsh (2006) 'A Fistful of Euros: Campaign Spending Effects Under the Single-Transferable Vote Electoral System'. Paper presented to the Annual Conference of the Midwest Political Science Association, Chicago, April.

Benoit, Kenneth and Michael Laver (2006) *Party Policy in Modern Democracies*. London: Routledge.

Blais, André (2000) *To Vote or Not to Vote? The Merits and Limits of Rational Choice Theory*. Pittsburgh, Pa.: University of Pittsburgh Press.

Blais, André, Elizabeth Gildengil, Richard Nadeau and Neil Nevitte (2001) 'Measuring Party Identification: Canada, Britain, and the United States', *Political Behavior* 23: 5–22.

Blondel, Jean, Richard Sinnott and Palle Svensson (1998) *People and Parliament in the European Union: Democracy, Participation and Legitimacy*. Oxford: Oxford University Press.

Bloom, Harold and H. Douglas Price (1975) 'Voter Response to Short Run Economic Conditions: the Asymmetric Effect of Prosperity and Recession', *American Political Science Review* 69: 1240–54.

Bochel, J. M. and D. T. Denver (1971) 'Canvassing, Turnout and Party Support: An Experiment', *British Journal of Political Science* 1: 257–69.

Bowler, Shaun and David Farrell (1991a) 'Voter Behaviour Under STV-PR: Solving the Puzzle of the Irish Party System', *Political Behavior* 13: 303–20.

Bowler, Shaun and David Farrell (1991b) 'Party Loyalties in Complex Settings: STV and Party Identification', *Political Studies* 39: 350–62.

Brady, Henry E. (1985) 'The Perils of Survey Research: Interpersonally Incomparable Responses', *Political Methodology* 11: 269–91.

Brandenburg, Heinz (2005) 'Political Bias in the Irish Media: A Quantitative Study of Campaign Coverage during the 2002 General Election', *Irish Political Studies* 20: 297–322.

Brandenburg, Heinz and Jacqueline Hayden (2003) 'The Media and the Campaign', in Michael Gallagher, Michael Marsh and Paul Mitchell (eds), *How Ireland Voted 2002*. London: Palgrave, pp. 177–96.

van der Brug, Wouter, Cees van der Eijk and Michael Marsh (2000) 'Exploring Uncharted Territory: the Irish Presidential Election 1997', *British Journal of Political Science* 30: 631–50.

Budge, Ian and Dennis Farlie (1983) *Explaining and Predicting Elections: Issue Effects and Party Strategies in Twenty-Three Democracies*. London: Allen and Unwin.

Butler, David and Donald Stokes (1969) *Political Change in Britain: Forces Shaping Electoral Choice*. New York, NY: St. Martin's Press.

Cain, Bruce, John Ferejohn and Morris Fiorina (1987) *The Personal Vote: Constituency Service and Electoral Independence*. Cambridge: Harvard University Press.

Campbell, Angus, Philip E. Converse, Warren E. Miller, Donald E. Stokes (1960) *The American Voter*. New York, NY: John Wiley & Sons.

Carey, John M. and Matthew S. Shugart (1995) 'Incentives to Cultivate a Personal Vote: A Rank Ordering of Electoral Formulas', *Electoral Studies* 14: 417–39.

Carty, R. Kenneth (1983) *Electoral Politics in Ireland: Party and Parish Pump.* Dingle, Co. Kerry: Brandon Press.

Carty, R. Kenneth and Munroe Eagles (1999) 'Do Local Campaigns Matter? Campaign Spending, the Local Canvass and Party Support in Canada', *Electoral Studies* 18: 69–87.

Chubb, Basil (1970) *Government and Politics of Ireland.* Oxford: Oxford University Press.

Clark, Harold D. and Marianne C. Stewart (1995) 'Economic Evaluations, Prime Ministerial Approval and Governing Party Support in Britain: Rival Models Reconsidered', *British Journal of Political Science* 25: 145–70.

Clarke, Harold D., David Sanders, Marianne C. Stewart and Paul Whiteley (2004) *Political Choice in Britain.* Oxford: Oxford University Press.

Collins, Stephen (2003) 'Campaign strategies', in Michael Gallagher, Michael Marsh and Paul Mitchell (eds), *How Ireland Voted 2002.* London: Palgrave, pp. 21–36.

Converse, Philip E. (1964) 'The Nature of Belief Systems in Mass Publics', in David Apter (ed.), *Ideology and Discontent.* New York: Free Press, pp. 206–61.

Converse, Philip E. (1966) 'The Concept of the Normal Vote', in Angus Campbell, Philip E. Converse, Warren E. Miller and Donald E. Stokes (eds), *Elections and the Political Order.* New York: Wiley, pp. 9–39.

Costa Lobo, Marina (2006) 'Short-Term Voting Determinants in a Young Democracy: Leader Effects in Portugal in the 2002 Legislative Elections', *Electoral Studies* 25: 270–86.

Crewe, Ivor (1976) 'Party Identification Theory and Political Change in Britain', in Ian Budge, Ivor Crewe and Dennis Farlie (eds), *Party Identification and Beyond: Representations of Voting and Party Competition.* Chichester: Wiley, pp. 33–62.

CSO (1986) *Ireland: Statistical Abstract 1982–85.* Dublin: Stationery Office.

CSO (2001) *Statistical Yearbook of Ireland 2001.* Dublin: Stationery Office.

CSO (2003) *Statistical Yearbook of Ireland 2003.* Dublin: Stationery Office.

Curtice, John (2003) 'Elections as Beauty Contests: Do the Rules Matter?' Paper presented at the International Conference on 'Portugal at the Polls'. Lisbon, Portugal.

Curtice, John and Sören Holmberg (2005) 'Leadership and Voting Decision', in Jacques Thomassen (ed.), *The European Voter.* Oxford: Oxford University Press, pp. 235–53.

Dalton, Russell J. (2000) 'The Decline of Party Identifications', in Russell J. Dalton and Martin P. Wattenberg (eds), *Parties Without Partisans: Political Change in Advanced Industrial Democracies.* Oxford: Oxford University Press, pp. 19–36.

Dalton, Russell J., Ian McAllister and Martin P. Wattenberg (2000) 'The Consequences of Partisan Dealignment', in Russell J. Dalton and Martin P. Wattenberg (eds), *Parties Without Partisans: Political Change in Advanced Industrial Democracies*. Oxford: Oxford University Press, pp. 37–63.

Darcy, Robert and Michael Marsh (1994) 'Decision Heuristics: Ticket Splitting and the Irish Voter', *Electoral Studies* 13: 38–49.

Denver, David and Gordon Hands (1997) *Modern Constituency Electioneering: The Case of Britain*. London: Frank Cass.

Denver, David and Gordon Hands (2002) 'Post-Fordism in the Constituencies? The Continuing Development of Constituency Campaigning in Britain', in David Farrell and Rudiger Schmitt-Beck (eds), *Do Political Campaigns Matter?* London: Routledge, pp. 108–26.

Denver, David, Gordon Hands and Ian MacAllister (2004) 'The Electoral Impact of Constituency Campaigning in Britain 1992–2001', *Political Studies* 52: 289–306.

Denver, David, Gordon Hands, Justin Fisher and Ian MacAllister (2002) 'The Impact of Constituency Campaigning in the 2001 General Election', *British Elections and Parties Review* 12: 80–94.

Dorussen, Han and Michaell Taylor (eds) (2002) *Economic Voting*, London: Routledge.

Downs, Anthony (1957) *An Economic Theory of Democracy*. New York: Harper & Row.

Duch, Raymond M. and Randy Stevenson (2008) *Voting in Context: How Political and Economic Institutions Condition the Economic Vote*. Cambridge: Cambridge University Press.

van der Eijk, Cees and Kees Niemoller (1983) *Electoral Change in the Netherlands. Empirical Results and Methods of Measurement*. Amsterdam: CT Press.

van der Eijk, Cees, Mark N. Franklin, Thomas T. Mackie and Henry Valen (1992) 'Cleavages, Conflict Resolution, and Democracy', in Mark N. Franklin, Thomas T. Mackie and Henry Valen et al. (eds), *Electoral Change Responses to Evolving Social and Attitudinal Structures in Western Countries*. Cambridge: Cambridge University Press, pp. 406–31.

van der Eijk, Cees, Wouter van der Brug, Martin Kroh and Mark N. Franklin (2006) 'Rethinking the Dependent Variable in Voting Behavior: On the Measurement and analysis of Electoral Utilities', *Electoral Studies* 25: 424–47.

Evans, Geoffrey and Robert Andersen (2005) 'The Impact of Party Leaders: How Blair Lost Labour Votes', *Parliamentary Affairs* 58: 818–36.

Farrell, Brian (1990) 'Forming the Government', in Michael Gallagher and Richard Sinnott (eds), *How Ireland Voted 1989*. Galway: Galway University Press and PSAI Press, pp. 179–91.

Fiorina, Morris P. (1981) *Retrospective Voting in American National Elections*. London: Yale University Press.

Fleming, Sean, Paul Bradford, Joan Burton, Fiona O'Malley, Dan Boyle, Aengus Ó Snodaigh and Liam Twomey (2003) 'The Candidates' Perspective', in

Michael Gallagher, Michael Marsh and Paul Mitchell (eds), *How Ireland Voted 2002*. London: Palgrave, pp. 57–87.

Franklin, Mark N. (1996) 'Electoral Participation', in Laurence LeDuc, Richard Niemi and Pippa Norris (eds), *Comparative Elections and Voting in Global Perspective*. London: Sage, pp. 216–35.

Franklin, M. N., Thomas T. Mackie and Henry Valen *et al.* (eds) (1992) *Electoral Change Responses to Evolving Social and Attitudinal Structures in Western Countries*. Cambridge: Cambridge University Press.

Gallagher, Michael (1978) 'Party Solidarity, Exclusivity and Inter-Party Relationship in Ireland 1922–1977: The Evidence of Transfers', *Economic and Social Review* 10: 1–22.

Gallagher, Michael (1981) 'Societal Change and Party Adaptation in the Republic of Ireland, 1960–1981', *European Journal of Political Research* 9: 269–85.

Gallagher, Michael (1987) 'The Outcome', in Michael Laver, Peter Mair and Richard Sinnott (eds), *How Ireland Voted: The Irish General Election 1987*. Dublin and Limerick: PSAI/Poolbeg Press, pp. 63–98.

Gallagher, Michael (1993) 'The Election of the 27th Dáil', in Michael Gallagher and Michael Laver (eds), *How Ireland Voted 1992*. Dublin: PSAI Press, pp. 57–78.

Gallagher, Michael (1996) 'Electoral Systems', in Constitution Review Group, *Report on the Constitution*. Dublin: Stationery Office, pp. 499–520.

Gallagher, Michael (1999) 'The Results Analysed', in Michael Marsh and Paul Mitchell (eds), *How Ireland Voted 1997*. Boulder: Westview Press in association with PSAI Press, pp. 121–50.

Gallagher, Michael (2003) 'Stability and Turmoil: Analysis of the Results' in Michael Gallagher, Michael Marsh and Paul Mitchell (eds), *How Ireland Voted 2002*, London: Palgrave, pp. 88–118.

Gallagher, Michael and Michael Marsh (1992) 'The Presidential Election of 1990', in Ronald J. Hill and Michael Marsh (eds), *Modern Irish Democracy: Essays in honour of Basil Chubb*. Dublin: Irish Academic Press, pp. 62–81.

Gallagher, Michael and Michael Marsh (2002) *Days of Blue Loyalty: the Politics of Membership of the Fine Gael Party*. Dublin: PSAI Press.

Gallagher, Michael and Lee Komito (2005) 'The constituency role of Dáil deputies', in John Coakley and Michael Gallagher (eds), *Politics in the Republic of Ireland* (4th edition). London: Routledge, pp. 242–71.

Galligan, Yvonne (1999) 'Candidate Selection', in Michael Marsh and Paul Mitchell (eds), *How Ireland Voted 1997*. Boulder CO: Westview in association with PSAI Press, pp. 57–81.

Galligan, Yvonne (2003) 'Candidate Selection: More Democratic or More Centrally Controlled', in Michael Gallagher, Michael Marsh and Paul Mitchell (eds), *How Ireland Voted 2002*. London: Palgrave, pp. 37–56.

Garry, John (2007) 'Making Party Identification More Versatile: Operationalising the Concept for the Multiparty Setting', *Electoral Studies* 26(2): 346–58.

Garry, John and Lucy Mansergh (1999) 'Party Manifestos', in Michael Marsh and Paul Mitchell (eds), *How Ireland Voted 1997*. Boulder CO: Westview Press in association with PSAI Press, pp. 82–106.

Garry, John, Fiachra Kennedy, Michael Marsh and Richard Sinnott (2003) 'What Decided the Election?', in Michael Gallagher, Michael Marsh and Paul Mitchell (eds), *How Ireland Voted 2002*. London: Palgrave, pp. 119–42.

Gerber, Alan S. and Donald P. Green (2000) 'The Effects of Canvassing, Telephone Calls, and Direct Mail on Voter Turnout: A Field Experiment', *American Political Science Review* 94: 653–3.

Gerber, Alan S., Donald P. Green and Ron Shachar (2003) 'Voting May be Habit-Forming: Evidence from a Randomised Field Experiment', *American Journal of Political Science* 47: 540–50.

Green, Donald P., Alan S. Gerber and David W. Nickerson (2003) 'Getting out the Vote in Local Elections: Results from Six Door-to-Door Canvassing Experiments', *The Journal of Politics* 65: 1083–96.

Gschwend, Thomas, Ron Johnston and Charles Pattie (2003) 'Split-Ticket Patterns in Mixed-Member Proportional Election Systems: Estimates and Analyses of their Spatial Variation at the German Federal Election, 1998', *British Journal of Political Science* 33: 109–27.

Harrison, Michael J. and Michael Marsh (1994) 'What Can He Do for Us? Leader Effects on Party Fortunes in Ireland', *Electoral Studies* 13: 289–312.

Heath, Anthony F., Roger M. Jowell and John K. Curtice (1985) *How Britain Votes*. Oxford: Pergamon Press.

Heath, Anthony F., Roger M. Jowell and John K. Curtice (2001) *The Rise of New Labour*. Oxford: Pergamon Press.

Huckfeldt, Robert and John Sprague (1992) 'Political Parties and Electoral Mobilization: Political Structure, Social Structure and the Canvass', *American Political Science Review* 86: 70–86.

Inglehart, Ronald (1977) *The Silent Revolution: Changing Values and Political Styles Among Western Publics*. Princeton: Princeton University Press.

Inglehart, Ronald (1990) *Culture Shift in Advanced Industrial Society*. Princeton: Princeton University Press.

Jenssen, Anders T. and Toril Aalberg (2006) 'Party-Leader Effects in Norway: A Multi-Methods Approach', *Electoral Studies* 25: 248–69.

Johnston, Ron and Charles Pattie (2003) 'Do Canvassing and Campaigning Work? Evidence from the 2001 General Election in England', in Colin Rallings, Roger Scully, Jonathan Tonge and Paul Webb (eds), *British Elections and Parties Review*, 13: 210–28.

Karp, Jeffrey A. and David Brockington (2005) 'Social Desirability and Response Validity: A Comparative Analysis of Overrepresenting Voter Turnout in Five Countries', *The Journal of Politics* 67: 825–40.

Karp, Jeffrey A., Susan A. Banducci and Shaun Bowler (2003) 'Electoral Systems, Party Mobilisation and Turnout: Evidence from the European Parliamentary Elections 1999', in Colin Rallings, Roger Scully, Jonathan Tonge and Paul Webb, *British Elections and Parties Review*, 13: 210–28.

Karp, Jeffrey A., Susan A. Banducci and Shaun Bowler (forthcoming) 'Getting Out the Vote: Party Mobilization in a Comparative Perspective', *British Journal of Political Science.*

Karvonen, Lauri (2004) 'Preferential Voting: Incidence and Effects', *International Political Science Review* 25: 203–26.

Katz, Richard S. (1980) *A Theory of Parties and Electoral Systems.* Baltimore: Johns Hopkins University Press.

Katz, Richard S. (1985) 'Measuring Party Identification with Eurobarometer Data: A Warning Note', *West European Politics* 8: 104–8.

Katz, Richard S. (1986a) 'Intraparty Preference Voting', in Bernard Grofman and Arendt Lijphart (eds), *Electoral Laws and their Consequences.* New York NY: Agathon Press, pp. 85–103.

Katz, Richard S. (1986b) 'Party Government: A Rationalistic Conception', in Rudolph Wildenmann and Francis G. Castles (eds), *The Future of Party Government.* Berlin: W. de Gruyter, pp. 31–71.

Kavanagh, Adrian and Richard Sinnott (2007) 'Voting age population versus the electoral register: Findings and implications from an analysis of turnout in recent Irish general elections', working paper in Public Opinion and Political Behaviour Programme. Dublin: UCD Geary Institute.

Kennedy, Fiachra and Richard Sinnott (2006) 'Irish Social and Political Cleavages', in John Garry, Niamh Hardiman and Diane Payne (eds), *Irish Social and Political Attitudes.* Liverpool: Liverpool University Press, pp. 78–93.

Key, Valdimer O. (1966) *The Responsible Electorate: Rationality in Presidential Voting, 1936–1960.* Cambridge, Massachusetts: The Belknap Press of Harvard University Press.

King, Anthony (ed.) (2002) *Leaders' Personalities and the Outcome of Democratic Elections.* Oxford: Oxford University Press.

King, Simon (2000) *Parties, Issues and Personalities: The Structural Determinants of Irish Voting Behaviour from 1885 to 2000.* Thesis submitted for the degree of Doctor of Philosophy, Oxford University.

Kirchheimer, Otto (1966) 'The Transformation of the Western European Party Systems', in Joseph LaPalombara and Myron Weiner (eds), *Political Parties and Political Development.* Princeton, NJ: Princeton University Press, pp. 177–200.

Kitschelt, Herbert (2000) 'Linkages between citizens and politicians in democratic polities', *Comparative Political Studies* 33: 845–79.

Kramer, Gerald H. (1970) 'The Effects of Precinct-Level Canvassing on Voter Behaviour', *Public Opinion Quarterly* 34: 560–72.

Krassa, Michael A. (1988) 'Context and the Canvass: the Mechanisms of Interaction', *Political Behavior* 10: 233–46.

Laver, Michael (1986a) 'Ireland: Politics with Some Social Bases: An Interpretation Based on Aggregate Data', *Economic and Social Review* 17: 107–31.

Laver, Michael (1986b) 'Ireland: Politics with Some Social Bases: An Interpretation Based on Survey Data', *Economic and Social Review* 17: 193–213.

Laver, Michael (1987) 'Measuring Patterns of Party Support in Ireland', *Economic and Social Review* 18: 95–100.

Laver, Michael (2004) 'Analysing Structures of Party Preference in Electronic Voting Data', *Party Politics* 10: 521–41.

Laver, Michael (2005) 'Voting Behaviour', in John Coakley and Michael Gallagher (eds), *Politics in the Republic of Ireland* (4th edition). London: Routledge in association with PSAI Press, pp. 183–210.

Laver, Michael and Audrey Arkins (1990) 'Coalition and Fianna Fáil', in Michael Gallagher and Richard Sinnott (eds), *How Ireland Voted 1989*. Galway: Galway University Press and PSAI Press, pp. 192–207.

Laver, Michael, Yvonne Galligan and Gemma Carney (1999) 'The effect of Candidate Gender on Voting in Ireland, 1997', *Irish Political Studies* 14: 118–22.

Laver, Michael, Richard Sinnott and Michael Marsh (1987) 'Patterns of Party Support' in Michael Laver, Peter Mair and Richard Sinnott (eds), *How Ireland Voted: The Irish General Election 1987*. Dublin: Poolbeg Press, pp. 99–140.

Lewis-Beck, Michael S. (1988) *Economics and Elections: The Major Western Democracies*. Ann Arbor: University of Michigan Press.

Lewis-Beck, Michael S. and Mary Stegmaier (2000) 'Economic Determinants of Electoral Outcomes', *Annual Review of Political Science* 3: 183–219.

Lipset, Seymour M. and Stein Rokkan (1967) 'Cleavage Structures, Party Systems, and Voter Alignments', in Seymour M. Lipset and Stein Rokkan (eds), *Party Systems and Voter Alignments*. New York: Free Press, pp. 1–64.

McAllister, Ian (2002) 'Calculating or Capricious? The New Politics of Late Deciding Voters', in David Farrell and Rudiger Schmitt-Beck (eds), *Do Political Campaigns Matter?* London: Routledge, pp. 22–40.

McElroy, Gail and Michael Marsh (2003) 'Why the Opinion Polls Got it Wrong in 2002', in Michael Gallagher, Michael Marsh and Paul Mitchell (eds), *How Ireland Voted 2002*. London: Palgrave, pp. 159–76.

Mair, Peter (1979) 'The Autonomy of the Political: The Development of the Irish Party System', *Comparative Politics* 11: 445–65.

Mair, Peter (1987) *The Changing Irish Party System: Organisation, Ideology and Electoral Competition*. London: Frances Pinter.

Mair, Peter (1992) 'Explaining the Absence of Class Politics in Ireland', in John H. Goldthorpe and Christopher T. Whelan (eds), *The Development of Industrial Society in Ireland*. Oxford: Oxford University Press, pp. 383–410.

Mair, Peter and Michael Marsh (2004) 'Political Parties in Electoral Markets in Postwar Ireland', in Peter Mair, Wolfgang Muller and Fritz Plasser (eds), *Political Parties and Electoral Change: Party Responses to Electoral Markets*. London: Sage, pp. 234–63.

Mansergh, Lucy (2004) Do parties makes a difference? The Case of Governments in Ireland 1977–1997 (PhD thesis, Trinity College, Dublin).

Mansergh, Lucy and Robert Thomson (2007) 'Election pledges, Party Competition and Policymaking', *Comparative Politics* 39: 3, 311–29.

Marsh, Michael (1981) 'Localism, Candidate Selection and Electoral Preference in Ireland', *Economic and Social Review*, 12: 167–86.

Marsh, Michael (1985a) 'Ireland', in Ivor Crewe and David Denver (eds), *Electoral Change in Western Democracies: Patterns and Sources of Electoral Volatility*, pp. 173–20. London: Croom Helm.

Marsh, Michael (1985b) 'The Voters Decide? Preferential Voting in European List Systems', *European Journal of Political Research* 13: 365–78.

Marsh, Michael (1987) 'Electoral Evaluations of Candidates in Irish General Elections, 1948–1982', *Irish Political Studies* 2: 65–76.

Marsh, Michael (1991) 'Accident or Design: Non-Voting in Ireland', *Irish Political Studies* 6: 1–14.

Marsh, Michael (1992) 'Ireland', in Mark N. Franklin, Thomas T. Mackie and Henry Valen *et al.* (eds), *Electoral Change: Responses to Evolving Social and Attitudinal Structures in Western Countries*. Cambridge: Cambridge University Press, pp. 219–37.

Marsh, Michael (2000) 'Candidate-centred but Party Wrapped: Campaigning in Ireland under STV', in Shaun Bowler and Bernard Grofman (eds), *Elections in Australia, Ireland and Malta under the Single Transferable Vote*. Michigan: Michigan University Press, pp. 114–30.

Marsh, Michael (2002) 'Electoral Context', *Electoral Studies* 21: 207–17.

Marsh, Michael (2006) 'Stability and Change in Structure of Electoral Competition 1989–2002', in John Garry, Niamh Hardiman and Diane Payne (eds) *Irish Social and Political Attitudes*. Liverpool: Liverpool University Press, pp. 94–112.

Marsh, Michael and Richard Sinnott (1990) 'How the Voters Decided', in Michael Gallagher and Richard Sinnott (eds), *How Ireland Voted: The Irish General Election, 1989*. Galway: Galway University Press, pp. 68–93.

Marsh, Michael and Richard Sinnott (1993) 'The Voters: Stability and Change', in Michael Gallagher and Michael Laver (eds), *How Ireland Voted 1992*. Dublin/Limerick: Folens/PSAI Press, pp. 93–114.

Marsh, Michael and Richard Sinnott (1999) 'The Behaviour of the Irish Voter', in Michael Marsh and Paul Mitchell (eds), *How Ireland Voted 1997*. Boulder: Westview Press in association with PSAI Press, pp. 151–80.

Marsh, Michael and James Tilley (2006) 'Golden Halos and Forked Tails: The Attribution of Credit and Blame to Governments and its Impact on Vote Choice', paper delivered at the Annual Meeting of the American Political Science Association, Philadelphia, 31 August–3 September.

Miller, Warren E. (1976) 'The Cross-National Value of Party Identification as a Stimulus to Political Inquiry', in Ian Budge, Ivor Crewe and Dennis Farlie, *Party Identification and Beyond*. London: Wiley, pp. 21–32.

Miller, Warren E. and J. Merrill Shanks (1996) *The New American Voter*. Cambridge: Harvard University Press.

Nadeau, Richard and Richard Niemi (1995) 'Educated Guesses', *Public Opinion Quarterly* 59: 324–46.

Nannestad, Peter and Martin Paldam (2002) 'The Costs of Ruling', in Han Dorussen and Michaell Taylor (eds), *Economic Voting*. London: Routledge, pp. 17–44.

Norris, Pippa (2002) 'Campaign Communications', in Lawrence LeDuc, Richard G. Niemi and Pippa Norris (eds), *Comparing Democracies 2*. London: Sage, pp. 127–47.

O'Halpin, Eunan (2000) ' "Ah, They've Given us a Good Bit of Stuff...": Tribunals and Irish Political Life at the Turn of the Century', *Irish Political Studies* 15: 183–92.

O'Malley, Eoin (2001) 'Apathy or Error? Questioning the Irish Register of Electors to Question Turnout Decline', *Irish Political Studies* 16: 179–90.

Palmer, Harvey D. and Guy D. Whitten (2000) 'Government Competence, Economic Performance and Endogenous Election Dates', *Electoral Studies* 19: 413–426.

Palmer, Harvey D., Christopher J. Anderson and Raymond M. Duch (2000) 'Heterogeneity in Perceptions of National Economic Conditions', *American Journal of Political Science* 44: 635–52.

Parker, A. J. (1982) 'The "friends and neighbours" voting effect in the Galway West constituency', *Political Geography Quarterly* 1: 243–62.

Pattie, Charles and Ron Johnston (2003) 'Hanging on to the Telephone? Doorstep and Telephone Canvassing at the British General Election of 1997', *British Journal of Political Science* 33: 303–22.

Pattie, Charles, Ron Johnston and Edward Fieldhouse (1995) 'Winning the Local Vote', *American Political Science Review* 89: 969–83.

Petrocik, John (1996) 'Issue Ownership in Presidential Elections, with a 1980 Case Study', *American Journal of Political Science* 40: 825–50.

Poguntke, Thomas and Paul Webb (eds) (2005) *The Presidentialization of Politics: A Comparative Study of Modern Democracies*. Oxford: Oxford University Press.

Powell, Jr., Bingham G. (2000) *Elections as Instruments of Democracy: Majoritarian and Proportional Visions*. New Haven: Yale University Press.

Powell, Jr., Bingham G. and Guy D. Whitten (1993) 'A Cross-National Analysis of Economic Voting: Taking Account of the Political Context', *American Journal of Political Science* 37: 391–414.

Ranney, Austin (1962) *The Doctrine of Responsible Party Government: its Orgins and Present State*. Urbana: University of Illinois Press.

Richardson, Bradley M. (1988) 'Constituency Candidates versus Parties in Japanese Voting Behaviour', *American Political Science Review* 82: 695–718.

Richardson, Bradley M. (1991) 'European Party Loyalties Revisited', *American Political Science Review* 85: 751–75.

Robson, Christopher and Brendan Walsh (1974) 'The importance of Positional Bias in the Irish General Election of 1973', *Political Studies* 12: 191–203.

Rorschneider, Robert (2002) 'Mobilizing Voters versus Chasing Voters', *Electoral Studies* 21: 367–82.

Roscoe, Douglas D. (2003) 'The Choosers or the Choices? Voter Characteristics and the Structure of Electoral Competition as Explanations for Ticket Splitting', *The Journal of Politics* 65: 1147–64.

Rudolph, Thomas J. (2003) 'Who's Responsible for the Economy? The Formation and Consequences of Responsibility Attributions', *American Journal of Political Science* 47: 698–713.

Sacks, Paul (1976) *The Donegal Mafia: an Irish Political Machine*. New Haven, CT and London: Yale University Press.

Sanders, David and Sean Carey (2002) 'Temporal Variations in Economic Voting: A Comparative Cross-National Analysis', in Han Dorussen and Michaell Taylor (eds), *Economic Voting*. London: Routledge, pp. 200–32.

Schattschneider, E. E. (1942) *Party Government*. New York: Rinehart.

Schmitt, Hermann and Sören Holmberg (1995) 'Political Parties in Decline?', in Hans-Dieter Klingemann and Dieter Fuchs (eds), *Citizens and the State*. Oxford: Oxford University Press, pp. 95–133.

Shively, W. Phillips (1979) 'The Development of Party Identification among Adults: Exploration of a Functional Model', *American Political Science Review*, 73: 1039–54.

Shugart, Matthew S. (2005) 'Comparative Electoral Systems Research: The Maturation of a Field and New Challenges Ahead', in Michael Gallagher and Paul Mitchell (eds), *The Politics of Electoral Systems*. Oxford: Oxford University Press, pp. 25–36.

Sinnott, Richard (1978) 'The Electorate', in H.R. Penniman (ed.), *Ireland at the Polls: The Dáil Elections of 1977*. Washington, DC: American Enterprise Institute for Public Policy Research, pp. 35–68.

Sinnott, Richard (1984) 'Interpretations of the Irish Party System', *European Journal of Political Research* 12: 289–307.

Sinnott, Richard (1987) 'The Voters, the Issues, and the Party System', in B. Farrell and H. R. Penniman (eds), *Ireland at the Polls Vol. II: The Dáil Elections of 1981–2*. Washington DC: American Enterprise Institute, pp. 57–103.

Sinnott, Richard (1995) *Irish Voters Decide: Voting Behaviour in Elections and Referendums since 1918*. Manchester: Manchester University Press.

Sinnott, Richard (1998) 'Party Attachment in Europe: Methodological Critique and Substantive Implications', *British Journal of Political Science* 28: 627–50.

Sinnott, Richard (2002) 'Cleavages, parties and referendums: Relationships between representative and direct democracy in the Republic of Ireland', *European Journal of Political Research* 41: 811–26.

Sinnott, Richard (2005) 'The Rules of the Electoral Game', in John Coakley and Michael Gallagher (eds), *Politics in the Republic of Ireland* (4th edition). London: Routledge, pp. 105–34.

Stevenson, Randolph (2002) 'The Economy as Context: Indirect Links between Economy and Voters', in Han Dorussen and Michaell Taylor (eds), *Economic Voting*. London: Routledge, pp. 45–65.

Stewart, Marianne C. and Harold D. Clark (1992). 'The (Un)importance of Party Leaders: Leader Images and Party Choice in the 1987 British Election', *The Journal of Politics* 54: 447–70.

Stokes, Donald E. (1963) 'Spatial Models of Party Competition', *American Political Science Review* 57: 368–77.

Stokes, Donald E. (1966) 'Some Dynamic Elements in Contests for the Presidency', *American Political Science Review* 60: 19–28.

Swaddle, Kevin and Anthony Heath (1989) 'Official and Reported Turnout in the British General Elections of 1987', *British Journal of Political Science* 19: 537–51.

Thomassen, Jacques (1976) 'Party Identification as a Cross-National Concept: Its meaning in the Netherlands', in Ian Budge, Ivor Crewe and Dennis Farlie (eds), *Party Identification and Beyond*. London: J Wiley and Sons, pp. 63–79.

Thomassen, Jacques (1994) 'Empirical Research into Political Representation: Failing Democracy or Failing Models?', in M. Kent Jennings and T.E. Mann (eds), *Elections at Home and Abroad, Essays in Honor of Warren Miller*. Ann Arbor: Michigan University Press, pp. 237–65.

Thomassen, Jacques (ed.) (2006) *The European Voter*. Oxford: Oxford University Press.

Tufte, Edward R. (1978) *Political Control of the Economy*. Princeton, NJ: Princeton University Press.

Wattenberg, Martin P. (2000) 'The Decline of Party Mobilization', in Russell J. Dalton and Martin P. Wattenberg (eds), *Parties Without Partisans: Political Change in Advanced Industrial Democracies*. Oxford: Oxford University pp. 64–78.

Weisberg, Herbert F. (1980) 'A Multidimensional Conceptualisation of Party Identification', *Political Behavior* 1: 33–60.

Whiteley, Paul and Patrick Seyd (2003) 'How to Win a Landslide by Really Trying: the Effects of Local Campaigning on Voting in the 1997 British General Election', *Electoral Studies* 22: 301–24.

Whyte, John H. (1974) 'Ireland: Politics Without Social Bases', in Richard Rose (ed.), *Electoral Behaviour: A Comparative Handbook*. New York: The Free Press, pp. 619–51.

Wielhouwer, Peter W. (1999) 'The Mobilization Of Campaign Activists by the Party Canvass', *American Politics Quarterly* 27: 177–200.

Wielhouwer, Peter W. (2003) 'In Search of Lincoln's Perfect List: Targeting in Grassroots Campaigns', *American Politics Research* 31: 632–69.

Wielhouwer, Peter W. and Brad Lockerbie (1994) 'Party Contacting and Political Participation, 1952–90', *American Journal of Political Science* 38: 211–29.

Wlezien, Christopher, Mark N. Franklin and Daniel Twiggs (1997) 'Economic Perceptions and Vote Choice: Disentangling the Endogeneity', *Political Behavior* 19: 7–17.

Index